VISIONARY PRAGMATISM

VISIONARY PRAGMATISM

Radical and Ecological Democracy

in Neoliberal Times

———————————

ROMAND COLES

DUKE UNIVERSITY PRESS

Durham and London

2016

Library of Congress Cataloging-in-Publication Data
Coles, Romand, [date] author.
Visionary pragmatism : radical and ecological democracy in
neoliberal times / Romand Coles.
pages cm
Includes bibliographical references and index.
ISBN 978-0-8223-6049-0 (hardcover : alk. paper)
ISBN 978-0-8223-6064-3 (pbk. : alk. paper)
ISBN 978-0-8223-7466-4 (e-book)
1. Democracy—United States—Citizen participation.
2. Democracy—Social aspects—United States.
3. Capitalism—Social aspects—United States.
4. Capitalism—Environmental aspects—United States.
5. Capitalism—Political aspects—United States.
6. Community organization—United States. I. Title.
JC423.C6476 2016
320.973—dc23
2015035886

Cover art: Detail of *80sw Iridescent / Flying Garden
/ Air-Port-City* (2011) installed in *Tomás Saraceno:
Cloud-Specific* at the Mildred Lane Kemper Art
Museum, Washington University in St. Louis
(September 9, 2011–January 9, 2012). Courtesy the
artist, Esther Schipper Gallery, Berlin; Pinksummer
contemporary art, Genoa; Tanya Bonakdar Gallery,
New York; Andersen's Contemporary, Copenhagen.
Photo by Whitney Curtis.

THIS BOOK IS DEDICATED TO

MY DAUGHTER AVIVA ASPEN HARO-COLES,

BORN ON AUGUST 5, 2015.

In the beautiful aura of her emergent, exuberant, and full-bodied efforts to live into the world, I marvel in deepest love at the traces of ancestors she will never know and future possibilities beyond the reach of my wildest imagination.

CONTENTS

ACKNOWLEDGMENTS

Visionary Pragmatism is profoundly indebted to conversations and engagements with countless students, faculty, and members of the broader community in the action research teams movement in Northern Arizona, as well as to conversations with scholarly colleagues at professional occasions across North America, Europe, and Australia for the past seven years.

In this overly abundant context I am inexpressibly grateful to the following people for their inspiring example, generosity, and insights: Paul Apostolidis, Frankie Beesley, Jane Bennett, Lauren Berutich, Craig Borowiak, Harry Boyte, P.J. Brendese, Danielle Celermajer, Gerald Coles, Maria Coles, Marianna ColesCurtis, Miles ColesCurtis, William Connolly, Kimberley Curtis, Ian Dixon-MacDonald, Jacob Dolence, Peter Euben, Coral Evans, Luis Fernandez, Laura Grattan, Joanna Hale, Lia Haro, Bonnie Honig, Ron Hubert, Chris Huebner, John Hultgren, Wahleah Johns, Nicholas Kompridis, Eli Lauren-Bernstein, Madison Ledgerwood, Jason Lowry, Sandra Lubarsky, Jane Marks, John Meyer, Leah Mundell, Robert Neustadt, Aletta Norval, Joel Olson, Melissa Orlie, Billy Parrish, Patrick Pfeifer, Nina Porter, Tamara Ramirez, Mark Reinhardt, Lizett Castruita Rivera, Blase Scarnati, David Schlosberg, Mort Schoolman, Sandy Schram, George Shulman, Nicholas Tampio, Frank Vander Valk, Marina Vasquez, and Miguel Vasquez. There are so many others whose ideas, lives, and imaginations have informed this work—sometimes in ways that are as profound as they were brief.

To Ella Myers and an anonymous reviewer at Duke University Press, I owe special thanks for reading the entire manuscript and making innumerable suggestions that greatly improved this work. I am grateful to Courtney Berger, senior editor at Duke University Press, for being an incomparable editor in every way.

A section of chapter 1 contains significantly revised and expanded material that was first published in an article entitled "The Neuropolitical Habitus of Resonant Receptive Democracy," *Ethics and Global Politics* 4, no. 4 (2011) (Creative Commons), that was later included in *Essays on Neuroscience and*

Political Theory, edited by Frank Vander Valk (New York: Routledge, 2012). I am grateful to the editors and reviewers of the journal and the book for their generosity and helpful suggestions.

Nearly every day during my six years in Flagstaff, I biked ecstatically from meeting to meeting—organizing, listening, teaching, learning, cowriting, reading. As I did, the San Francisco Peaks modulated amidst the shifting light, the snows, the monsoon clouds, the seasons, and continually informed and energized my sense of why I am here. I am grateful for this land and for those who have lived on the Colorado Plateau for ages far better than most of us who do now.

During this time, my life has become wonderfully intertwined with the life of Lia Haro. We have read each other's every word, begun to cowrite together, and embarked upon parallel and resonant action research projects. We have greeted countless days with poetry, and witnessed the poetry of countless days. *My voice because of you* (La voz a ti debida), Lia.

Theorizing from and Traveling toward a Radical Democratic Habitus

A catastrophe is under way. A hypermalignant form of capitalism is entangled with ecological collapse, unfathomable inequality, ruthless privatization of the commons, the dismantling of democracy, intensifying xenophobia, "new Jim Crow" racism, permanent war, and the destruction of higher education as a space for critical and creative inquiry. This malignancy often manifests remarkable capacities to outmaneuver even modest efforts to avert the worst, let alone more ambitious movements to generate powerful alternatives that lean in fundamentally better directions. Formal politics are confined to narrowing channels that keep shifting rightward, while a vast portion of what goes on even in the "critical" portions of the academy has become hyperprofessionalized in ways that often lack *both* transformative vision *and* serious contact with movements trying to make real change. Pragmatic sensibilities too often lose connection with the creative provocations, affective intensities, and expansive horizons of radical vision. Scholarly sensibilities increasingly focus on discursive industries of hermetic tertiary literature that shed less and less light on matters of increasing urgency. For a long time, powers that might resist neoliberalism and generate alternatives have grown less creative and less powerful, while vicious game-changing dynamics of rapacious powers are modulating and on the move. As hopeful movements around democratizing education, climate justice, racism, austerity, solidarity economics, migration, and broad-based community organizing are beginning to rumble, how might we regenerate more promising forms of academic work and politics?

This book is written in the midst of scholarly, pedagogical, and activist movements along various edges between scholarship and practice. My aim has been to inhabit these edges as ecotones—rich evolutionary zones of tension and pregnant commingling between different-yet-related ecological communities, rather than locations where one is reduced to the myopic imperatives of the other. I have sought to provoke theoretical and scholarly shifts in the midst of the imaginative openings and the challenges of grassroots political life, and I have sought to inform the latter by means of ideas that have had freer range in spaces where the pressures of immediacy are not (yet) quite as severe. At every point in this uncertain yet exciting journey, I have tried to tune my ears and direct my gaze toward possibilities of creating transformative theories and practices for radical and ecological democracy. How might we generate new patterns and interactions, charged at the edges between myriad fields within the academy and the broader world of democratic practices that might gather and generate transformative powers of a visionary pragmatism?

This book is unusual, insofar as it is not merely *about* such edges between theory and practice, it is also written *from* some of those edges, and it is a call *for* reworking the scholarly habitus in ways that make such edgework an integral part of the ecology of endeavors necessary for visionary pragmatic thinking and acting. As such, I begin with some vignettes from my often-meandering journeys beyond certain ruts and walls of the academy. These travels have repeatedly provoked me to explore the practice of theory in relation to political pedagogies of receptive and catalytic movement in places typically avoided by scholars. I consider these journeys and explorations to be indispensable conditions of nearly everything else that follows.

———————

The sky is gray, the falling rain is gray, and the pavement is gray. As I open the car door and thank my colleague for giving me a ride home on a day when my bike has failed me, he glances at the shabby houses along the street and says, "Rom, I could never live in a neighborhood like this—it is just too dreary and depressing."

It is the early 1990s, my political theory tenure clock at Duke University is ticking, and with my family I have moved here on the edge of this Durham ghetto out of a vague sense that this is where I should be thinking. This turns out to be easier said than done, as gunshots interrupt most nights and a gang of drug dealers moves into the house across the road.

One late afternoon, several feet from our front room, about a dozen guys with sticks and knives face off against about a dozen others similarly armed. Some have guns. The worst does not happen, but along the edge of the road is a child who is four or five. He has a stick, and during the entire event he is banging the hell out of a metal garbage can close to the scene. I sometimes say that my life moves to the beat of Martin Luther King Jr.'s voice as I heard it boom while riding on my dad's shoulders before I could stand up for long. Yet the truth is that for more than two decades now, the main beat moving me is that stick on the can.

There is a widely shared sense among radical democrats of many stripes that what matters in politics, theory, and other kinds of scholarship is the journey—the performance and practice—far more than the destination. Yet the very ease with which we circulate this too-common wisdom risks turning it into a destination. As we settle into this sense that our vocation is an odyssey, we may obscure how difficult it is to move—the intellectual, experiential, and ethical energies, depths, and agonies that theoretical, scholarly, and political journeys require. Our sense of odyssey may conceal how narrow the horizons of our journeys have become, or our sense that we are moving may itself become a soporific that draws us unaware toward an unfortunate rest. The journey of which this book is a part is propelled by uneasiness about such possibilities. It is born of a sense that the hyperactivity and professionalization of much radical political theory and critical scholarship in many disciplines is becoming a vehicle for going nowhere, or at least that *I* was becoming stuck.

I move to the edge of the ghetto to mix in the neighborhood in whatever way differences of class and race might allow, and so to keep my fingers on the pulse of difficult life that, I was thinking, is what radical democratic theorists should be animated by, even when we are not thinking about it directly. Yet the first thing that the near riot and the stick on the can move me to do is to search for a home in a safer neighborhood. Just as we are about to sign a lease on a new place, a former student of the populist historian Larry Goodwyn who has recently started organizing in the neighborhood shows up at the front door, manages to claim a chair in our living room, and somehow convinces us to stay put, talk with the neighbors about the confluence of slumlords and drug dealers, and become politically active in the hood. Before I know it, I am spending a lot of time organizing in the living rooms of grandmothers one street over who sleep on the floor to avoid bullets that might come through the windows. I do a lot of listening. I am among a small group of people creeping into run-down vacant houses to record and report unenforced housing code violations, holding up large pictures of a slumlord's mansion in front of the shacks he owns, building a network of relational power to address problems in the neighborhood. We begin to organize against the slumlords and for affordable housing, a land trust, a community center, a preschool for kids in the neighborhood, drug rehabilitation programs, a different kind of policing—but the issues matter less than the engagements. Without realizing it at first, and in ways I never anticipated, I am beginning to think in relation to how things unfold in the living rooms, the conversations and actions in the streets, the community center. I begin imagining the world through the anxious and excited movement of our bodies through smashed windows in and out of dilapidated houses. I am reading, teaching, and writing about Merleau-Ponty, Foucault, Gadamer, Adorno, Kant, Wolin, Derrida, among many others, but I am increasingly reading them from the broken windows, the differences and dreams in the living rooms, the streets—reading more to the beat of that stick on the garbage can, and less to the textures of life in the library, the departmental and professional meetings, and the academic rituals of making it at an elite university (even as these continue to matter).

Across many disciplines, epic traveling has long been constitutive of theorists' imagination of our vocation, as the Greek etymological roots linking theorists, theory, traveling, and even the ships that carried such travelers suggest.[1] In more tacit ways, I think this undergirds many less theoretical scholars' sense of their work as well. We imagine ourselves struggling our scholarly ways out of and back into caves in which the rest of humanity remains stuck and bound to illusion. We journey in time—while others are merely swept along without reflection and agency—whether we spread our wings of comprehension as the sun sets on an age, or march knowingly in an avant-garde pushing history's revolutionary edge. Where others reside in and think from one position in a political order, we move, think, and forge vision from multiple perspectives afforded by travels across the rugged geography of high peaks and deep valleys of our polity. We move restlessly to and from the gatherings of the herd and our places of solitude, becoming, while others are stuck in reified misapprehensions of being. Though most are mired in tribalism and patriotism, we imagine ourselves soaring to heights from which we forge cosmopolitan perspectives in which humanity is one. Or we connect the heart of theory and other scholarship to arteries and capillaries through which we circulate across borders of polis, culture, nation, and religion to offer an essentially comparative wisdom. Or we forge political imagination, judgment, and action through world traveling, as we attentively visit—yet keep a certain distance from—various perspectives around the tables at which we gather in speech and deed.

I am inspired by several of these images of political theory, even as I am highly suspicious of others, and seek to resist the (sometimes absurd) hubristic pretensions that are associated with most of them. Yet I increasingly doubt that the aspirations guided by these metaphors hold up well in the ritualized movements of most professionalized theorists' daily lives. If fresh thinking and acting is so deeply linked with metaphors of movement, and if the first theorists actually were geographic travelers whose capacities to theorize were thought to be inseparable from the manifold experiences and perspectives associated with their journeys, might we not have reason to suspect that the kinds of movements we engage in day in and day out may indeed influence our capacities to think—and not necessarily for the better? My unease here concerns not only what I take to be an exaggerated sense of the mobility of our imagination in the absence of unwonted experience and corporeal movement, but even more so the extent to which the routinized movements of our daily lives powerfully guide and constrain our capacities for political imagination and vision. For a vocation so shaped by metaphors of movement, are we not remarkably inattentive to the actual movements that make up the quotidian life of most theorists (and scholars more generally) in the academy? If metaphors of sweeping, grand, and attentive movements often orient our aspirations, what happens to our vocation when our bodies circulate in deep, overworn ruts of movement, avoidance, attention, and inattentiveness?[2]

We theorists and scholars of politics across many disciplines tend to be very busy people in perpetual motion. Many different drives and pressures propel our movement, ranging from intrinsic love of theoretical questions and scholarly work, to passionate concerns about politics, to a desire for scholarly expertise that may enhance our engagements as public intellectuals, to tenure pressures of elite universities, to massive teaching loads of contingent faculty who are simultaneously scrambling to publish their way out of these most precarious faculty positions in corporatized institutions, to love of academic camaraderie, to desires for—and fears of—the judgment of one's peers, to desires to move into administrative positions and try one's hand at shaping higher education, to earning salary increases associated with "highly meritorious" evaluations. Thus, we find ourselves moving among classrooms, to our offices, to faculty meetings, to libraries, to attend or give guest lectures, to professional conferences and corporate hotel rooms, to our middle-class homes and higher-end supermarkets in comfortable neighborhoods, to restaurants where we dine with people a lot like us, to long hours of sitting in our studies.

We have fantasies about the powers of our imaginations to embark on vast disembodied journeys with texts. Yet we are profoundly embodied beings so often swept up in frenetic motions myopically focused on the concerns of a professionalized environment—disengaged from and oblivious to most of the world around us, harboring ourselves within a small range of spaces, experiences, types of energy, modes of activity, cultural productions, ways of being and doing. Insofar as capacities for theory and scholarship are in any way linked to attentive travels beyond the familiar, it is tempting to say that the professionalized movements of academic governmentality may be among the most antitheoretical and antischolarly conditions of impossibility imaginable for fresh thinking and political acting.[3] Pierre Bourdieu formulated the idea of "habitus" to express the ways in which dispositions, perceptions, affect, expectations, thought, and bodily engagement in practices and institutions are closely articulated, correlated, and cogenerative of each other.[4] Highly critical of theories of free subjectivity and intersubjectivity, he argued that the everyday practices of our habitus generate and are reproduced by a very structured and limited repertoire of improvisations. Our "flights" of imagination are mostly propelled by and adhere to the contours, requirements, and limits of this moving structure of behavior—including the necessary fantasy that we are free travelers.

The stick, the can, and the kid laid in a beat that made me feel increasingly uncomfortable with the rhythms, flows, interactions, productions, and limits of academic practice. They cast me forth along other paths. I found myself spending a lot of time organizing in the basements of black churches across uncanny lines of race, class, and religion, and walking attentively in unfamiliar parts of Durham, North Carolina, with many others, as we listened to stories of challenge and aspiration in an attempt to fashion a radically democratic epistemology, community, and form of power. As I taught and wrote, these experiences increasingly animated and infiltrated my work. Yet at the same time, even my most philosophical writings and conversations animated and infiltrated my organizing experiences and orientations. If I felt uncomfortable and claustrophobic in the midst of academic rituals and productions, these feelings developed less as negation and more as a growing taste for the generative-if-difficult intertwinements between these very different modes of being and reflection. For me, this intersection seemed to engender more receptive and expansive journeys—and these seemed to give birth not only to political possibilities that I found more hopeful but also to theory that seemed to move anew—to find many of its richest possibilities in these movements. Some of my writing began to change, and many of my students began to move about and become involved in the community in new ways at the same time they became involved in radical democratic theorizing. Their flights of inquiry and imagination became more courageous and interesting—to themselves and to me. I developed an insatiable hunger to explore and experiment with these edges, to proliferate them in pursuit of a new educational culture and set of practices. I began to wonder if it might be possible to cocreate a radical democratic habitus that would become conducive to fresher, more potent thought and action in the face of the monumental crises of our times.

For Bourdieu, habitus is a principle of reproductive practice and improvisation whose tendencies are centripetal. Insofar as we are animated to venture beyond the limits of the order, it is due to crises, internal contradictions, cultural confrontations from without, and so forth. Yet a central question that animates this work is whether we might be able to generate practices that are, in a sense, more centrifugal in character. Might we fashion corporeal and theoretical practices that move attentively with the tensions, differences, strangeness, suffering, and suppressed yet very present possibilities of the world in ways that tap into and cultivate energies more conducive to what Foucault called a "limit ethos," that questions the "necessities" that so often "go without saying because they come without saying"?[5] Might we engender transformative conducts in which patient labors give form to our impatience for freedom and commonwealth? How might we cocreate a habitus of durable transformative patterns and interactions that I shall refer to as game-transformative practices?

Along with a few colleagues and a couple of organizers in the Southeast Industrial Areas Foundation organizing network, we began to experiment with one modest incarnation of this hopeful possibility. We gathered organizers, grassroots leaders, and scholars from across the southeastern United States for a couple days of intensive conversation a few times a year around issues and texts concerning race, democracy, religion and politics, immigration, unions and community organizing, and so forth. The idea was to generate a radically different kind of encounter that might throw all of us a bit off balance, toss us out of comfort zones, and stir up creative energies. On the one hand, folks who spent most of their time in scholarly settings would engage the narratives and living theory of folks who spent a lot of time in the trenches. On the other hand, folks in the trenches would have an opportunity to pause, reflect, and discuss scholarship pertinent to their struggles with those who had the luxury to spend countless hours reading and writing.

We called this initiative the Third Reconstruction Institute. The idea was that the first Reconstruction was in the process of creating an enormously transformative and promising radical democratic movement when it was crushed in the nineteenth century. Almost a hundred years later, the organizing tradition of the civil rights movement of the 1960s arose to reinvent U.S. democracy in unprecedented ways but was driven back once again. Amid so much promise and retrenchment, it was long past time to strive to generate a third reconstruction. Inspired by how important the intersections between scholars and activists had been in the 1960s, we wanted our engagements to be like watering holes, wellsprings—whirlpools where we would all commingle and jostle each other out of our dogmatic slumbers. The Third Reconstruction Institute, in other words, would be an effort to cocreate an indispensable part of a radical democratic habitus.

Move each other we did. Most of us with our heavy foot in academia quickly came to realize that the organizers and grassroots leaders from across the Southeast not only brought textured and gritty narratives to the table but also brought a trove of reflection and theorizing. To be sure, this theory was often not of the scholarly kind, but rather was born of repeated reflection at the intersection of their own experiences, those of others in their communities, as well as those in communities across the Southeast and beyond. A number of academics felt rumblings of inspiration and no small uneasiness at how good some of those outside the academy were at our own game. Maybe they were more interesting than we were. A mutual appreciation and respect began to develop across these differences that was—as we had hoped—a source of revitalization and uneasy jostling. And different people had different experiences and reflections in the gatherings. Some of the newer and less formally educated leaders in the grassroots organizing network felt put off by abstract academic language and references. Others were comfortable with and hungry for the different lenses these afforded. Many of us from various backgrounds started to make new connections and ask new questions that seemed crucial to and engendered by this distinctive kind of conversation. Most of the academics in the midst felt an increasing sense of narrowness and staleness in the more conventional discussion practices to which we returned, and went back to seek ways to change things.

The Third Reconstruction Institute was a modest effort to form a game-transformative practice that might press and midwife new possibilities for democratization and justice into being. I suspect that such practices have been integral to every genuinely transformative movement of theory and practice. The idea of changing the game in the struggle for a better world is not new, but rather is an enduring (if episodic) pulse in many traditions. Lao-tzu, Jeremiah, Jesus, Buddha, many Native American trickster figures, and numerous others can each be read to (pre)figure such possibilities.

In this light, I think it is useful to begin our inquiry by considering a biblical story that has repeatedly been a source of inspiration and guidance for transformative movements, in order to glean insights into how underdogs and social movements can alter the spacing, timing, and practices of encounter in ways that change the conventional contestation—or game—to enable victories deemed highly improbable.

When Goliath, a gigantic, highly skilled, and heavily armed (and armored) fighting champion, steps out of the Philistine camp to challenge any Israelite to battle him to determine which nation will become enslaved, Saul and all the others are terrified. They have good reason. Goliath stands just a few inches shy of ten feet tall; he wears a coat of armor that weighs 125 pounds; the iron tip of his spear alone weighs 15 pounds. For forty days, twice each day, Goliath stands forth and shouts his challenge, and each time the Israelites "all fled from him in great fear" (1 Samuel 17:24 [NIV]). The king of Israel has offered the man who can kill Goliath great wealth and his daughter in marriage, but it makes no difference. There is no earthly measure that can overcome the trembling terror and hopelessness each soldier feels in the depths of his being. Goliath is the best at this game, and no one can conceive of beating him.

Except David, a young shepherd with no military experience, who volunteers for the battle and insists on fighting in spite of Saul's resistance and others who dismiss him. When he is given the go-ahead, a string of game-changing events is under way. At first, David attempts to play the anticipated game, steps up, and dons armor and sword. Yet he quickly realizes that this will lead to defeat and then proceeds to dramatically alter the expected engagement: swapping his coat of mail and blade for five smooth stones and a slingshot, he steps forth, proclaims his purpose, slings a stone, and knocks that giant dead—thus releasing Israel from threatened servitude.

Marshall Ganz, an unusual scholar who dropped out of Harvard to join the civil rights movement, has fashioned his five smooth stones from five decades of involvement in grassroots political organizing. He is fascinated by David's "unusually unconstrained approach to learning" and wonders how David is "so strategically resourceful," "unlike anyone else on the battlefield."[6]

What sets him apart? David draws from an incomparable depth of enthusiastic commitment—he perceives what he is about to do as a divine calling. In response, he moves beyond his comfort zone, puts on armor, and picks up weapons. Yet their impossible weight and demands press his imagination toward "new pathways, often employing bricolage to combine familiar elements in new ways."[7] As an outsider to combat, he reimagines the battlefield. In a responsive interplay of body and mind, he refuses the compartmentalized assumptions of the embattled polity, removes armor from his body, rearticulates what to most are separate spheres of pertinent capacities, and draws on body practices and movements he developed as a shepherd charged with protecting flocks from predators. As Ganz mixes insights from this narrative with those he gleaned as a leader in the United Farm Workers movement, he suggests that responsive enthusiasm is key. To become powerful, a social movement must combine extraordinary commitment with the commingling of extraordinary differences in ways that repeatedly propel it beyond the comfort zones of settled practices and assumptions. For a time, he suggests, the United Farm Workers gathered laborers, priests, rabbis, students, civil rights workers, lawyers, consumers, and more into a dynamic mix that forged new political vision and potent strategies of engagement that overwhelmed corporate forces that had far greater conventional resources.

There appear to be elements of wisdom here that have broad significance. In Ivan Arreguin-Toft's study of every war in the past two centuries in which strong combatants were at least ten times as powerful as their weaker counterparts, he finds that the underdogs win 29 percent of the time.[8] Even more remarkably, he finds that when Davids acknowledge their disadvantage and invent an unconventional strategy, they win nearly two-thirds of the conflicts. In other words, when people acknowledge that they can't win the traditional contests and pursue radical alternatives, they can change the game and win far more often than not. Observing that "Davids win all the time," Malcolm Gladwell suggests that what distinguishes Davids is that they discern and enact radical modulations of the spaces, times, and modes of engagement that most others take to be sharply delineated and immutable.[9] When Lawrence of Arabia led Bedouin fighters who were (in conventional military senses) poorly trained and poorly armed in their uprising against the occupying Ottoman army, their success was due to the fact that they refused to wage a concentrated assault on the heavily armed Turkish garrison at Medina. Instead, they spatially dispersed the conflict by repeatedly attacking telegraph and railroad lines in unexpected places across hundreds of miles of desert. To enact this strategy they deployed cognitive, imaginative, and physical abilities they gleaned from traveling in other contexts. Hence they deployed their incomparable knowledge of the land and capacities to move across uncanny distances at high speeds on camels in order repeatedly to confuse the Turks' sense of timing.

Examining a totally different terrain of contest, Gladwell arrives at similar conclusions in the case of his twelve-year-old daughter's basketball team in Silicon Valley, coached by a man from Mumbai. A cricket and soccer player profoundly puzzled by why basketball teams would usually rapidly retreat to their end of the court when the other team would inbound the ball, the coach decided to deviate from the accepted common sense and play intense full-court press "every game, all the time." With this dramatic alteration (imaginatively drawn from cricket and soccer) of the space, timing, practices, and intensities of conventional basketball, his team of nerdy "little blond girls" totally confused the strategies of other teams, utterly broke their rhythm, and made it all the way to the national championships.

What the protagonists in each of these stories have in common is a profoundly mobile imagination that is intertwined with bodily movement: as they move into new engagements, they draw on movements from other spheres of activity, to move in new ways. In each case, where most people perceptually appropriate a given terrain of encounter through an unquestioned and rigid lens, these Davids sense and imaginatively enact tremendous potentials that transform the very character of the contest. They sense and enact the hope of the hopeless.

Of course, the conventional patterns—and patterns of being myopically conventional—have a remarkable capacity to reassert their dominance, as shepherd David becomes King David and then reassumes a too-common sense, lords his sovereign power in relation to Uriah, commands an abusive census, and so forth. Ganz tells a parallel story of the ascent and descent of Cesar Chavez and the United Farm Workers.[10] Thus, what interests me in these narratives is not that they are compelling examples of "game changers"—a term that typically indicates little more than the reversal of probabilities and outcomes in a given game due to an unexpected strategy, tapping into unsuspected sources, a wild card, and so forth. Such readings confine the significance of the events within the teleological narratives provided by the basic games and who wins them. What interests me, rather, is to modulate the temporality of reading; to tarry with the zone in which the actors are imagining and doing a new thing; to take *this emergence itself* as the focus of what is significant; to explore how that newness happens; and, whirling with the vertiginous possibilities that unfold then and there, to ask questions concerning how we might gather insights from the event of game changers in order to create game-transformative practices. I read the protagonists as prototheorists, intertwining travel and theory in ways that give birth to imaginative and incisive thought and action.

These events go to the far edge of what we typically mean by "game changer," insofar as they do more than implement an exceedingly smart strategy. Rather, they profoundly deviate from and challenge conventions that are taken for granted by nearly all who play. Yet their transgression of these conventions lacks resilience and also leaves the more elemental basics of the game unquestioned. In what I am calling a game-transformative practice, both commonsense conventions *and* basic institutional rules and orientations are altered, *and* the energies, sensibilities, and modes of moving, imagining, thinking, and acting associated with such transformations become partially embodied in practices through which they acquire significant resilience and regenerative powers. Sometimes game-transformative practices alter things dramatically and quickly; sometimes their processes are more incremental. Usually game-transformative practices involve a complex interanimation of multiple processes across a broad spectrum of transformative tempos, spaces, modes, and intensities.

The game-transformative practices of a radical democratic habitus for theory and politics that I seek in what follows would engender persistent patterns, practices, dynamics, and sensibilities that tend to further nurture our receptive and cocreative powers in relation to differences and collective possibilities typically unacknowledged by the dominant rules and common sense of any given time. These dynamics would in turn tend to enhance our capacities for radical reformations that further enhance our powers for receptive creativity and complex commonwealth. Clearly there is something paradoxical here, insofar as such game-transformative practices would hinge upon a profoundly receptive democratic common sense that seeks to radically reform itself in order to intensify these very capacities. Yet I will try to show in the chapters to follow that this paradox is neither a contradiction nor impossible, but rather a tension that can be negotiated through the vitality of political theory, vibrant scholarship, and democratic life—particularly in relation to practices of resonance, circulating movement, autocatalytic system dynamics, and the alternating electrical currents of radical democracy.

———————

As I moved to and fro between practices of grassroots organizing and political action, on the one hand, and those of academic life, on the other, two things became particularly tiresome. There was a too-frequent tendency on the part of my scholar-colleagues to dismiss the pertinence for "genuine theory" of movement in the world of political engagement. Being politically active was a "nice" thing, and perhaps a good thing to do as a member of the polity. Yet too few took seriously the idea that it might be integral to revitalizing political theory and scholarship. At the same time, there were many who inhabited the world of grassroots politics in flat-footed ways who had very little patience for theory that could not prove its immediate "relevance" and "applicability." In both cases, it was easy to understand a moment of truth in some of their dismissive postures: there were types of action that did little to stretch, inform, or inspire inquiry; and there were types of inquiry that were so hermetically sealed in arcane bureaucracies of secondary and tertiary commentary that their broader significance seemed a stretch. Yet more often than not, such dismissive insistence also seemed tightly intertwined with defensive dispositions to constrain or even eliminate unorthodox gestures and unfamiliar possibilities. One result of my fatigue in the face of such responses was the emergence of a predisposition of my own, namely, the sense that endeavors to proliferate movements beyond the stultifying habitus of academic scholarship and stagnant politics should proceed by way of multiplication and juxtaposition, rather than truncation, new uniformities, and separations. A radical democratic habitus for theory, scholarship, and politics would require a complex and dynamic ecology of practices, not a new monoculture.

Insofar as the emergence of the energies, imagination, and cognitive shifting of game-transformative practices is intertwined with bodily travels and attentions that move beyond our comfort zones, the vision of a radical democratic habitus—for theory, for politics—would not consist of a new discipline founded on newly discovered "*right* movements." The (cl)aim should not even be that every theorist and scholar must be deeply engaged in *unwonted* movement of some sort, in order to theorize well. In myriad relationships, each of us may be fed variously by the energies, comparisons, collaborations, insights, and wonder of others who theorize attentively in relation to journeys in proximate or distant places tabooed, maligned, or ignored. Receptive physical journeys may stimulate imaginative journeys; imaginative journeys may dispose us toward more receptive physical journeys; and the imaginative journeys of some feed those of others. The generative movements to and fro among these different types of traveling theory are as important as the movements within any single mode. Journeys toward critique, insight, wonder, new modes of democratic collaboration and struggle are many. Many are oblique. And movement in each typically requires movement in others. Yet anyone who is half honest knows how unimaginative we often are, even as it is easy to overestimate our capacities. This concern here isn't to form a new uniformity but to move beyond the stultifying limits of the uniformity that is so pervasive in the academy today in ways that enhance radical democratic imagination and practice.

We would be terribly ill-served by a new regime that has no taste for the delights and fruits of endless hours in libraries buried in difficult scholarly texts (which remain among my favorite things). Rather, we *also* need a collaborative effort that cares—and cares profoundly—for the *ecology* of bodily movements and political involvements of political theory, scholarship, and pedagogy as a whole. We need collaborative initiatives in which we ask questions about this ecology from vantage points that are almost entirely ignored in most places today. Are we cultivating among ourselves and in our relations with the broader world an ecology of practices that nurture radically democratic imagination capable of moving beyond the ruts and walls of a professionalized habitus that render us increasingly dull—sometimes even as we perform our most radical posturing? Are we engendering an ecology of practices for theorizing that is conducive to vital and capacious responses to questions of commonwealth, earth, difference, and democracy? Are the practices and discourses of political theory favorable to an expansive, powerful, and pluralizing democratic "we"— the "we" of theory, the "we" of broader commonwealth? Or are we performing a shrinking "we" that moves, sounds, and looks more inward and administrative in modality and tone?

To tend to the ecology of our practices would mean considering these questions as elemental to the development of theory and politics. We would do so in collective decisions regarding hiring, promotion, tenure, teaching, institutional support, refashioning campus spaces, rethinking who counts as credible collaborators in scholarly inquiry, rearticulating the textual genres we engage and create, curricular design, and so forth.[11] We would care for this diverse ecology as a condition of possibility for theory and scholarship that has some chance to contribute to intensifications of democracy that can journey beyond enclosures, insane inequalities, and ecological catastrophe to cocreate commonwealth.

———————

Black clouds and strong storm bands moved off across the desert. In the distance ahead, golden setting sunlight cast beams in every direction from behind Northern

Arizona's San Francisco Peaks that rise above Flagstaff, creating a dark and mysterious silhouette towering many thousand feet above us. Along this last stretch of interstate I was teeming with a giddy mix of anticipation, hopes, and aspirations, as well as some uncertainties and doubts. This journey felt right to me, but it was haunted by months of questions from many friends, colleagues, and family members, for whom my move from a top theory program to a "second-tier" public university in a state with a far-right-wing legislature that regularly expressed animosity toward education was unintelligible. Each evening for the previous few days, the car raced toward sunsets, and in the mornings, the sun was rising in the east as we were driving away. The intersecting movements of car and sunlight seemed to mirror my difficulty responding to people's consternation.

Beginnings are easier to imagine in relation to where you've been and experienced other beginnings. But as you move toward a markedly different future in a place you don't know much about, when you try to express it—not only to those who aren't going and haven't been, but even to yourself—the words you toss toward whatever glimpses of miracle you may have seen seem to either fall into a darkening horizon or to turn "biblical" in a sense that only the worst artists can portray. And so, the better part of what I had to say floated in a future that was necessarily quite indeterminate, somewhat improbable, and that always sounded (to me) a lot more grandiose than what I actually felt and imagined. Still, this sunset over a land of new beginnings was as compelling as any I've seen.

Months before this trip, in a job interview at Northern Arizona University, I had boisterously declared that if they were to offer me the directorship for the Program for Community, Culture, and Environment, I would spend a lot of my time engaged in attentive traveling in the community, seeking receptive collaborations with people in the poorer neighborhoods around town, many of whom were undocumented immigrants and Native Americans—and I would try to take a lot of students with me to community centers, schools, churches, and organizing centers because I suspected these people and places might be integral to teaching and learning about community, culture, and environment. This could get uncomfortable for the university, I noted, but generating democratic political thought and action with a vast range of people that universities typically try to exploit or ignore was vital to why I was interested in the job. I loved many of my students, colleagues, and opportunities at Duke, and I loved the political engagements in Durham that were a vital part of my daily life, but I was drawn by possibilities to help create a very different set of practices for political and ecological thought and action. And I thought the openings for such institutional change in higher education might be greater at a university that had a more regional identity, professed commitments, and set of relationships, as well as fewer pressures to be an academic in the narrower disciplinary sense of the term.

During the six years since I came to NAU, *many of my skeptical friends' and colleagues' concerns have been borne out, and this has posed great challenges: Arizona shifted farther to the right, and the sharp economic downturn of 2008 happened just as I arrived. This intersection of politics and economics led to massive budget cuts, virulent legislative attacks on ethnic studies, bills to allow concealed handguns on campuses, an unrelenting assault on all things public, and the harshest anti-immigrant regime in the nation. This shock politics has contributed to a climate of widespread fear, anxiety, cynicism, and exhaustion, as the number of tenured faculty has taken a plunge, while the number of contingent faculty and the size of the student body have grown enormously. Most of the colleagues with whom I had anticipated long-term interesting relationships have left for other universities.*

At the same time, however, the last six years have been absolutely exhilarating, as initially indeterminate aspirations developed more quickly and profoundly than I could have ever imagined and morphed into myriad forms in relationships with diverse communities. Many elements of a radical democratic and ecologically resilient habitus for thinking, teaching, learning, and acting are being created and woven together in a process that is dynamic, interdisciplinary, and supple. Each semester, many hundreds of students, faculty, and community partners are involved in action research teams that combine academic knowledge and democratic engagement with community partners on issues ranging from grassroots democracy and sustainability education in K–12 schools; to energy efficiency and renewable energy; to water conservation and rights; to alternative agriculture on campus, in community gardens, and in K–12 schools; to immigration; to public spaces; to indigenous environmental justice; to cooperative and sustainable economics; to climate change; to alternative health practices; to art and political action; to velocomposting; to queer politics; to animal oppression, and more. This is to say that hundreds of students and many faculty members find themselves moving between seminars and K–12 schools in diverse neighborhoods, community centers, social movement meetings, agricultural plots, city council meetings, congregations, neighborhoods many would otherwise likely never visit, occasional street protests, and so on. In close conjunction with action research teams and seminars, a host of other spaces and practices are emerging—from self-organizing residential learning communities, to a green café, to sustainable student-organized gardens, to poetry jams, to a solidarity economy center called Mercado de los Sueños. For all the challenges we face, there is a level of enthusiasm for this work among students and faculty that is incomparable on campus: growing numbers of people are getting involved; modest yet significant resources are flowing our way; and promising forms of theory, scholarship, pedagogy, and political practice are pressing into being. Similar enthusiasms for this work are growing among members and groups in the wider community and to a lesser but significant degree among some in the university administration.

I am an avid cyclist, and I find myself cycling an hour or two each day back and forth across town (a person who has trouble being on time, I am always sprinting) to meetings where we are in dialogue, imagining, organizing, learning, thinking anew, frequently discovering "smooth stones" and different ways to use them. The habitus we are creating is coursing with movement—people walking attentively and listening to stories in unfamiliar neighborhoods, struggling to bridge histories of colonialism, hostility, and indifference through attentive conversations and collaborations for a complex, plural, and dynamic commonwealth. We are relearning how to regenerate ecological resilience through macro and micro political movements, and also by tending to the soil, plants, and creatures that live here—the way water moves across the land, how plants grow near the south faces of stones.

Why am I telling you all this? As I have said, this book is not simply about these things, this pedagogy, the specifics of this political work and action—it is also *from* this work and action. It is imagined, theorized, practiced, and written from this strange and evolving habitus, as well as the intersection of this habitus and the habitus that still prevails in most universities and conferences where I also regularly collaborate. Hence, when I am discussing mirror neurons, resonance, circulation, complex dynamic systems theory, democratic natality, hope, and social movements—even in the most philosophical moments, I am often thinking from this work and these intersections, informed and inspirited by them in ways that offer something that I think is somewhat distinctive among scholars. I am also a strange radical evangelist *for* these types of habitus. I hope my account is interesting.

It is intentionally polyvocal, in the sense that it is written with more than one audience in mind. On the one hand, I continue to engage in the scholarly conversations and communities that have excited me for decades in spite of the detrimental limits discussed here. This book seeks to make a contribution there, even as no minor part of this contribution is to call the habitus of conventional academia and politics into question—to call many of those who inhabit it to move and attend to the world differently. On the other hand, the book is also written *to* and *for* those engaged in or searching for alternative modes of theorizing, pedagogy, and political practice. It seeks to make a contribution concerning *a way* of pulling these endeavors into new relationships that may enable us to become more capable of initiating new and more hopeful paths before it is too late—or perhaps even after that. In this text I interweave these endeavors, but I also give each the space I think it needs in order to do its work and sing its own song.

———————

I conceive of the work that follows as *visionary pragmatism*. One important way to think of visionary pragmatism is as an energetic refusal of how these two words have so often been opposed to each other, by people on more than one side of more than one antagonism. Visionary pragmatists seek the resonance *and* dissonance of this pairing, even as others generate contradictory frames to secure various borders of theory and politics.

Consider the terms. On the one hand, people invested in politics and theory that adheres to the textures, flows, and limits of the present often marshal pragmatism to dismiss far-ranging critique and alternative vision as impractical, irrelevant, and hence of no value to the world that matters. Unjust suffering is happening now, and we should attend to it in ways that have short- and medium-term impacts on the current order of things. We should work with the standard tools that are available, even as we make some adjustments. This kind of pragmatist often uses this argument to fence his or her work off from calls for more "transformative" theory and practice.[12] On the other hand, many who are invested in projects for radical critical thought and political action explicitly refuse the demand that theory (and political engagement) be oriented by ambitions that are practical and relevant according to the present horizons of time, spatiality, and meaning.[13] Often the most important work we can do may be to question those horizons and seek possibilities—however indeterminate and distant—beyond their dead ends of violence, injustice, and ecocide. Such disruption, whether by means of theory or political practice, can be extremely important, long before an alternative horizon and political strategies have been articulated. "Pragmatism" here names a line to be criticized rather than crossed.

In refusing this binary, visionary pragmatism is *pragmatic* insofar as it relentlessly thinks, works, and acts on the limits of the present, drawing forth and engendering new resonances, receptivities, relationships, movements, circulations, dynamics, practices, powers, institutions, strategies, shocks, and so forth, in an effort to contribute to desirable changes in our lived worlds. Yet it is *visionary* in the sense that it maintains an intransigent practice of peering underneath, above, around, through, and beyond the cracks in the destructive walls and mainstream ruts of this world. It lingers in eddies, catches cross-currents, and cultivates new flows that spill through these cracks and flood beyond the banks. It has an unquenchable appetite for visions that come from beyond hegemonic common sense or exceed it from within, and it devotes itself to looking for clues of these, listening to whispers near and far that articulate suggestive possibilities beyond the assumed boundaries, and seeking modes of political engagement that help inspire, energize, inform, and enact them. The ways that we think, work, and act are forever informed and inspired by visions—both immanent and transcendent—that again and again call us to "do a new thing" that nurtures democratic possibilities and ecological flourishing. And doing new things may nurture such visions.

Visionary pragmatism is oriented by a profound sense that the alternative resonances, flows, and system dynamics associated with the political work and action of a radical democratic habitus can be indispensable for opening our senses and enhancing our capacities for theorizing and scholarship. Moreover, I shall argue that when such work and action is done well, it can create self-regenerating dynamics that enliven rather than vitiate the richly emergent characteristics of game-transformative practices. For visionary pragmatists, then, vision and pragmatism must often be dynamically interwoven in order to avoid quickly taking reified forms that become increasingly functional for the dominant order. Visionary pragmatists recognize ways in which each side can also threaten and undermine the other, but we believe that it is necessary to take these risks because the binary alternatives (when they are pursued in ways that intensify homogeneous academic ecologies on either side) are almost always employed in ways that lead to theoretical and political dead ends.

When I say that this book is written from the radical democratic habitus we are generating, I mean that it is opened, oriented, energized, and informed by the mobile intersections of theory and practice that are pressed into being there, in ways that may be integral to radical democratic and ecologically resilient transformations. Insofar as we take seriously at least some of the ways in which theory and travel have been closely associated for eons, this claim should not be so preposterous as to be met with dismissal. What is involved is not a claim to epistemological privilege, but rather a theory of some of the conditions of movement and practice that are conducive to and generative of alternative and promising insights. Like all insights, these need to be examined, explored, criticized, and extended from a variety of angles and in a variety of engagements. To make a claim for certain possibilities of insight that may occur in the movements of a radical democratic habitus is not to make pretenses to epistemological invulnerability, but just the opposite. Only by undergoing vulnerable encounters and criticism is there any hope of learning how we might live less poorly—or even well. Yet visionary pragmatists will insist that critical self-reflection upon the habitus in relationship to which one thinks, works, and acts becomes an integral part of the conversation, for in the absence of such reflection, our endeavors will be "precritical" in the worst possible manner. This insight is as old as traveling theory.

The chapters that follow offer a visionary pragmatic account of an emergent habitus of radical and ecological democracy. Both critical and generative, each chapter analyzes a dimension of power that is an elemental aspect of the contemporary catastrophe and explores emergent counterpractices and alternative practices in relation to it that are beginning to generate ethical-political powers that I take to be indispensable to promising movements for democracy, ecological resilience, and commonwealth. Of course, these different aspects of power are not isolated from each other but rather interconnected in amplificatory webs—in both their catastrophic and their more hopeful forms. My discussions in each chapter move back and forth between theory and scholarship drawn from many fields and from participant-observer accounts from the democracy and ecology movement in which I have been a leader during the past six years at Northern Arizona University and in Northern Arizona.

In chapter 1, "The Neuropolitical Habitus of Resonant Receptive Democracy," I begin with a critical analysis of the contemporary right-wing resonance machine and turn to how we might theorize and practice a politics of radically receptive resonance that animates rather than euthanizes democratic relationships and power. I was drawn to this theme as I experienced and reflected upon face-to-face interactions both in political organizing contexts and in classrooms. Anyone who teaches young adults who have been subjected to overcrowded, underfunded, test-driven education is familiar with blank faces. The same could be said for the faces of many faculty members grown weary from shock doctrine attacks on higher education. Yet one of the most profound manifestations of radically democratic engaged pedagogies is the emergence of resonant faces: faces of university students lit up by attentive curiosity, empathy, questions, unexpected possibilities, and enthusiasm in the midst of an encounter in a nearby impoverished neighborhood, and long after; faces of k–12 students as they begin to work in a grassroots action research team, learning concepts of democracy as they explore and enact them together; faces of parents and community members challenging an elected official or a police officer in a public meeting; faces of faculty working together on a new action research network, or faces of faculty seeing their college students' faces light up in relation to the faces of third graders and their parents practicing democracy; faces of people around a table of conversation on emerging collaborations and possibilities for cooperative economics—seized by mimetic energies of excitement they can barely contain, and sometimes can't; faces of students, faculty, and community members gathered around a table deeply engaging a text that is pertinent to this action.

Early in my work at nau, I became fascinated with the interactions among excited faces because, when this work is going well, this buzz is more frequent and energetic than in most other kinds of pedagogical contexts. Often, this resonance is intertwined with the birth of public relationships, the conceptualization of new political strategies, and the imaginative articulations of emergent sensibilities and vision. My interest in the power of expressive faces was magnified as I myself frequently felt swept up and charged—theoretically and politically—when I encountered them. And so, a few passing comments on mirror neurons sent me into a rather extensive investigation of these one-fiftieth-of-a-second resonant mimetic relationships between faces and bodies that are integral to cognition and (inter)action, yet are rarely given serious attention in considerations of political life. At the intersection of moving encounters in our theory and practice, it was becoming clear that we were in the process of cocreating elements of an alternative to what William Connolly calls the "capitalist evangelical resonance machine."[14]

When nau students succeeded in getting the university to provide space and support for a sustainable café that would be a site for democratic engagement, we quickly approached Shonto Begay—a brilliant Navajo (Dine) artist whose work is expressive of many aspects of the ethos that animates engaged pedagogy—to see if he would be willing to work with students to do a large mural in the café. Through a process of extensive conversation and collaboration, an electrically beautiful painting now greets all who work and dine in this space. When Shonto and I were discussing the mural, he told me that he conceives of all his painting as a process of visual drumming—a tapping on the canvas (or wall) that resonates with the broader world to engender a visual expression that at once embodies and enlivens the vibrant interconnections among things. In a most profound sense, then, the resonance of the mural both registers and contributes to the resonant interactions of people in the café. This chapter explores these resonant relationships at the heart of our work—from the cellular level, through bodies, assemblages of bodies, specific democratic practices, and (less extensively) a variety of communications media. Through a careful—if nonexpert—engagement with the neuroscience of mirror neurons, I begin to construct an argument for the possibility of a radical democratic habitus at the cellular level that can engender and support game-transformative practices, rather than practices that are merely reproductive, as Bourdieu would suggest. I argue that these processes and mimetic energies have the potential to dislodge and provide a radical democratic alternative to the dominant resonant machine.

Chapter 2, "From Mega-circulatory Power to Polyface Flows," pursues themes of resonant *movement* that begin to emerge in chapter 1, in order to consider counterconducts and alternative conducts to the vast arteries and capillaries of circulatory power that are integral to contemporary forms of governmentality. The mirror neurons that undergird our capacities of perception, recognition, and comprehension develop in relation to the movements of our own bodies and those of others with whom we are engaged. This chapter tends more carefully not only to the character of these movements but also to the movements of our bodies in relation to the world of beings and things that is set into circulation (or already moving) all around us. The chapter begins with a discussion of Foucault's interpretation of ways in which contemporary power operates through the proliferation, management, and juxtaposition of massive circulations, and develops these insights in the context of gargantuan flows of oil, corn, factory-farmed animals, water, people, finance, capital, political power, military, soil, and so forth. I understand the increasingly hybridized and fluid forms of political economy that Sheldon Wolin calls superpower and inverted totalitarianism as institutional articulations of this circulatory regime. In the context of a world and people increasingly being reengineered according to the imperatives of this malignant circulatory apparatus, this chapter examines a plethora of new—yet often unrecognized—social movements that are creating an assemblage of "new materialist" counterflows and alternative flows of things, beings, energy, people, capital, and radical democratic practices of moving democracy.[15]

I examine and theorize these new materialist social movements primarily through the lens of alternative agriculture and food politics (and to a lesser extent, renewable energy) initiatives that are proliferating at impressive rates, developing a notion of "polyface" flows inspired by Emmanuel Levinas's notion of the "face" and radical eco-farmer Joel Salatin's practices of cultivating receptive flows on his Polyface Farm. In the form of thousands of farmers' markets, community-supported agriculture (CSA) arrangements, grassroots community gardening initiatives, food policy councils, farm-to-school collaborations, fair trade practices—as well as inflections of each by environmental justice initiatives that address issues of class and race—alternative patterns of material flows and powers are emerging that increasingly contest the neoliberal regime of governmentality. In a project focused solely on circulatory politics, there would be space to develop similar accounts in relation to emergent flows of people and things in the realm of energy, water, soil, clothing, capital, finance, medicine, transportation, new monasticism, and so forth.

The ethics and politics of movement and new materialist flows are a vital element in our public work, political action, and theoretical reflection at NAU, and these surely inform the work that follows. Indeed, before I came to NAU, my political involvements with Durham CAN (Congregations, Associations, and Neighborhoods, an Industrial Areas Foundation affiliate)—particularly the ways in which receptive movement across the city was integral to the organizing process—played an indispensable role in theorizing "moving democracy," which developed related insights.[16] In our action research teams, we are continually imagining, theorizing, and enacting an alternative politics of circulation based on attentive movements. In our grassroots democracy education initiative, scores of students travel to schools in neighborhoods in Flagstaff, where they form relationships by listening attentively and coaching K–12 students to work together in ways that are similarly attentive. Meanwhile broader community organizing efforts with which we collaborate practice a similar politics of receptive relationship building across myriad differences of places, people, and so forth. In the campus, community, and school garden action teams, attentive and careful movement with plants, soil, compost, and water forms the heart of our work—as do experiments with establishing healthy symbiotic microflows and relationships among all these elements and among the diverse peoples involved in the gardens. Hence, quotidian experiences with people who are reflectively involved in such flows have played a vital role in giving birth to the theoretical work that follows.

This habitus of emerging flows (at NAU and in many other places as well) also importantly informs the writing that follows insofar as I write (partly) to those involved in these practices. Specifically, in this chapter I am concerned to provide a narrative and theoretical understanding of this work and action that suggests an alternative to more territorial and nostalgic readings and self-interpretations. It is not uncommon in the literatures on environment and place to inflect this work toward *rooting*, reestablishing deep connections with localities, creating a relocalized dominion of land stewardship, and returning to a nostalgic sense of the simplicity of an earlier time. In contrast, it is crucial to supplement rooting narratives with narratives that accent *routing*—a political ecology of receptive and generous movements in the midst of a world teeming with human and nonhuman complexities, migrants, and differences.[17] A new materialist politics of tending ought to be understood and practiced as deterritorializing, nurturing relationships across myriad scales and dimensions of being, becoming inventive and imaginative of complex dynamic practices, and cultivating hospitality as a central motif in our thought, work, and action. The theory of receptive circulation—or polyface flows—seeks to illuminate and intensify what I take to be most hopeful in new materialist movements, at a time when problems of ecological catastrophe and human dislocation are growing rapidly along with dangers of resurgent racism, xenophobia, and class-war-from-above politics.

While chapter 2 builds on chapter 1 by focusing on movement more than resonant receptivity—even as the two are utterly intertwined—its most distinctive contribution is to show how cocreating a radical and ecological democratic habitus greatly hinges upon how we both craft and tend to flows of beings and things around us, and how we let be vast portions of the circulations of air, water, soil, insects, flora, and fauna in ecological systems in which we are immersed. The question of how we move attentively (or not) in relation to the flows of beings and things we let be, and how we foster, interweave, and tend to flows of other beings and things we set in motion is integral to the kind of ethical-political powers we are able to bring forth in human and nonhuman communities.

If we accept that radical democratic and ecologically resilient pedagogies and politics are emerging that contest and venture alternatives to dominant forms of contemporary power, are there reasons to be hopeful that these still comparatively small movements might suggest possibilities with any significant chance of engendering systemic transformation? Given that such movements are often radically precarious and short-lived, is there reason to think that recent democratic initiatives might engender a degree of resilience? And if so, what sorts of insights and theoretical analyses might enhance these possibilities?

In chapter 3, "System Dynamics and a Radical Politics of Transformative Co-optation," I argue that systems theory can make indispensable contributions to the potential and transformative power of radically democratic initiatives. It enables us to understand emergence, duration, resilience, and self-organizing transformation as immanent conditions of each other's possibility and power, and it offers a compelling heuristic for theorizing and organizing.

While my interest in systems theory dates back to my undergraduate fascination with Gregory Bateson, Irvin Laszlo, Ludwig Bertalanffy, and myriad articulations in ecology, physics, chemistry, sociology, economics, and political theory, I leave most of that to the side in this chapter. For my ambition here has nothing to do with providing an extensive scholarly engagement with the terrain of systems thinking as such. Broad overviews of core ideas have been provided many times, including discussions of insights that have become widespread, as well as those that are the subject of intense contestation. In her classic work, *Thinking in Systems*, Donella Meadows focuses on introducing "core ideas" while leaving "the leading edge" for others to address.[18] In contrast, in chapter 3, I focus my engagement on one "leading edge" of complex dynamical systems theory, namely, Stuart Kauffman's theory of self-organization, and examine what it might offer to the theory and practice of organizing resilient forms of democratic emergence. I am particularly interested in Kauffman's ideas on autocatalysis—or the ways in which processes generate conditions of their own reproduction and thereby acquire self-generative characteristics.

Ultimately, I think that Kauffman's work in complex dynamic systems theory suggests ways of understanding and seeking to cocreate democratic transformation that make significant advances over much contemporary democratic theory and practice. Kauffman de-reifies systems so that they no longer appear a priori as closed totalities. Instead, they are complex assemblages of processes in relation to which it may be possible to generate emergent autocatalytic dynamics that tip systems toward alternative equilibriums, transformed patterns, and so forth. If systems are mutable in these ways, then antidemocratic systems of political economy ought to once again become a focus of our transformative energies, rather than forces we accept as immutable—attempting merely to hold them somewhat "accountable" from the terrain of "civil society."

One of the most significant insights in this chapter concerns a theory and practice of *co-optative systems dynamics*. The idea here is that we can link certain aspects of radically democratic autocatalytic systems dynamics to particular dynamics of non- or antidemocratic systems in order to co-opt them in ways that intensify our own powers. As we connect with certain nondemocratic system dynamics in order to advance autocatalytic features of our own, we can exponentially expand our capacities to resist and transform neoliberalism. Indeed, this co-optation has been one of the most important innovations—and an elemental condition—of the radical and ecological democracy movement at NAU and in Northern Arizona. If it were to spread to other institutions of higher education and regions, it would be nothing short of revolutionary.

Kauffman's work adds significant insight into how emergence and duration ought to be conceived as conditions of each other's possibility—rather than antitheses, as many strands of contemporary political analysis and theory would have it. In this way, his thinking further contributes to our effort to theorize the possibility of cultivating a radical democratic habitus. Moreover, if natality and persistence may be best understood as potentially cogenerative, then theoretical reflections concerning specific modes of organizing radical democracy can move beyond the antinomy in which organization is either ignored or gestural, on the one hand, or so foundational that the basic modes of organizing are themselves largely removed from democratic processes of contestation and emergence, on the other. My sense is that Kauffman's theory of modular "patchwork" learning processes provides a compelling heuristic for reflecting on democratic organizing in theory and practice.

As with the other chapters, my engagement with Kauffman stems from our efforts to create a radical democratic habitus. His theory of autocatalysis drew my attention in the way that it did precisely because I found myself involved in numerous initiatives in which we were attempting to catalyze democratic energies and dynamics that might become more self-sustaining and resilient. Kauffman provided a theoretical lens that both made sense of and has powerfully informed some of our efforts. At the same time, our efforts predisposed some of us to read his work on chemical reactions and biological dynamics in ways that developed radical democratic implications that move significantly beyond his own forays into politics and economics.

In the last chapter of this book, "Shock Democracy and Wormhole Hope in Catastrophic Times," I step back to reassess possibilities for political transformation in the context of neoliberal shock politics and the likelihood of climate catastrophe. I argue that Naomi Klein's work ought to become more salient in contemporary theories of power. In a grim supplement to the complex intertwinements and modulations of circulatory biopolitics, disciplinary power, and sovereignty, shock politics repeatedly sends devastating charges through political bodies. Contemporary power works by means of alternating currents: it sends shocking surges of power that tend to level old and new resistances, followed by mega-circulations that proliferate capillary flows, microresonances, and autocatalytic dynamics in ways that reengineer people, things, urban spaces, and finance, followed again by additional shock surges that further decimate resistance and create conditions for renewed intensifications of governmentalized circulations, resonances, and so on.

If we return to the narrative of David and Goliath, in which David's performance intimates key themes that are characteristic of game-transformative practices, we might say that in contemporary times, Goliath has become a masterful David. Goliath has learned the arts of radical and relentless game transformation. In the form of global neoliberal capitalism, Goliath is no longer a dumb giant but a dynamic malignancy that has developed transformative powers of an alternating current that are nearly unfathomable. In this context, we must supplement the work we have done in earlier chapters. It is not enough to learn from David in our efforts to initiate the game-transformative practices of a radical democratic habitus. We must also learn from the Goliath who has learned from David, without becoming ourselves what is horrendous about Goliath.

I theorize this in terms of the need to carefully interweave the shocking politics of outrageous ephemeral protest performances—such as Occupy, the Battle of Seattle, the nationwide immigrant marches, 350.org rallies—with the quotidian politics and receptive flows of broad-based community organizing. While others have called for making such connections in order that the momentary characteristics of the former can be channeled into the more durable modalities of the latter, I accent another aspect of the relationship between these two political modalities. In my view, the most profound reason that the two modes must be intertwined in a complex and subtle strategy is that the political natality of each mode hinges on the political natality of the other. Hence the democratic political capacities of each are greatly hampered when disconnected from the other. Nevertheless, one of the most common moves in contemporary democratic theory is to "take sides"—affirming one modality over the other. This unwittingly unplugs the powers of each. What we can learn from the Goliath who has learned from David is that when dramatic surges are connected with micropolitical flows and resonances in the politics of alternating currents, each grows more powerful as it empowers the other. In the context of our discussion of movements for radical democracy and ecological resilience, this means that the politics of receptive resonance and attentive circulation can greatly enhance its autocatalytic system dynamics if it can connect the natalities of dramatic action with those of quotidian politics of tending. This is, I think, indispensable for cultivating transformative power in our times.

Nevertheless, even if we make significant headway on this latter front in order to effectively counter shock politics, we will still face the overwhelming likelihood that climate change will radically erode the stability that has characterized the Holocene period during which human civilizations of the past ten thousand years have taken form. We will face a storm-shocked Eaarth (to borrow Bill McKibben's term).[19] My sense is that this will require that we develop capacities to modulate genres in order not to succumb to cycles of self-reinforcing despair. Visionary pragmatism orients us toward working with our chin up to build expansive imagination and a movement that enhances radical democratic power and ecological resilience. However much this work always faces setbacks and discontinuities, visionary pragmatism accents a kind of at least modestly hopeful politics in which prospects for imagining and building a movement with substantial continuity are not unreasonable. I take it that this genre is an indispensable aspect of radical democracy, even as long-term horizons, wild patience, and the unanticipatable must be a constitutive part of the strange perspective it offers.

Nevertheless, my guess is that though necessary, this will not be sufficient. Human beings will likely face a world in which storms, droughts, floods, fires, and so forth, will far more often destabilize much that we seek to build, and repeatedly create massive numbers of climate refugees—all of which will likely pose monumental challenges that not infrequently overwhelm our capacities to cope well and maintain desirable continuities. In the context of a storm-shocked Eaarth, then, we will likely also require something like what I call "wormhole hope," in order to cultivate passage across especially bleak periods to come. Wormhole hope is a faith that the better intensities of movements for democratic communities and ecological care can survive underground, across vast stretches of time and space where they appear to be absent, and resurface with an uncanny power to establish resurgent relationships for democratic and ecological renewal across apparently impossible and discontinuous times and places. It is a faith that our best works will endure in this way, even if they "fail" according to more continuous coordinates of time and space, by which we must also continue to orient our endeavors. It is a faith in strange future possibilities that is born of histories in which we have seen retrospectively, time and again, how unfathomable—and unfathomably powerful—connections happen across vast expanses of time and space in which continuities (of democracy, freedom, equality, etc.) were not discernible. Such connections, then, rapidly develop powers to disrupt and transform the continuities (of hierarchy, subjugation, inequality, ecocide, etc.) that we had come to think were immutable.

This happens; we know it does. It may seem bleak to raise the need for cultivating such faith in the context of a visionary pragmatic work. Yet I don't see it this way, partly because the darkness stems not from the theory but from the conditions in which we will likely find ourselves, and partly because visionary pragmatism will be neither visionary nor pragmatic if it fails to address a world in which continuities will more frequently be disrupted. When lines of vision, work, and action that we may presently take for granted are broken, we will need to cultivate ways of seeing, working, and acting that can harbor and unfold different kinds of power across especially dark times. This is to say that a visionary pragmatism that fails to address tragedy will almost certainly succumb to it, whereas one that cultivates wormhole hope may have significant resources for generating words and deeds that make indispensable contributions to maintaining Ralph Ellison's "raft of hope" when the seas become especially stormy and wash across much of the land—or when the waters depart.[20]

Once we recognize the ways in which ricocheting trajectories often unexpectedly connect struggles across the most disparate times, territoriality comes undone insofar as these connections leap far beyond spatial borders in ways that are impossible to control. Consider how the theory and practice of nonviolence leaps from Jesus in the Middle East, to Thoreau in New England, to Tolstoy in Russia, to Gandhi in India, to Martin Luther King Jr. and the Student Nonviolent Coordinating Committee across the U.S. South, and beyond. These movements cannot be controlled by the master narratives of nation-state sovereignty. Like ecosystems whose flourishing depends on what Rebecca Solnit poetically refers to as "weightless seeds" that come from far away—literal seeds, and metaphoric ones like rain, water, birds, fish, insects, and migrating mammals—so too does the flourishing of human communities. In a world that will soon be populated by many hundreds of millions of climate refugees, nothing will be more important than deterritorializing radical and ecological democratic sensibilities and practices. To this end, I argue that the "hospitality for weightless seeds"—for all those tossed into motion by shock doctrine and a storm-shocked planet—is indispensable if we are to avoid absolute barbarism.

These reflections on wormhole hope and the hospitality for weightless seeds, too, emerged in the context of our efforts to create political and pedagogical transformation, examining questions of what and how we ought to "pass on" to younger generations, dwelling as we are in the U.S. Southwest, which by all accounts is likely to become one of the epicenters of climate catastrophe—and is already the epicenter of migration from the south and neofascistic responses to it. What does it mean to learn and teach to live well—to speak, love, work, tend, and act politically in ways that cultivate relationships and a world we want to see, and help us survive the storm-shocked world we want not? Such questions come with nearly unbearable poignancy from younger people awakening both to theories and practices of radical hope and to a human and ecological catastrophe in their midst of proportions they had never dreamed. A broadening and deepening "we" is learning and struggling to respond. Much of what follows is emerging in this process.

CHAPTER I

The Neuropolitical Habitus of Resonant Receptive Democracy

It is early in the evening, and dozens of people are beginning to pack a class-room in San Francisco de Asis Catholic School in Flagstaff, Arizona. As the circle of chairs fills, people begin to gather behind them—standing, sitting on tables, propped on windowsills, leaning against walls—wherever we can squeeze ourselves in. Our bodies are shifting frequently as we wait for the meeting to begin. Some people are making eye contact; some are avoiding it altogether. Some are conspicuously outgoing, while others are trying to fold their bodies into shadows of anonymity. There is that palpable mix of solidarity, giddy courage, uncertain hope, and trepidation that characterizes the outset of many political meetings where grand aspirations engage age-old suffering across entrenched axes of power. At last the police chief and one of his officers walk in. As promised, they are without their badges and here to listen.

Most of the people in the room are either undocumented immigrants or people who are in familial, friendship, or political relationships with them. For months we have been organizing in one-to-one meetings, house meetings, and action team meetings leading up to this event, gathering stories, developing a frame for our work, cultivating our networks, strategizing about how to tackle the problem of racial profiling and harassment of people who look to police like they may come from south of the border. The problem is intense: youth walk the streets with their eyes to the ground as if they could avoid the police—yet still get stopped; people are pulled over and interrogated for no apparent reason; people are arrested, sent to Immigration and Customs Enforcement (ICE), and deported—leaving behind families that are separated and desperate. Frightened people are refusing to call the police when real crimes occur and better modes of policing might be useful.

Yet this evening the feeling in the room is remarkably not that of people trembling before the arbitrary forces of the law and lawlessness. There is a sense of emergent democratic power: people coming together to publicly tell their narratives, render their accounts of an intolerable situation, and act in ways that begin to address discrimination and tend to the abused commonwealth. One after another, people stand up and speak in detail—some in English, some in Spanish—about how they or their loved ones and friends have been repeatedly harassed. Some step forward and hover over the seated chief of Flagstaff's police as they speak powerfully and at full volume, even as they remain respectful. People in the room embrace and amplify the words of those who speak with affirmative nods, attentive postures, sighs of compassion, and expressions of collective frustration. Importantly, people are attentive across lines of difference that have frequently shut down receptive relationships and solidarities. Not only are they listening across lines of race and class, but Hispanics whose families have been residents for generations are listening to and working with recently arrived Latino/as, and though people are assertive and firm with the police chief, they listen to him when he speaks, and many sense that he is actually listening to them (a sense borne out when his testimony later convinces the Flagstaff City Council to lobby in Phoenix against the infamous anti-immigrant bill, s.b. 1070). There is a vibe in the room, a receptive and powerful resonance that starts to shake the foundation of the house of "dry hate" that Arizona has built. The vibe travels across and opens political time—from sparks of illumination and enthusiasm in meetings past, into this meeting, through ongoing political action and potent senses of possibility continuing over the years, to the moment I write—even as the problems remain huge. Moreover, the vibe has traveled across myriad issues of a growing democracy movement in Northern Arizona—from immigration, to schools, to green energy, to LGBTQ rights, to water, to cooperative economics, to composting.

Around the same time that this resonant work and action were happening, I was biking to Killip Elementary School in the Sunnyside neighborhood (where some of the worst police abuses frequently take place) to discuss a grassroots democracy education project that we had recently launched there. On the way, I was hit by an SUV that hurled me twenty feet and then slammed into me again. Luckily, only my knee suffered serious injury. Nevertheless, during the following months I found myself spending a fair amount of time in medical waiting rooms subjected to FOX and other news stations prior to the surgery and many appointments that followed the accident. Though I was, of course, familiar with many intellectual critiques of media misinformation, the affective degradation of the culture industry, and the ways in which the resonant practices of the virtual sphere are integral to contemporary power, the visceral experience was nevertheless overwhelming. There were scary portrayals of Mexicans creeping across the Arizona border; angry sheriffs and politicians claiming they were coming to do "us" harm; far-right pundits furious about how liberals and even moderate Republicans were failing to protect us; conjured images of dirty mothers who were seeking to plant "anchor babies" on our soil; law enforcement glorifications of militarized police raids; early accusations from Tucson School Board members and legislators that those who taught ethnic studies were engaged in a tribalist plot to de-Americanize our country. This drumbeating about "illegal aliens" created a rhythm that insinuated itself into inane commentary on insidious communist climate scientists lying to us about global warming in order to destroy our way of life and freedom. The continuous audiovisual resonance of loud voices, angry faces, mad gestures, and scary portrayals of creeping brown people contributed to a powerful affective undertow across the state whose surface effects could be seen as voters and elections began an extreme rightward shift. The pulsating fury of these audiovisual performances appeared to be shutting down human capacities for paying attention, receptivity, and curiosity and tarrying with the complexities of different people's lives.

Meanwhile, this resonance machine was having profound effects in the largely Hispanic, Latino/a, and Native American Sunnyside neighborhood where Killip Elementary is located. Undocumented parents were working two or three jobs, often beneath the radar suffering miserable working conditions and illegally low wages, and barely able to support their families. Some fled inside their homes when they saw me—a white man—walking door-to-door in the neighborhood to discuss voter registration and political organizing. The NAU students who were "coaching" kids in the arts of grassroots democracy were increasingly seeing tears on the faces of students whose parents had been taken away in the middle of the night by ICE and panic among those who feared that their parents would be next.

Yet there were more hopeful sorts of resonance emerging as well, such as those I described around immigration organizing. Parents often volunteered together to improve the infrastructure of the school, and their bodies manifested a certain collective confidence and pride in their work. When a group of fourth- and fifth-grade students led adult members of the Killip Elementary community before the Flagstaff School Board in a successful defense against threats to scrap the year-round school calendar that worked best for the community, the stories of that meeting buzzed for a long time: the excitement of children enacting powerful citizenship; the sense of hope and utter amazement on the part of the adults who witnessed and stood in solidarity with them; the enthusiastic affirmations of the dialogical organizing processes that led up to the action. When brown, black, red, and white people from the Sunnyside neighborhood began listening to each other

*and working together in response to problems they faced, one could sense differ-
ent energetic connections emerging. Maybe it was something like what the NAU
coaches reported that they sensed in the elementary students as they facilitated
grassroots democracy teams on issues that mattered to the children. Maybe it was
like what faculty sensed when talking with the NAU coaches. Faces were lighting
up; faces and bodies were manifesting vital signs of democratic receptivity with
each other—leaning forward, twisting, turning, tilting, in ways that seemed to
manifest energies of opening. It wasn't just individual bodies, it was something
that seemed rooted in vibrant relationships among them, and I became obsessed
with trying to understand this phenomenon that appeared to be elusive yet indispensable to energetic democracy.*

Democracy—as the gathering of people across differences to contest arbitrary
and damaging inequalities; to respond to new movements, events, and situations;
and to cocreate responsive, complex, and dynamic forms of commonwealth—
hinges upon radical receptivity. By *radical* receptivity, I mean the difficult arts
of moving with responsive creativity in the face of entrenched and blinding
challenges and unfamiliar opportunities. These are arts we cultivate through
practices of learning to pay full-bodied attention, listen deeply, exercise hospitality, dwell with patience, and potentially shift our being at very deep levels
in the midst of others, events, and barely emergent possibilities that may be
unwonted, unwanted, and disturbing because they trouble our more stubborn
obtuseness, misperceptions, and assumptions about order, justice, and power.
In a rapidly changing world on the brink of collapse, where people of different traditions, new movements, and emergent experiences are tossed together
more frequently and need to generate democratic power together in order to
address problems, it is difficult to think of a more important ethical and political art. It is crucial because it is the basis for cocreative democratic solidarities
and dynamic political visions that are necessary for navigating the shifting
terrains and tiny crevasses of possibility through which we need to pass if we
are to generate pathways and powers beyond the catastrophes of the present.

Yet as these discrepant vignettes suggest, our receptive capacities may be,
variously, profoundly shut down or enlivened by resonant sounds, images,
expressions, postures, movements, interactions, and other intensities amid
which we live. In the examples of both corporate media resonances and democratic resonances of collaborative work and political action, we see that
power—whether radically democratic or steeply hierarchical—can in different

ways amplify, diminish, or inflect our receptive capacities in markedly different ways. This would suggest that at very deep, practiced, interbodily, and visceral registers we may become more or less democratic—in the sense of how well we are able to stretch ourselves receptively across differences and newness with which we are unfamiliar to seek possibilities of commonwealth we had not imagined.

As I shall explore in this chapter, contemporary neuroscience suggests that our capacities for conscious reflection and even perception are greatly shaped, oriented, limited, and propelled by resonant relationships among our bodies. Our mirror neurons "fire" preconsciously in relation to other bodies (or don't) in small fractions of a second, transmitting vast amounts of information (or not). It turns out that these relationships are profoundly intertwined with the practices in which we engage. Our capacities to perceive and think, thus, are intertwined with corporeal relationships that precede and greatly condition our perception and thought, and this conditioning influences our abilities to reflect on and modify these practices themselves.

This would appear to put us in a potentially impossible bind that impedes democratic freedom, or perhaps reveals it to be an illusion altogether. This problem is further compounded by the fact that these intercorporeal resonances are not innocent of inequalities and the toxic politics of (in)difference but rather *are themselves targets and products of modes of power invested in dampening, orienting, and limiting our receptive and reflective capacities.* This has likely always been true, but in present times the relationship between our capacities for intercorporeal resonance and contemporary practices of power is particularly salient and intense due to the ways in which such power is enmeshed with and borne by audiovisual political technologies of resonance that proliferate inequality, domination, and exclusion. In other words, contemporary modes of power operate upon and through what neuroscience increasingly reveals to be elemental registers of our cellular being. Moreover, they do so by deploying instruments, relationships, and strategies that are at once sophisticated, intense, amplified, and nearly ubiquitous in "developed" societies.

Does this mean that radical and receptive democracy is merely an illusion? If this were the case, rather than beings capable of becoming freer—individually, collectively, dialogically—we would be thoroughly engendered by what Pierre Bourdieu calls our habitus, or the coarticulation of our perceptions, thoughts, dispositions, and improvisational capacities with daily practices through which our lives are integrated into larger institutions and systems of power. "Freedom," then, would become the name for our highly limited and programmed capacities to improvise in ways that fulfill the functional requirements of our orders; and, where there are "democracies," it would also serve an ideological function that simultaneously legitimates and conceals the dense and dominating operations of power. If we are much more corporeality than consciousness, and if bodies are ensconced in practices saturated by power, would we not be trapped in ways that are nearly ontological?

In contrast, I shall argue that the paradoxes of receptive democracy and the daunting challenges we face in relation to resonant techno-practices of power need not lead us to despair. Instead, I venture here that recent work on mirror neurons helps illuminate the character of our capacities for a politics of resonant receptivity in ways that suggest indispensable possibilities for ethical and strategic modes for organizing a powerful radical democratic movement. *In so doing, neuroscience simultaneously contributes to our understanding of the possibility and importance of a more durable (less fugitive) radically democratic habitus.* While the trope "radically democratic habitus" may seem oxymoronic in light of Bourdieu's extensive rendering of "habitus" in a nondemocratic key, I suggest that research on mirror neurons discloses ways in which iterated practices and dispositional structures are crucial for democratic freedom. Indeed, the evidence suggests that bodily practices can open and enhance biocultural powers for receptivity, reflection, and radical democratic engagement, even as such powers are most often incorporated into practices of the sort that Bourdieu describes. In what follows I explore this possibility in multiple and intersecting modes—from the cellular level, to reflections on corporeal practices, to participant observations in the democracy education movement at Northern Arizona University and Flagstaff, to theoretical formulations of possibilities for a radical democratic habitus. Each register of reflection and practice both illuminates and offers support for what is most promising in the other registers. Together they disclose what I take to be promising pathways and possibilities.

In the next section, I set pertinent aspects of the political stage with an overview of what William Connolly has insightfully coined the "evangelical-capitalist resonance machine." The following section explores research on mirror neurons in order to better illuminate the phenomena of intercorporeal resonance. This exploration opens onto the third section, where I examine neurological dimensions of compulsive political closure and consider how more receptive and generous democratic initiatives might open beyond such dispositions. In the fourth section, an engagement with Pierre Bourdieu allows us to see how an alternative habitus might—somewhat paradoxically—be cultivated so that dynamic democratic openings and resonant receptivity could be rendered at once more powerful, creative, and durable. In the final section, I gather together the threads of participant observation that are interwoven in this chapter in order to further explore ways in which a radically democratic and resonant habitus might be given textured prefiguration in a series of democratically engaged pedagogical initiatives in which faculty and students at NAU are organizing with a variety of partners in broader communities in Northern Arizona.

Evangelical Capitalist Resonance Machine

At the intersection of neuroscience, political theory, and democratic practice, I am interested in exploring possibilities for cultivating capacities and powers that might both disrupt the dominant resonance machine and play an indispensable role in an alternative democratic politics characterized by increasingly receptive and generous relationships. We might call this horizon of inquiry a democracy of resonant receptivity, insofar as I am suggesting that intercorporeal resonances—energetic sensual neurological relationships among people and other beings—are a condition of radical receptivity, and such receptivity is a condition of both democratic vision and power. Yet the challenges to this project are great, as William Connolly's analysis of the "evangelical-capitalist resonance machine" makes clear.

Connolly—indebted to Gilles Deleuze and others—writes of capitalism as a resonant "*assemblage* composed through relations of imbrication [overlapping of edges], infusion [the emergence of a new thing, by immersing one substance in another, like ground coffee in water], and intercalation [creating a change by inserting one thing into the structure of another] between heterogeneous elements that simultaneously enter *into* one another to some degree, *affect* each other from the outside, and generate residual or torrential *flows* exceeding the first two modes of connection."[1] Key elements in this assemblage include corporations, financial institutions, "state policies, educational institutions, media practices, church proclivities, class experiences, and scientific practices." This assemblage supports a commonly recognized "capitalist axiomatic" and also engenders a spiritual ethos in which extreme inequality, fundamentalism, generalized *resentiment* toward difference and ambiguity, as well as bellicosity and indifference toward future generations, the poor, foreigners, and the planet often intensify one another.[2] Connolly characterizes the relationships between diverse elements in terms of "resonance" where they "*infiltrate* each other, metabolize into a moving complex. Spiritual sensibilities, economic presumptions, and the state priorities slide and blend into one another, though each also retains a modicum of independence from the others. [It is a] causation as resonance between elements that become fused to a considerable degree. Now causality, as relations of dependence between separate factors, morphs into energized complexities of mutual imbrication and inter-involvement, in which elements heretofore unconnected or loosely associated fold, bend, blend, emulsify, and resolve incompletely into each other."[3]

The language of causality as resonance suggests how, for example, theologies of a punitive god, economic theories that blame the poor for their poverty, xenophobic nationalist tendencies to demonize people slipping through walled states, and proclamations about communist climate scientists are drawn into mutually amplifying relations that then "morph into energized complexities." Affective intensities from several different loci of practice resonate with each other in ways that engender alignments exceeding those that could be formed through explicit articulations (say, between secular economists and fundamentalist Christians). Resonance often operates beneath and between explicit articulations by means of images, music, tone of voice, facial expression, bodily posture and gesture, tempo, types of aesthetic objects, modalities of genuflection, and collective performances of hostility. In this type of "machine," resonant relationships happen as our bodies move through and experience the myriad institutions, practices, energetic flows, and representations that mobilize and intensify one another through operative relationships of visceral similitude. The virtual world of electronic media—network news, televangelists, press conferences, blogospheres, TV and radio talk shows, Internet, Twitter, movies, YouTube, corporatized tele-education, infomercials, and so forth—is powerfully implicated in and often constitutive of our experiences of different domains and their relationships. While the electronic sphere conveys, infuses, and mediates resonances among elements that are irreducible to itself, this sphere *is itself an elementally resonant audiovisual medium.* By this I mean that its existence consists of resonant waves of light and sound that vibrate through our bodies and surroundings—from living rooms, to classrooms, to offices, to waiting rooms, to sporting events, to churches, in our cars, on airplanes, in shopping spaces, at restaurants, and so on—engendering experiences, dispositions, attention, inattention, and intensities of feeling, as well as practical engagements, relationships, and interactions. We are increasingly vibrated into being by these visceral practices of technopolitical resonance. In short, in Connolly's account, resonance refers *both* to amplificatory affinities of affect, bodily comportment, and spiritual sensibility among multiple sectors *and* to the resonant audiovisual technologies that fold them together and proliferate their presence.

While most of the democratic left in recent decades has missed this aspect of political life, the right wing has invested its time, money, and organizing efforts across a wide array of resonant venues with great success. An effective challenge to this evangelical-capitalist resonance machine requires "a countermachine": "a political assemblage composed of multiple constituencies whose diverse experiences resonate together, finding expression in churches, schools, factories, neighborhoods, the media, occupational groups, the electorate, a segment of the capitalist class, state policy and cross-state movements."[4] Such a counterresonance machine, Connolly suggests, would cultivate a spiritual ethos of pluralization that is more capacious toward difference, more egalitarian, experimental, and ecologically responsible.

I too seek to contribute to a theory and practice of resonance that disrupts and disestablishes the dominant exploitative resonance machines of our day and simultaneously enhances relational capacities for receptive generosity, dialogic power, and vital ecological sense. Part of such a project involves considering ways in which we may employ currently dominant modalities and practices of resonance in different ways and toward different ends. Yet my focus here is to inquire into how resonance *as such* might be reconceived and reworked—even *re-resonated in radically receptive democratic modes*—in ways that are vital for the relationality, ethos, and power of an engaged, hospitable, and ecological democracy. We tend to think of resonance primarily in amplificatory terms, asking how our powers to express, broadcast, and convey might be enhanced. Though I am interested in relationships and energies that increase the projective volume and affinities of radical and ecological democracy, I am even more interested in how we might generate resonant relational energies that enhance our *receptivity*—or, as bass player Victor Wooten puts it, modes of resonance that "*turn up . . . our receiving volume*" (my emphasis).[5]

Might it not be possible and indeed necessary to reimagine resonance *in radically receptive democratic terms*, such that we would work with resonance *less* as a relatively stable *type* of energy we must redeploy (though surely we must) and *more* as a phenomenon that must *itself* undergo elemental transformations if we are to advance radical democracy? Such transformations, I suggest, would involve modulating and intensifying the receptive aspects of the resonant intercorporeal networks of mirror neurons. Here resonance would be less about what is already shared and more about our capacities for developing a hospitable sense and disposition toward differences we do not yet quite perceive and understand, as well as for emergent phenomena. I suggest that such *transformations in the very character of resonant energy* are among the *most vital conditions* for the counter-ethos, counterconducts, countermovements, and counterpowers through which a distinctly radical, ecological, and hospitable democracy might emerge. In a nutshell, such changes would involve a type of receptive resonance toward opening, questioning, and ground transformation.

Mirror Neurons and Receptive Intercorporeal Resonance

There are important ways in which neuroscience can shed light on intercorporeal receptive resonance in relation to ethics and politics. Elsewhere, I have employed many genres of inquiry to illuminate this theme—from political theory, to philosophy, to theology, to historical and participant observer work on social movements, to ecology, and more. I do not employ neuroscience here as a determinative or privileged discourse in relation to ethics and politics, but rather as one that is suggestive and informative in ways that must be dialogically mediated with a variety of other modes of inquiry and practice. Indeed, mirror neurons are a biocultural phenomena; moreover, scientific inquiry is always already entangled with other modes of inquiry in patterns of world disclosure that inflect scientific efforts even as we have significant capacities to mediate these over time. Processes of illumination, in this context, require that we explore the reciprocal implications of different modes. My discussion here seeks to contribute to and inspire further inquiries that draw upon multiple modes of reflection.

To situate my earlier suggestion about the possibility and importance of transforming resonant energy, first consider a couple of reflections on resonance from complex dynamic systems theory. Ilya Prigogine and Isabelle Stengers (advancing a line of inquiry initially formulated by Henri Poincaré) argue that resonant relationships among the energetic frequencies of all moving bodies disrupt Newtonian trajectories and thereby provoke elemental events analogous to Epicurus's *clinamen*—or contingent atomic swerves. Such interactive energy plays a vital role in the birth, sustenance, and disruption of many orders of things, and its presence challenges the false dichotomy between a universe governed by Newtonian causality, on the one hand, and pure human freedom, on the other. According to Prigogine and Stengers, "human creativity and innovation can be understood as the amplification of laws of nature already present in chemistry and physics," when the latter are understood to be fundamentally infused with resonant energies that introduce probabilistic contingency into being and becoming.[6] At their most radical, they argue that resonance is "at the root" of thingness in a most basic sense, insofar as resonance not only is what happens among, to, and in things but also is constitutive of the very emergence of things. They make this case not only with regard to observable phenomena ranging from the subatomic to the cosmological but also in terms of speculations on the origin of the universe, in which they suggest that the very birth of space, substance, and the irreversible "arrow of time" may be a consequence of instabilities of resonant energy that provoked the big bang.

Yet if Prigogine and Stengers help us understand the centrality of resonant energy in the universe and its *continuity* with specifically human freedom, it is also true that the resonance between and among humans beings (and among humans, nonhuman beings, and things) is profoundly *different* from that among subatomic particles. Inquiry into resonant energy and radical democratic transformation requires that we attend to *both* the continuities *and* the changes undergone by resonance in various processes of emergence. To gain insight here, it is helpful to draw on the work of John Holland, a theorist of complexity who has played a leading role at the Santa Fe Institute.

Holland is much less attentive to resonance than Prigogine and Stengers, yet he is wonderfully insightful about ways in which simple laws enable new relationships and "persistent patterns" that "*generate emergent behavior far beyond the individual [unrelated elements'] capacities*" (my emphasis).[7] Each emergent pattern transforms the capacities and possibilities of the materials from which it is made. When emergence happens, in vital respects the "same stuff" does not remain the same—as, for example, when we shift from subatomic to atomic to molecular to organic materialities. Moreover, at new levels of combination in which responsive capacities for adaptation and learning emerge, the "*possibilities for emergence [themselves] increase rapidly* as the flexibility of the interactions increases" (my emphasis).[8] Human capacities amplify and transform such possibilities for emergent recombination, particularly our facility for discerning metaphoric relationships of similarity—and, I argue later, registering resonance—amid differences. Though Holland does not explore the possibility, his discussion of our metaphoric capacities and pleasures suggests that new patterns of relationship generate *emergent characteristics* not only in relation to constitutive elements, but also in regard to *resonant energies and relationships*—especially when read in light of Prigogine and Stengers. *With sentient life-forms and human beings, resonance acquires*

distinctive, emergent, particularly receptive, and amplificatory potentials: reso-
nance re-resonates.

Yet how might we understand specifically human-related resonance? What role might it play in human receptivity, cognition, reflexivity, ethical-political community, and the arts of transformative political organizing? These questions become particularly complex and salient if, as I have suggested, the character of such energy both provokes emergent patterns and may itself repeatedly undergo changes in relation to them. If human resonance harbors highly dynamic receptive potentials (to others, otherness, and futurity), then illuminating these might aid our political imaginations of radical democratic practices that in turn cultivate receptive learning and thus intensify the opening or emergent character of political time. They might, in the words of Ernst Bloch, develop a more potent relation to presently unactualized possibility—the *not yet*—which is so integral to human freedom and flourishing.[9]

Recent developments in the science of mirror neurons illuminate the centrality and distinctiveness of resonance in human being.[10] Marco Iacoboni sharply articulates this when he writes of "the fundamentally intersubjective nature of our own brains": "Mirror neurons put the self and other back together again. Their neural activity reminds us of the primary intersubjectivity."[11] Thoroughly intertwined with the birth of human perception and preconscious communication, mirror neurons infuse and enable our emergence in the world of human and more than human relationships, and they are in turn multiplied and transformed in these relationships, in cycles of ongoing development. We are born, formed, carried along in, and transformed by waves of intercorporeal resonance that precede all recognition. Our perception of the world is born in resonance.

Drawing from empirical evidence, as well as speculating beyond that which is currently available, Iacoboni surmises that our most elemental sense of self, as well as the mirror neurons that facilitate this sense, develop in affective-sensual interactive responses between the bodies of babies and those of adults. We are born with undeveloped sensual fields, some active mirror neurons, a mimetic propensity, and a capacity to further develop mirror neurons: we are born *to* engage the interworld. Yet these rudimentary conditions for self and brain development processes are highly interactive: they and we are, thus, also born *in and of* the emergent interworld of resonant energies. Here is Iacoboni's basic sketch of our capacity to recognize self and other in the process of smiling: "Baby smiles, the parent smiles in response. Two minutes later the baby smiles, the parent smiles again. Thanks to the imitative behavior of the parent, the baby's brain can associate the motor plan necessary to smile and the sight of the smiling face. Therefore—presto! Mirror neurons for a smiling face are born. The next time the baby sees somebody else's smile, the neural activity associated with the motor plan for smiling is evoked in the baby's brain, *simulating* a smile . . . 'self' and 'other' are inextricably blended in mirror neurons."[12] As babies, we come to sense the identity of our smiling—and sense the identity of *ourselves* smiling—through the smiles of *others* who are affectively resonating with and responding to our faces smiling! Then we draw upon the resonant receptive capacities of mirror neurons born in such interactions further to perceive and understand others in a circular biocultural development in which "the mirror neuron system is largely shaped by imitative interactions between self and other."[13] Of course, a smile is by no means a simple thing.[14]

The key insight here is less that we rely on mirror neurons to interpret and empathize with the faces we perceive, and more that intercorporeal affective resonance is intertwined with the very birth of perception. As infants with basic perceptual fields, we have capacities for sensuous receptivity to waves of light and sound, but it is through the affective, mimetic, responsive intercorporeal relationships that these biocultural capacities are launched on their journeys of emergence. As another smiles in response to my smile, the energetic configurations in that person's face evoke a relationship with energetic configurations in mine, and through these energetic resonances my biocultural capacities to perceive others and myself, and to affect all, begin to acquire texture and subtlety. Biologically, mirror neurons develop that "fire" in fractions of a second in response to the energetic "firing" of the neurons of an other, and we emerge in a very elemental sense in these resonances.

When we clench a pencil tightly between our teeth, it profoundly disrupts the mimetic facial dance that ceaselessly occurs in fractions of a second between people who are before each other. This disruption, in turn, greatly reduces the efficiency of people's receptive capacity to detect emotional changes in others' facial expressions. In other words, the resonant relationship of affective "mimicry precedes and actually helps the recognition."[15]

In addition to both enabling and developing through relations among human beings, mirror neurons play a fundamental (and related) role in disclosing the world of things: things are born in association with resonant possibilities for action. In a manner that would come as no surprise to Merleau-Ponty (and as disclosed by scientists explicitly indebted to him), when we see a cup, "the cup functions . . . as a *virtual pole of action*, which, given its relational nature, both defines and is defined by the motor pattern that it activates."[16] We don't see the cup and then consider possibilities for grasping it: the cup emerges for us with the firing of mirror neurons and "appears as graspable in this or that manner"—it appears as energized "invitations to act":[17] "crisscrossed with viable paths and more or less surmountable obstacles."[18] We haunt the space we see, and we are haunted by it: virtual possibilities for action and possible futures emerge at the intersection where self and perceived world are born. This is one way in which Bloch's claim that possibility is every bit as real as the world of present actuality appears to be profoundly true.

This action schema in which the perception of things originates is simultaneously entangled in resonant relations with the possible actions of others, and this intercorporeally crisscrossed world is in turn elemental to our disclosure of others' movements, which we perceive as intentionally related to it. When the other acts, our mirror neurons energize nearly simultaneously with those engaged by the other's action (though there are control mechanisms that generally prevent this firing from leading to action in our own body). This resonant recognition is tightly intertwined with the action-charged context in which the movement takes place. Hence, our neurons fire differently depending on the object and context toward which a grasp is directed, and in this way we register the otherwise invisible intentionality of the other. Vision of the same hand movement in different contexts (e.g., in relation to a cup versus a pencil) energizes our neural circuits very differently. All of these observations lead Vittorio Gallese to theorize what he calls a "shared manifold" in which actions, contexts, and intentions of self and others cogenerate the world we experience in a primordial way by means of resonant energetic relationships.[19] Moreover, these resonant relationships and capacities are highly dynamic. Underscoring the way in which resonance alters the quality of resonance itself, Giacomo Rizzolatti and Corrado Sinigaglia write that "mirror neuron activation changes depending on the specific motor competences of those who are observing specific actions being performed by others" (e.g., the mirror neurons of dancers fire differently than do those of nondancers when watching a dancer).[20]

Monkeys' and humans' neuronal systems both fire in witness to the object-directed movements of others. Yet human beings' resonant mirror systems have an additional characteristic: our mirror neurons fire in the presence of *intransitive* movements.[21] Noting that human mirror neurons fire at the sight of pantomime while monkeys' usually do not, Iacoboni observes that "our mirror neuron areas are activated by more abstract actions than are those of monkeys."[22] This would appear to afford humans a greater capacity for coparticipating in resonant tracking of more indeterminate actions that are not (yet) anchored in specific goals. This capacity in turn opens possibilities for gestural communication that both guide and intensify the intercorporeal activity of the mirror neuron system, so that we can not only receptively "read" others' gestures but also *anticipate* the effect of our gestures upon them, modify our gestures according to such anticipations, read others differently in this light and their own capacities to do the same, and so forth.

It becomes apparent here that the resonant energies of our mirror neuron system infuse our being with dynamic qualities that harbor richly receptive and transformative potentials. In light of earlier reflections by Prigogine, Stengers, and Holland, we could say that with the sensual-mirror neuron characteristics of human beings, resonant energies that are an elemental aspect of the universe have acquired particularly receptive, interactive, and adaptive powers through which resonance can reflectively modify resonance in ways that demonstrate remarkable capacities to alter systems within and between selves, as well as in relation with the world. Our perceptual world emerges as imbued with possibilities for action, and our resonant receptive capacities develop in relation to how our interactions with the world actualize some of these possibilities. People who dance a lot disclose the world of dancers differently than those who do not. What of those who engage in the resonant practices of radically receptive democracy?

Insofar as we have developed capacities for registering movements that are intransitive, abstract, and communicatively (hyper)interactive, the quality of time-as-opening-of-possibility that infuses each context *intensifies, because movement and action can become significantly unbound from the givenness of relatively closed contexts in ways that afford visceral experiences of indeterminacy, manifold potential relationships, and transformative interactions that can act receptively not only within the world but upon the world-disclosive context itself—the basic dimensions of how the world appears.* The more we engage in receptively accented activity and experience, it appears that the resonant capacities of our neuronal system may often undergo development and transformations that further enhance our capacities for resonant receptivity. Thus our resonant capacities for emergence, in Holland's sense, would appear pregnant with capacities for learning and adapting that rapidly increase what he alludes to as "possibilities for emergence [themselves] . . . as the flexibility of the interactions increases."[23]

In the following, I explore the political implications of this for grassroots democratic practice in significant detail. Yet we can get a preliminary sense of the horizon of such an inquiry into our potential for enhancing democratically receptive, flexible, and generative relationships in light of the following example. At the end of each semester, several hundred first-year college students gather to present and discuss their work with the broader community on Action Research Teams (ARTs). In a breakout discussion to evaluate the implications of this work, a student who had been coaching an action team of mostly Hispanic children at Killip Elementary School in the theory and practice of grassroots democracy began to speak from a deeply reflective place. Elbow on the table, he raised his forearm to a vertical position, gazed at it, and said, "You know, before working with these kids—seeing them get together, really talk with each other, identify an issue, research it, then move to make it happen even though everyone would say they are the most disadvantaged and powerless—before this, everywhere I saw a problem that needed change, the whole world seemed like a wall."[24] Then, lowering his forearm flat on the table, he said more excitedly, "Now, when I see problems, I see possibilities, pathways." What this student was getting at in the most profound terms, I think, is how the world appeared fundamentally different to him; how through his immersion with others in radical democratic practice, the world previously disclosed as a series of immutable barriers had substantially transformed in ways that made it appear as a tissue of countless and untold possibilities for critical interrogation and imaginative action. With others, in a pattern of radically receptive democratic practice, he inhabited and intensified an emergent set of biocultural possibilities in a way that cultivated his powers for sensing and coacting responsively.

At least *this* aspect of our biocultural being would seem charged with revolutionary receptive potentials in which both our sense for, and the actuality of, the "not yet" character of becoming might deepen as we interactively work the horizons of the present with others. This suggests that the resonant capacities with which we are born enable relationships that in turn qualitatively shape, transform, and may intensify these very capacities.[25] Indeed, as Susan Blackmore argues, evolutionarily, human practices that are imitatively learned and transmitted appear to transform our brain's imitative capacities themselves (here, our mirror neuron system), such that these elements of culture depend on a human mind that, in Daniel Dennett's words, "is itself an artifact created when memes [elements of culture passed on by imitative learning] restructure a human brain in order to make it a better habitat for memes."[26] I will return to this point later when I consider the implications of all this for cultivating radical democratic resonance. The key point for now is that *resonance appears to transform resonance* not only with shifts from level to level (e.g., subatomic to atomic to organic) but also within the development of human individuals, cultures, and evolution over different scales of time. This biocultural quality confirms and encourages the emergent sense of the first-year student indebted to it.

Yet, of course, the potential for ethico-political relationships and powers of receptive resonance often seems dimly manifest—at best. In our earlier discussion of the evangelical-capitalist "resonance machine," we sketched a few of the myriad ways in which power can dampen and subvert these energetic potentials. Insofar as contemporary neuroscience sheds light on how this resonance machine operates upon us, it may also inform our struggles to resist and transform it.

Recall the study in which the interpretive capacities of people who clenched their jaws around a pencil were significantly impaired in comparison to those of people who were relaxed as they viewed the faces that appeared before them on a screen. Jaw clenching diminished the capacities of their mirror neurons to resonate with pictures of those firing in other faces, and so they had difficulty perceiving and interpreting others' corporeal expressiveness. If my experience in waiting rooms subjected to FOX News and other stations has any merit, it would suggest that a significant portion of both the substance and the corporeal performativity of this resonant programming likely works to undermine our corporeal capacities for resonant receptivity. Not only were a variety of others regularly framed as objects demanding our anger and fear, but the faces of those conveying the news and being interviewed were often clenched as well. Insofar as regular viewers tend to resonate (in different ways) with both the corporeal performances and substance of these shows, it seems likely that their own faces—and bodies more generally—would become tensed in relation to targeted others in ways that would significantly diminish capabilities for resonant receptivity, as well as those cognitive capacities that are profoundly indebted to it. This could help explain how people on the upper side of racial hierarchies, for example, can repeatedly encounter people on the underside exhibiting all sorts of affective and cognitive activity that is profoundly at odds with dominant stereotypes and yet remain utterly insensible to it—frequently across many generations.

Compound these problems with the recent neurological studies suggesting that such sociopolitical oblivion likely anchors itself—and then intensifies—in the mirror neuron system's basic tendency to activate differentially in relation to patterns of "social relevance." Part of this is due to great differentials in mirror system activation based on filtering due to visual discriminations that have an automatic dimension. Thus, when moving, people facing away from us activate our mirror neurons far less than those doing the same movement who are facing us. In this way, "signals about the actions of other people are filtered, by modulating visuospatial attention, prior to the information entering the 'mirror system' allowing only the actions of the most socially relevant person to pass."[27] Another study indicates that (beyond visual attention differentials) "social relations modulate action simulation": "Motor activation during action anticipation depends on the social relationship between the actor and the observer formed during the performance of a joint action task. Simulation of another person's action, as reflected in the activation of motor cortices, gets stronger the more the other is perceived as an interaction partner."[28]

This research seems to suggest that, in addition to power-laden patterns of clenched closure, the oblivion of those on the topsides of power becomes lodged in neurological patterns that filter appearances visually and raise the thresholds required to activate motor cortexes—at least when the interaction contexts would involve the equality of persons.

In elemental ways—corporeal, sensual, affective—those in privileged positions are likely to have a difficult time sensing they are genuinely *with* those on the lower sides of social hierarchies. They will be challenged to feel these others' affects and emotions, and they will often inhabit a world in which those more subjugated do not appear, or appear only dimly or episodically.

One does not have to speculate wildly to suspect that this would be intertwined with politically debilitating deficits that strike not only at empathy as a capacity to receptively acknowledge *specificities* of another's presence—affects, intentions, activities—but even more basically at our propensities and capacities *to receptively resonate with targeted others in ways that allow us to register and acknowledge their copresence as singular-yet-similar "others" in the first place*. This dampened resonance, in turn, would be cyclically entangled with an extremely dimmed sense for relational possibilities—be they cooperative, agonistic, or both—that are at the heart of democratic political dialogue, reflection, and action. And so, this would be far from conducive to possibilities for entering into democratic relationships that might bend the world toward justice and cocreate commonwealth.

On the whole, the research on mirror neurons suggests that we conceive of the resonant receptivity that is a condition of democratically ethical and political relationships neither as "affective merging" (in the sense Hannah Arendt fears) nor as a relationship that is formed among selves who "world travel" in ways that emotionally interact only in the sense that they ask, "How would I feel where you are?"—while assiduously maintaining a fundamental distance (in the sense Arendt affirms).[29] Rather, in elemental registers, democratic ethical and political relationships are born/e through the receptive resonances of an intercorporeal fabric in which we both become and are disclosed as singular-yet-similar coexistent beings. This resonant tissue of intercorporeal being is at once highly fecund and extremely precarious. Tending to conditions in which this fabric—and thus *we* ourselves—may flourish is consequently perhaps our most elemental ethical and political task, for only insofar as it is vital are we capable of fashioning perceptive judgment concerning desirable political modes of drawing near, remaining apart, world traveling, and cocreating through which we may open the future miraculously beyond the blind, closed, and compulsive automaticity that sets in when such resonance is dampened. No doubt tending to this resonant intercorporeal tissue, in turn, also hinges upon such judgments and political modes in what amount to circles of reciprocal implication. Yet one upshot of this discussion is that in a world born, carried, inflected, and often damaged by intercorporeal resonance, transformative care for the political world of embodied practices shifts to the foreground. What might be the implications of this insight for theorizing and enacting practices of a radically democratic habitus?

Toward a Democratic Habitus of Resonant Receptivity

Democratic political relationships are distinct from many others in that they are drawn by and engender a sense of the future as more open to transformative possibilities through collective engagement. While a basic characteristic of all (inter)action is that we intend to make a difference that would not otherwise occur in a future moment, most action at present accepts the basic social structures of the world as immutable frames: the temporal character of such frames appears frozen, as a closed context within which our actions take place. Typically when you play soccer, for example, you play according to established rules. Playing the game does not involve questioning and possibly transforming those rules. The context of social orders, as Bourdieu puts it, typically *"goes without saying because it comes without saying."*[30] From a radical democratic vantage point, political orders that seal themselves from possibilities of interrogative perception, dialogue, and action can appear quite similar to compulsive repetitive-motion disorders—tracing the contours of the given over and over again as if they were immutable. Democratic temporality involves a heightened receptive sense of the emergent, transformable, relational character of the future *even in regard to aspects of social structure that are typ-ically considered unalterable.* It is not that democratic time is somehow "pure openness" or "pure plasticity." The closing and opening qualities of time are not dichotomous but rather more matters of degree, intensity, and mixture that are greatly affected by many kinds of resonant practices, habits, capacities, knowledge, and institutions in relation to which people develop. In situations where embodied receptive democratic engagement is widespread, however, the character and limits of the order of things tend to be disclosed as more open and capable of undergoing (sometimes dramatic) transformations.

The white NAU student who was coaching elementary students and began to sense a world of walls transforming into possible pathways regularly moved his body receptively into a poor neighborhood to spend time in a school con-sisting predominantly of students of color. His task was to pay deep atten-tion to the passions and interests of the students; to facilitate their capacities both to give expression to their sense and yearnings in relation to their sur-roundings and to pay deep attention to others' expressions as they did so; to teach them how to identify common issues of significance around which they then conducted research, developed a strategy, generated power, and acted for change; to midwife a culture that robustly celebrated their engagement in this process as well as their tangible achievements. In other words, he was immersed in and co-tending an embodied fabric of resonant interrogative and transformative relationships through which unexpected and promising things were emerging. Remove bodies, places, and things from this picture (say by reducing it to "deliberation"), and you miss much of what nurtures the vitality of democratic sensibilities.

Like a soccer player whose regular practice gives her a sharp eye for the movements and possibilities of the game, the NAU democracy coach and his students were developing a sharp eye for ethical and political movements and possibilities by practicing the arts of receptive democracy. Yet these movements and possibilities made incursions into some of the basic conditions of the field of interaction that are frequently taken to be immutable—like immigration issues, or a disadvantaged playground, or a library in which they previously had no say that hadn't been replenished in far too long, or the assumption that they were just poor undocumented kids of color who ought to basically focus on learning how to stay in line rather than on becoming the next generation of grassroots leaders transforming and cocreating their common world. The library, the playground, bullies, the meaning of grassroots democratic citi-zenship, as well as their relationships of agency and accountability with each other, their school, and their neighborhood started to become terrains that might be refashioned, rather than crappy conditions according to which we must conform our lives. The "walledness" of the world began to crack, crumble, and come down.

Recall the earlier reflections on how perceptual capacities are essentially born and develop in intercorporeal relations of affective resonance in relation to bodily expressions, gestures, movements, and intentional relations with our surroundings. Resonance creates possibilities for further interaction that in turn enhances resonance. This circular development fosters a perceptually enriched and more open disclosure of a world that is increasingly "crisscrossed" with more—and more textured and resonant—possibilities for action. Hence, for example, what appears as an insurmountable wall of impossibilities to those who do not climb rock may be receptively disclosed to a community of practiced climbers as a surface of dynamic possibilities for movement, exuberant pleasure, and health. Similarly, with practice, we increasingly disclose a checkerboard as manifold networks of possibility rather than disorienting complexity.

I suggest that radically democratic perception and sensibility is likewise born and developed in *relationships* of public work and political action. In such relational practices, however, the emergent transformative possibilities of the future—the future *as* possibility—are experienced, solicited, and cultivated in broader, deeper, and more intense ways. Radically democratic practices likely deepen and broaden resonances that disclose the world as more temporally open, because democracy involves distinctively *game-transformative practices* in which those engaged experience each other—in gesture, expression, movement—questioning, testing, modifying, cocreating, challenging, and transforming topographies of power, suffering, outcome, and possibility that most people not thus engaged accept as immutable. Such practices "crisscross" our perceptual world with possibilities for action in a manner that differs from the crisscrossing that happens in relation to action in practices that take the basic structure of the world as given. The interactivity of questioning, challenging, and changing situations likely engenders resonant perceptions we might think of as *crisscrossed in depth*. Here, possibilities for action burrow *into* the basic terrains, patterns, interactions, structures, and flesh of the political-social world, such that they tend to render its primordial appearance more mutable—more elastic, malleable, *possible*—in ways that resonate with our bodies and thus energetically solicit further interrogative and game-transformative interactivity with each other and the world.

Reconsider the narrative about the meeting between many undocumented people and the police chief. To be sure, they were deliberating. Yet the action was a resonant and embodied event. The police chief and his officer consented to the community's extensive work and its call for a relationship without their badges, so as soon as they entered the room, the basic structure of power modulated a bit. Things began to bend further when people stood to talk—sometimes towering over the chief—and the chief leaned forward and listened with postures of respect. The community members' resonance with speakers, and also their physical gestures of agonistic respect for the chief, inflected individuals' senses of who, how, and what they could become as public beings, as well as the community's sense of itself as a whole. Later in the year, when the chief's testimony before the Flagstaff City Council joined the voices of many undocumented people and their allies in persuading the council to lobby against s.b. 1070, rounds of enthusiastic celebration further intensified a deepening sense of a world pregnant with possibilities—even as the forces opposed to them are powerful, persistent, often horrendous, and this all remains precarious.

Public corporeal experiences of intense efforts to question and openly imagine basic alternatives; or experiences of frequently journeying into neighborhoods you may have feared, in order to engage in collaborations and political actions that were inconceivable to you just months earlier; or experiences of organizing viscerally charged powerful networks to advance fundamental alternatives to the suffering that is regularly shared in narratives accompanied by tears and anger; or experiences of engaging and witnessing great deeds that open horizons hitherto unimaginable; or experiences of solemn remembrance or ecstatic celebration of such performances, achievements, and possibilities with artwork, dancing, music, and poetry; or experiences of having been tossed into a highly unexpected perception of what you took to be fundamental structures of the world by voices, questions, movements, and initiatives of others around you—all these experiences of intense affective resonance likely cultivate a poignant and increasingly general sense of ourselves, others, the world, and time as fecund with the "not yet." This type of resonant sensibility and perception, in turn, also likely nurtures and intensifies the development of human capacities we mentioned earlier for mirroring relatively intransitive and abstract movements, gestures, and affective intentions in ways that enable and solicit more democratic work and action infused with a sense of receptive possibility, *and* thereby stimulate further affective neurological development in a circular process. Through such practices, we gradually become beings with greater capacities to see, hear, and feel the solicitation of "not yet" realized possibilities for world-changing initiatives, as well as more robust propensities to work and act our way toward such possibilities. Insofar as such resonant malleable perceptual fields are powerfully intertwined with solicitations of democratic work and action, our polities not only would *appear* more elastic and open to possibility but also would actually *become* more elastic and temporally open to the resonant potency of Bloch's "not yet." This is part of what I meant by radical democratic transformations of resonance itself. Resonance would increasingly involve not simply a relationship between two or more bodies but also the possible not yet futures of bodies, relationships, contexts. The vibrations and energies would extend to futures (if Prigogine and Stengers are right) whose possibilities are opened by resonance. Yet the "not yet" would itself become part of the resonance of now (through bodies that open beyond themselves in space and time)—energizing and energized by it—as a strange capacity that amplifies our capacities for intransitive and indeterminate mirroring. My gesture toward specifically radical democratic resonance of mirror neurons calls us to this possibility for *enhancing the experience and actuality of political possibility as such.* It is a call to cultivate dynamic practices through which receptive democratic resonance enriches and creates a polity more hospitable to receptive democratic resonance: a radically democratic *meme.*

My intention is not to cast the role of mirror neurons here in ways that occlude the vast and important role of more explicit modes of teleological reasoning and cognitive inference, for clearly the latter are also fundamental aspects of democratic engagement. Indeed, recent studies indicate that when we are faced with "nonstereotypic implausible actions," we utilize "context-sensitive inferential processing," while, "the mirror system [is] more strongly activated for intentionally produced action" in contexts where the action is more readily plausible.[31] Yet the activities of resonant democratic practice mentioned in the previous paragraph likely tend to do two things in relation to these findings. First, they extend the range of "the plausible," such that democratic intensities of questioning, imagining, exploring, advancing, struggling, and cocreating tend to be witnessed with greater affective receptivity—or visceral comprehension. Second, through this extension of the viscerally "plausible" to include activities that proliferate our engagement with the "not yet," our bodily being is in turn likely more receptively drawn to engage (and countenance others engaging) the *edges* of radically *unusual possibilities.* Inference, teleological reasoning, and a range of affective responses will all be drawn upon to engage these edges in any democracy worth its salt. My wager here is that the mirror resonance associated with practices of democracy can prepare and predispose us to employ these manifold modalities in ways more solicitous than fearful—more drawn by resonant energies of opening and less so by intensities toward closure.

Such experiences and sensibilities are not—and ought not be—homogeneous in focus, scope, or intensity within vibrant and sustainable democracies. Rather, they stem from *ecologies* of practices in which the temporal orders of our world are pushed and pulled in different registers and modalities, across diverse sectors, with different effects. Mutually informing and transforming each other, these different kinds of practice contribute to disclosures of the world that are "crisscrossed in depth" with diverse possibilities for collective action. Hence, for example, everyday political engagements in what Harry Boyte insightfully analyzes as "public work" (engaging, bending, and reorganizing our institutions and practices of daily life in order to cocreatively produce commonwealth) engender relationships, knowledge, and capacities that enable people to sense themselves as powerful democratic agents receptive to the constructed mutability of the world.[32] Such work typically involves a mix of cooperative and agonistic aspects, and takes the textures and limits of the present to be objects of reflection and gradual transformation—sector by sector, site by site. They build deep and broad senses of collective agency. Yet while such practices are profoundly indebted to and sometimes entwined with more intense modes of radical democratic challenge to the present, public work typically involves modalities that are more modest, slower burning, much less contestational, and more durable. Though they don't usually take Foucault as an inspiration, they nonetheless give profound expression to his line about "patient labor giving form to our impatience for freedom."[33]

Looking from another vantage point in the ecology of democratic practices that engender sensibilities for temporal opening, we see a variety of more intense, interruptive, and directly contestational activities against war, inequality, racism, ecocide, anti-immigrant politics, and so forth. These practices benefit greatly when they draw on political sensibilities of people who have developed in more modest forms of collective action, and vice versa—a theme I discuss in chapter 4. Yet intensifying movements frequently must invent modalities that importantly exceed the repertoire and sensibilities of those formed through public work, as they engage in actions with higher temperatures, greater risks, more radical disruption, targeted polarization, and more irruptive relationality. The opening of time requires a dense and variegated matrix of supportive relational sensibilities that enable us to palpate, push, pull, ply, and sometimes pound at and pour beyond the edges of the polity.

Hence radical democracy ought to nurture tensional ecologies of practices and associated resonant capacities that engender selves who are responsive to the mutability of the world and can supplely move among a variety of agonistic political modalities: rooting in many domains and at many depths, working the limits of the world in different ways and with manifold intensities, and forming networks of resonances across differences in order to engender more receptive, complex, and temporally open modes of commonwealth. Such would be the conditions of possibility for an organized, durable, resonant democratic movement.

All this is to say that a radically "democratic resonance machine" requires a sense of resonance that exceeds the terms and connotations of sympathetic or harmonious vibrations of shared common sensibilities and spiritualities—though these are an important part of the mix. Radical democratic resonance is also often more like the resonance of Jews around a table (or at least the Jews in my family and Woody Allen's), buzzing in many ways through the complex dissonances of heated argument; or the resonance of Jews with Yahweh, contesting not only each other but sometimes even Yahweh, and sometimes even the existence of Yahweh.[34] The assemblage constitutive of radically democratic resonance will be significantly enlivened by dissonances within itself, as well as those antagonisms between itself and that with which it is in deepest contestation. This internal dissonance is at once a *condition* of radical democratic vitality and opening toward the not yet, and must be recognized and cultivated as one *aim* of such vitality. The complex character of democratic resonance must be cultivated from the interactions of both sympathetic and discordant vibrations. Anyone who is attentive to blues experiences this possibility at the deepest level.

This analysis suggests the paradoxical possibility of cultivating a radically democratic habitus. Yet Bourdieu, the foremost theorist of this concept, is largely skeptical about such prospects, and we need to take his concerns seriously. Bourdieu conceives of habitus as "the durably installed generative principle of regulated improvisations, [that] produces practices which tend to reproduce the regularities immanent in the objective conditions of the production of their generative principle, while adjusting to the demands inscribed as objective potentialities in the situation, as defined by the cognitive and motivating structures making up the habitus." He sees a degree of flexibility and play, but habitus profoundly delimits this range insofar as the perceptions and dispositions generated by practices in objective conditions tend to be reproductive of and purely functional for the latter. Bourdieu's theory of practice concerns "the *dialectic of the internalization of the externality and the external-ization of internality*, or, more simply, of incorporation and objectification."[35]

This dialectic proceeds primarily through daily practices of "em-bodiment" that precede and frame consciousness, such that "the fundamental principles of the arbitrary content of the culture . . . are placed beyond the grasp of consciousness, and hence cannot be touched by voluntary, deliberate transformation, cannot even be made explicit; nothing seems more ineffable, more incommunicable, more inimitable, and, therefore, more precious, than the values given body, *made* body by the transubstantiation achieved by the hidden persuasion of an implicit pedagogy, capable of instilling a whole cosmology, an ethic, a political philosophy, through injunctions as insignificant as 'stand up straight.'"[36] The generative relations of practiced habitus are analogous both to the "art" of producing art and to how art itself communicates: in both cases there is "a *mimesis*" that is profoundly corporeal: "*something which communicates, so to speak, from body to body, i.e. on the hither side of words or concepts, and which pleases (or displeases) without concepts*" (my emphasis).[37] Bourdieu's account emphasizes how the historical and the arbitrary pass in and out of us such that doxa sediments so deeply into our unconscious being as to become self-evident and unquestionable.

Of course, Bourdieu not infrequently calls our attention to the fact that habitus is not the only factor that affects the limits, possibilities, and directions of practice. Cultural contact, class and generational conflicts, double binds, and various crises of disadjustment can throw doxa into question by presenting people with "competing possibles." In such situations, there is a dislocation of subjective structures of disposition and perception that previously "fit" with objective conditions, and this dislocation can "destroy self-evidence practically," thereby opening new spaces for a degree of autonomy for symbolic contestations in which we have a "margin of freedom" that can alter practices. Indeed, Bourdieu emphasizes that he first theorized habitus precisely "as a way to understand mismatches." Nevertheless, there is precious little in his writing to suggest that body practices themselves can be structured in ways that tend to generate imaginative critical interrogations, flexibility, energetic quaking of and push-back against the limits of the self-evident, and radical transformation. These spaces of possibility open only when and because gaps, blips, and mismatches—failures of articulation—occur. Bourdieu appears, in a sense, to read theories in which democracy engenders such possibilities as too *weightless*: too indebted to paradigms of subjectivism, ahistorical interpretivism, and communicative relations that all misconstrue consciousness as disembodied and thus exaggerate our symbolic freedom. Such paradigms and their associated intellectualist virtues of distance "simply transmute into an epistemological choice [and project onto practices one observes] the anthropologist's [or theorist's] objective situation," which is spectatorial, disengaged, and so forth.[38] Such transmutations and projections conceal the intricate and resonant crisscrossing of flesh by practices through which power sediments the perceptions and dispositions required for reproduction of subjugation. In this way, these paradigms participate in diminishing the very phenomena (freedom) they take to be the relatively weightless essence of our being.

I find Bourdieu's concerns and much of his theory of practice to be compelling. Yet the work on mirror neurons and resonance discussed here suggests that—to the extent that we cultivate them—our dispositions and capacities for generous perceptions of difference, receptive sensibility and dialogue, intense questioning, imaginative interpretation, radical challenges to injustice, and the cocreation of commonwealth, as well as a profound sense of political time as pregnant with possibility, are *themselves born in and cultivated by mimetic intercorporeal practices*, rather than disembodied subjective powers of cognition and autonomous symbolic interpretation. Bourdieu's skepticism toward the possibility of a *radically democratic habitus* appears to be entwined with his own undefended assumption about a tight association between the qualities associated with it and a problematic disembodied (inter)subjectivity that is all too often taken as the mythical principle of their origin. Indeed, this ready acceptance is part of the doxa that "*goes without saying because it comes without saying*," as he says. Yet just as Bourdieu argues that the subjectivist paradigm is a transmutation of the spectatorial practices and objective conditions of scholars, I suspect that *Bourdieu's own sense* and dismissal of these capacities, as well as associated possibilities for radical democratic habitus, is itself a transmutation of a pervasive scholarly posture which (for all we owe to his profound insights) too infrequently engaged in the textured practices of radical democratic body politics. Just as disembodied (inter)subjectivists underplayed the dense embodiment of social power, Bourdieu for analogous reasons underplays the dense bodily character of radical democratic *practiced sensibilities and enlivened possibility*. He failed to grasp how practice might engender the latter because he too infrequently experienced it or studied its fine-grained specificities.

This is not to say that enlivened senses of democratic possibility borne of democratic practices can completely free themselves from the powerful sedimentations of embodied subjugative power with which they always seem to be intertwined in messy relationships. Reform and revolution always work in unending tensional relation to problematic sedimented regularities, as Bourdieu illustrates most profoundly. Yet just as practices embody and animate subjugative regularities, so too my discussion of the science of mirror neurons suggests they may also embody and animate the public work and political action of receptive resonance, through which we democratically tend to each other and the world by means of practices of more dynamic reciprocal freedoms. Practiced habitus may be generative of both—the point is to enact shifts toward the latter.

My indebtedness to and divergence from Bourdieu here can be expressed in a different way that sheds additional light. Recall that he theorizes habitus as "the *durably* installed generative principle of regulated improvisations, [that] produces practices which tend to reproduce the regularities immanent in the objective conditions of the production of their generative principle" (my emphasis).[39] Even as we seek to cultivate a practiced habitus that accents democratic *improvisational* capacities in opposition to subjugative regularities, *both* Bourdieu *and* the neuroscientists suggest that a certain profound durability is both a condition for and a consequence of flourishing improvisational practices. Improvisational practice in the best democratic senses relies upon and embodies itself in our brains, perceptions, dispositions, and capacities for action and reflection. Such sedimented durability, it seems to me, is a *good* thing, for it indicates that where conditions and practices of resonant receptive democracy gain a foothold, humans are likely endowed with a biocultural being that can sediment *democratic* regularities—among which are precisely the regularities of practices and dispositions conducive to innovative action for both uncommon justice and complex commonwealth. This suggests that our biocultural makeup allows that embodied democracy can become more than "fugitive"— or ephemeral, episodic—in Sheldon Wolin's terms.[40] Indeed, our capacities for spontaneity, collaboration, improvisation, disruption, and transformation would likely be most intense and powerful when durable democratic practices and associated dispositions are vital aspects of a richly diverse political ecology.

Democratic Habitus and Engaged Pedagogy
Transformations at NAU

As I noted earlier, it was something electric and mimetic in the faces and gestures of many who began seriously engaging the ecological democracy movement in Northern Arizona that first drew me to investigate mirror neurons and theorize possibilities for a radical democratic habitus. It is worth discussing this movement further, in light of these theoretical reflections, in order to provide a more textured account of our experiences of resonant receptivity in this emergent habitus.

For the past half-dozen years, a broad movement for engaged democracy education has been under way at Northern Arizona University and surrounding communities. There are many ways to think about what we are doing (and each chapter will analyze this initiative through different interconnected lenses), but among the most significant is that we are cocreating a radical democratic resonance machine or (to avoid misleading mechanistic connotations) a resonant democratic habitus. In an effort to counter the dry hate of "Arizona" and provide an alternative, growing numbers of faculty, students, administrators, staff, and members of the broader community are collaborating to cocreate a new ecology of engaged and politically powerful pedagogical and community practices accenting resonant receptivity. Here I discuss several of the elements that constitute this assemblage and the resonances forming among them.

One of the most formative elements of the democratic education movement at NAU is called Public Achievement (PA), which is part of an international youth education movement that has also sprung up in South Africa, Eastern Europe, Palestine, and beyond. At NAU, first-year students who opt into PA seminars learn theories of democracy and democratic education as they participate in an Action Research Team through which they work as "coaches" with K–12 students in surrounding schools. Collaborating with several schools in Flagstaff, coaches typically work in pairs with about eight students in after-school programs or in classes during the day. They facilitate democratic relationship building, mutual accountability, action team formation, receptive dialogue amid differences, issue selection, power mapping, strategizing, public expression, and collaborative action, and celebrate their public work. Through the intertwinement of theory and practice, coaches and K–12 students learn the arts of grassroots democratic citizenship.

Many of the K–12 students are in fact practicing citizenship and community building in ways that complicate and conflict with official designations of legality and state-sanctioned citizenship. At Killip Elementary School many students are members of families who have crossed the Arizona-Mexico border illegally. They (and their parents) have no officially sanctioned rights of citizenship, yet they are full-fledged democratic leaders in the PA teams, taking responsibility for actions they collectively deem to be of vital importance to the community as they experience it. Over a third of the students at Killip are Native Americans (primarily Dine [Navajo] and Hopi) and thus are both U.S.

citizens *and* citizens of nearby sovereign Nations (reservations) with which most have significant ongoing affiliations. Other students are simply U.S. citizens. In sharp contrast to Arizona politics, where harsh vilifications of immigrants happen regularly and Native Americans have been on the underside of colonial power since the nineteenth century, students in Killip PA learn practices of democracy together that enact a radically different kind of community. Within PA they do not look to resonant alignments of (often xenophobic) nationality, race, and legality for the direction and boundaries of their political community, but rather engage in attentive discussions of their commonalities, differences, and challenges as the indispensable medium for learning how to live, work, and act politically toward a better future together. They identify and discuss issues of concern, ranging from school gardens to garbage, to diabetes, to bullying, to playgrounds, to graffiti, to old and torn library books, to safety, to school infrastructure, to public support for school programs, to immigration—and then they figure out how to work together to generate power and make changes that are important to them. Sometimes they work in teams to publicly advocate with school board officials on issues like the school calendar; sometimes they collaborate with adult grassroots leaders in an Industrial Areas Foundation affiliate, Northern Arizona Institutions for Community Leadership (NAICL), in public actions that address the mayor, city council members, and state representatives to advocate for public education funding, and so forth. They are a powerful force prefiguring a radically different kind of citizenship in a community constituted through receptive relationships across tremendous differences to build commonwealth.

The children and youth are crafting a radically democratic and resonant habitus far beyond the limits of the resonant political nightmare that has been bequeathed to them. Across multiple lines of inherited hostility and numbing indifference, they are attentively facing each other and their world and are cultivating dense fields of mirror neuronal relationships through which they are acquiring capacities to sense each other as unique human beings participating in a shared fabric of intercorporeal resonant receptivity. Consider the bodily character of this work to get a better sense of this.

In the spring of 2009, several of us launched a pilot PA project at Killip (where PA continues to this day). We met with several teams of about half a dozen students, gave them cameras, and asked them to lead us around the school and neighborhood, tell us what they loved, feared, wanted to change, and how. Before I knew it, I was heading with a group of excited students into a dusty arroyo-alley behind the school that was full of trash, obscene graffiti, and angry dogs pressing against the fences that bordered it. Together, they excitedly began to imagine fruit trees, a basketball hoop, a bench, beautiful artwork they might do on the walls, maybe a garden. With some prompting, they were beginning to sense and imagine their world with a certain utopic spirit. As we popped out of the arroyo onto a street, the conversation turned to a house that had had some scary activity, a corner where the year before there had been police violence that caused a ruckus in the community, and other topics. Emotions, faces, and gestures spanned a wide range, but we were all moving about together with a lot of intensity resonating among us. The following week, the students made collages of the pictures they had taken, and when I revisited the school, they were walking around to each other's desks discussing artistic pictorial renderings of different problems, interests, passions, and dreams. With great coaching from an undergraduate, they were also beginning to reflect on what their collages might have in common, as well as their differences. For some kids this was not easy, as their attention flitted about from one thing to another, but over the semester they began to pay attention to each other and more often direct their faces and bodily curiosity toward someone else who was speaking or perhaps bear themselves with more confidence and dignity when they themselves spoke. I noticed how the NAU coaches were modeling these bodily comportments with a youthful energy themselves, often squatting low to listen deeply at face level as a student was talking, using bodily gestures to draw the group's attention to someone who was talking, holding themselves in ways that were expressive, powerful, enthusiastic, hopeful, and deeply respectful of all involved. As a variety of small projects got under way, the NAU coaches were reporting a new sense of self-esteem and empowerment among many of the students. And the NAU coaches themselves had a whole new sense of things that was not unlike the student mentioned earlier who began to sense a world teaming with pathways of possibility.

Where there may otherwise have been fields of clenched jaws, grinding teeth, and numbed sensibilities, the students were cultivating a biocultural field of faces and bodies that were increasingly capable of the fraction of a second intercorporeal dance that is the powerful infrasensible tissue from which reflective and transformative political life becomes possible. If we abstract from the embodied character out this activity, we miss the way the practices of this emergent habitus were establishing resonant relationships that can scramble, contest, and displace the sound chambers of stupidity and partitioned fields of (in)sensibility of the dominant resonance machine.

Collectively, in Killip and Kinsey elementary schools and at Kinlani Dormitory (where many Native American youth who attend Flagstaff High School live), each semester there are nearly twenty PA teams in which six to ten youth practice the arts of radical democracy. Each of these teams is a powerful field of intersubjective resonance disrupting, ventilating, and transforming the systematic corruption of the broader polity and its dominant resonant machine with different sounds, sights, bodily bearing, and powers. These are engendering different capacities for listening, seeing, moving, working, and acting—together. Within the schools, each of the resonant fields of the several teams is beginning to resonate with the others in both collaborations and school-wide celebrations of the work; and related interactive fields of resonance are beginning to occur among the K–12 schools and NAU, and among a variety of sympathetic and collaborative groups, organizations, and movements across our community. When each field participates in and becomes witness to interactive fields, there tend to be remarkable amplificatory effects—growing enthusiasms, a sense of reinforcement, kindred efforts among people spanning vast differences of race, ethnicity, class, nationality, ideology, sexuality and gender orientations. A new resonant habitus is forming and struggling to radically transform the political oblivion, hostility, and impossibilities of the antidemocratic world we have inherited.

Yet, as we have seen, democratic resonance not only concerns *spatial* topographies of power (in this case, say, the geographies that separate and relate people[s], the geographies of where and how "democracy" is supposed to happen and not happen, who can and should participate and who not, etc.). It is also a set of body practices through which futurity—the *not yet*, time's *possibility*—can be acknowledged and tarried with, emerge more intensely, and move powerfully into political becoming. Recall that beings (e.g., cups) are disclosed as *fields of possibilities* related to histories of practice—grabbing, drinking, passing, throwing, being grabbed, drunk from, passed, thrown by others, broken, and so forth. This perceptual emergence of possibility and impossibility is in many ways prior to our explicit reflections about beings: perceptual fields of actuality-possibility are born with the firing of mirror neurons in relation to body practices and interactions. Because actuality and possibility are co-emergent, it is no wonder that antidemocratic configurations of power invest enormous amounts of resonant energy in efforts to wall off whole regions of democratic futurity. Yet as K–12 students coached by NAU students practice democratic arts of changing the world, the perceptually ensconced reification of situations according to a very narrow range of possibilities that create suffering, degradation, fear, a sense of immutability, and so forth, began to thaw.

Consider the third graders who had been moved from a school that had exciting playground equipment to a school that had greatly inferior equipment (and appears to be where the district has placed many kids from neighborhoods that other schools don't want to include). When the kids complained about this fact and flagged it as an issue, an NAU democracy coach asked, "Well, what do you want to do about it?" The kids discussed this viscerally important matter and decided to do research on playground equipment in order to organize an action with the school superintendent to get funding for better equipment. At the meeting with the third graders, the superintendent was so impressed by the research, organization, courage, and power of the action that he agreed that the school district would match all money the school raised for playground equipment improvements.

This may seem like a small victory—and in the scope of material inequality and resource shortages at the school, it certainly is. Yet in terms of eight-year-olds practicing democracy together and making a significant change in relation to a problem they found troubling, it is huge in a way that far exceeds playground equipment. What they learned was that the world that seems immutably given is capable of being changed when they work together democratically and muster the power to change it. And they learned this at the level of perception, sensibility, self-apprehension, and relationality as well as at the level of more explicit cognition. For many of these kids, the world begins to resonate as a terrain of possibilities: a site of questioning, vibrant conversation, exciting research, intense power building, collective action, and celebrated victory. The aura of democratic engagement and transformation begins to shift from "that's crazy" to "that's interesting and exciting, let's gather a bunch of different people, listen to each other, work together, and push to see what's possible for us to do." The world moves from being disclosed as a static, fixed game and acquires a resonant malleability as a terrain for potentially powerful democratic game-transformative practices.

Simultaneously, the world of one's fellow beings becomes newly resonant as fraction-of-a-second sensibilities are acquired that disclose one's peers as potentially cocreative people with whom world-transformative democratic action may be possible, rather than mere competitors on a fixed field of scarcity. Deep habits of being, perception, and affect are cultivated through which the others, the world, and time are increasingly disclosed as teeming with possibilities rather than moving on automatic pilot. So too are animating sensibilities that facilitate engaging the game-transformative practice of democracy well enough to actualize some of these possibilities and change the world—sensibilities such as attentive receptivity; a capacious relationship with ambiguity, tension, and difference; hunger for and delight in unexpected political relationships and strategies; creative imaginations for engendering complex commonwealth against the odds. Sensed, yes, and *more real because sensed*. Resonant democratic possibility becomes more than a philosophical concept as third graders learn it at the cellular level, explore its openings and textures, and generate power and political vision to actualize processes and goods hitherto unimaginable to them. Call this the resonant neurological infrastructure of democratic abundance. As resonance among different action teams and myriad groups across the community increases, so too does this abundance.

This process typically has a very profound impact on the NAU student coaches as well. As they move among, facilitate, and witness diverse children and youth (the majority of whom are on the undersides of more than one axis of power) working together on action research teams in increasingly exemplary fashion, many coaches gain an expansive sense of the transformative potential of grassroots democratic agency, the amazing blossoming of potentials in kids who may have been disaffected and silent at the beginning, as well as their own unexpected possibilities for cocreating change. For many NAU students, these sensibilities ignite their academic work with an excitement, seriousness, inquisitiveness, and sense of personal and public purposes through which they come alive in seminars as semesters unfold. A growing number of students seek additional avenues for democratic initiative beyond the seminars and official Action Research Teams in what appears to be an increasingly proliferative process.

Growing numbers of faculty who are increasingly buzzing from these experiences in the classroom and in a variety of community contexts are devoting more—and more imaginative—energy to this work. The Public Achievement seminars discussed here are but one example of engaged pedagogy opportunities among a quickly growing multitude of first- and second-year seminars that employ action research to engage a wide variety of issues—ranging from energy efficiency and renewable energy, to water conservation and rights, to public free spaces, to alternative agriculture, indigenous environmental justice, climate change, grassroots democracy in the schools, immigration, cooperative economics, alternative health, veterans' issues, civil discourse, LGBTQ themes, composting, animal rights, art and social justice—with dozens of community organizations and emergent movements. As several of the faculty and graduate students involved in crafting the original half dozen Action Research Teams realized that there was an undeniable resonance among multiple themes, sites, and modes of democratic engagement, we decided to gather in an ARTs Symposium at the end of each semester to present, discuss, and enthusiastically celebrate together. There is always a great deal of excitement at these events, and many of the hundreds of students, faculty, staff, and community members who attend them express a remarkable sense of enthusiastic activist hope, as team after team demonstrates ways in which they are creating significant changes—both on the issues and problems on which they are doing action research and on themselves as many are becoming democratic coagents of transformation. The auditorium becomes a resonance machine in which there is a shift from a world that appears largely immutable in its injustice, ecological destruction, and antidemocratic powers toward a radical democratic habitus in which myriad problems and issue domains appear to be sites where we are cultivating increasingly durable and intersecting practices, habits, and sensibilities for radical democratic innovation, resilience, and a complex, flourishing commonwealth. No small dimension of this resonance and enthusiasm concerns *the rapid expansion and intensification of this democracy education movement itself*, as we sense, learn about, and celebrate the work of generating new capacities for more significant change, new action research initiatives and teams, and so forth. The ARTs symposia thus generate a sense that growing expanses of the political and ecological geography of our time are becoming subject to democratic game-transformative practices and relationships of embodied critical reflection, dialogue, public work and action; *and* they generate a sense that the rate at which this shift toward democratic mutability is occurring *is accelerating*. In multiple registers—from the infrasensible, to the sensible, to interpretive research, to political imagination, to questions of strategy and substantive direction, to powerful actions that impact the world—we are becoming aware of and called to democratic action by an intensifying experience of a world of emergent possibilities.

Yet this intensifying experience of accelerating democratic transformation is not born of, nor borne by, pressures of simplification and efficiency so common (and self-defeating) in many political organizations and movements, increasingly under the sway of neoliberal "metrics." Rather, it is flourishing precisely as a blooming and buzzing complexity working on myriad problems, with a variety of community groups, organizing according to a wide range of modalities (from civil discourse, to education and outreach, to public work, political advocacy, artistic actions, community gardening, solidarity economy networking, dramatic public assemblies, street protest, and more) in relation to diverse interests, traditions, passions, and visions. We are accelerating in part because we are a *pedagogical* complexity, learning our ways, repeatedly modulating in light of critical evaluations and a healthy dose of tension. Our cohesion stems from a sense that broad-based democratic body politics, dialogue, work, and action negotiated in this undomesticated manner are precisely how we will forge a better future. By means of a resonant ecology of diverse pedagogical and political practices we are cultivating a sense—and a taste—for intensities and accelerations that are deeply intertwined with fierce urgencies and patient labors in the labyrinths of complexity.

While the ARTs symposia each semester provide particularly rich experiences of resonance among the diverse initiatives, the deeper challenge in terms of constituting a democratic habitus is how to cultivate similar experiences more frequently. To this end, we are creating numerous free spaces on campus—democratic residential learning communities, alternative gardens, a café—where students can gather, bump into each other, become acquainted with numerous initiatives, forge creative intersections, generate new visions, and celebrate their growing collaborations through visual arts, music, poetry, shared food, and debates. Exemplifying the spirit of these efforts, in the new Green Scene Café there is a large, colorful mural that evokes themes of ecological resilience, community building, mutuality, and intergenerational solidarity. This mural was created through dialogues and close collaboration between regionally loved and world-famous Dine (Navajo) artist Shonto Begay and NAU students involved in action research. Begay describes his painting process, in which he taps on the canvas (or, in this case, the wall) as *visual drumming*. His paintings often have echoes of van Gogh that incarnate the resonant process of creation on surfaces that appear to vibrate rhythmically with light and life. As one enters the café, one comes face-to-face with a resonant evocation of resonant democratic ecological engagement—the radical ordinary.

At the same time as we are beginning to fashion spaces for face-to-face encounters, we are also venturing into the virtual. Students are at the cutting edge of these initiatives as they utilize a wide variety of electronic media in ways that extend, disseminate, proliferate, intensify, and react back upon the resonances forming in more physically proximate encounters. Increasingly they are generating videos, audio recordings, Facebook sites, emergent websites like Democracy U (associated with the American Commonwealth Project), radio and television spots, electronic theses, blogs, open source technologies, cloud computing, and other media in ways that suggest great possibilities for developing a profoundly democratic populist resonance machine beyond contexts in which people can easily gather together—one that is decentralized, decentered, interactive, pluralizing, and empowering of diverse sites and networks of civic agency.

Debates about democracy sometimes revolve around axes that dichotomize face-to-face democracy, on the one hand, and virtual electronic democracy, on the other. In contrast, what we are seeing emerge are intertwinements of the two in which each modality relays, intensifies, amplifies, and serves various prosthetic functions for the others. Face-to-face resonance creates energies that draw people to resonances in the virtual sphere of electronic media, which in turn amplify the former. An inventiveness is starting to manifest here that suggests that possibilities of working at larger scales (e.g., translocal, national, transnational) may not necessarily engender the antidemocratic pressures many fear. Or it may do so to significantly lesser degrees at the same time that it creates democratic pathways that are indispensable given the large-scale ecological, economic, and political crises we face. I suspect that students now at Killip and Kinsey elementary schools may write some pathbreaking books on this that far exceed the limits of my imagination.[41]

Yet in all of this, are we really creating a game-transformative political practice? Or are we merely experimenting with a democratic pedagogy that may be admirable, yet barely approaches the radical promise of the theoretical vision conjured up at the intersection of neuroscience and Bourdieu? Part of this question concerns possibilities for creating broader transformation in the midst of complex dynamic systems that are very powerful and render our efforts precarious, in spite of their increasing power and durability. The chapters that follow explore different aspects of these challenges.

Yet insofar as the question addresses the character of the dynamics within this democratic movement during its first six years, I think there are reasons to be profoundly hopeful. One of the most powerful strands of evidence for the idea that the habitus of receptive radical democracy is indeed a game-transformative practice is that we *repeatedly critically reflect upon, rework, and reform the ground of our own movement.* In part, we do this by making "critical evaluation" a regular component of our practices, as do many broad-based community organizing initiatives today.

Yet the game-transformative dispositions significantly exceed the critical and reformative practices we try to build into our basic democratic processes. During the half-dozen years of our democracy education movement, mini-movements have repeatedly sprung up in more feisty tension with a specific political mode, or vision, or practice, or even orientations taken by some to be basic to the project as a whole. Undergraduates in particular ARTs have rebelled when they thought the graduate students who were facilitating their ART were doctrinaire or stifling undergraduate initiative; graduate students have launched initiatives to democratize leadership practices that they thought were becoming cliquish; faculty in different units have pushed back in different ways in resistance to developments they worried did not speak to the vision and interests of their programs; students, faculty, and community members have variously launched challenges that the ARTs were too radical, or not radical enough, or that they failed to take seriously in a transformative way crucial issues of power, diverse ways of organizing, or horizons of freedom. Typically these contestations have had heated moments, and we have developed new zones of dialogue, reassessment of different sorts, new ways of doing things, new ARTs, and so forth.

In my view, what has been most interesting in this dynamic evolution is that the radical democratic habitus we are cocreating seems to be engendering four virtues that, on the whole, are keeping things at once lively and powerful, *and* holding them together so that we learn from and cohere amid our differences and dissonances. First, the *more insurgent* game-transformative sensibilities and dispositions cultivated by the ARTs themselves are a significant part of what gives rise to and thrives in these more dramatic challenges, through which we often learn and are energized. Indeed, undergraduates often note that it was when they *challenged* (in ways that the ARTs as a whole encouraged) that they became most politically *fired up about and invested in* the ARTs. Second, this resulting commitment is related to the *radical receptivity* that is also integral to the game-transformative aspect of the ARTs, for such receptivity enables many who are more established in the process to listen, learn, bend, and reform in light of challenges, in ways that prevent contestation from breaking the movement into sectarian fragments. Third, as the ARTs have developed over time, many of us have cultivated a capacious sense that these more dissonant and heated elements of contestation are actually a healthy process that is integral to the resonance of our movement for radical democracy. This dampens our human propensities to get overly worked up when such contestations begin to simmer. Fourth, most of those who have been involved in this process for several years come to realize through experience that multiple modes, visions, and propensities are *part of* the radically democratic political condition, and that each has a range of things that it does relatively well, and a range where it is weaker. This tends to encourage a pluralizing view: namely, that a *rich ecology of differences*—in both collaboration and tension—is actually integral to bringing about transformation, rather than a single "line" or narrower bandwidth. So far, this habitus we are cocreating seems to be engendering each of these sensibilities in ways that are sufficiently energetic, resonant, and intertwined to sustain an unusually vital, transformative, broad, and resilient movement.

Of course, resonance, as we learned from Poincaré and Prigogine, emerges from the interacting frequencies of bodies in motion. With whom and with what the bodies of our polity (and our world) resonate hinges very much on where and how we move—and the character of movement itself as less the simple displacement of given bodies, and more the constitutive modes of receptivity through which bodies are brought into being. No mode of power has ever been more indebted to, invested in, and intent upon managing and controlling the political economy of circulations than the current neoliberal regime of corporate capitalism, as Marx and Foucault help us understand. Any politics that seeks to cultivate a resonant radical democratic habitus, yet which fails to engender counterconducts that resist and create alternatives to the mainstreams of circulation and governmentality that wreak havoc on democracy and the planet, is hardly worth considering. The politics of resonance—whether in the form of capitalist-vitriolic-fundamentalist resonance machines or of radical receptive democratic habitus—engenders flows of bodies driven and cultivated variously by desires, pleasures, hostilities, and visions. The political economy of flows, in turn, engenders resonance by fashioning and moving bodies and things through particular places, in particular modes, according to particular juxtapositions and interactions (or not).

What kinds of circulatory politics might disrupt the neoliberal order of gargantuan exploitative flows and nurture radically receptive, democratic, and ecologically resilient polities and networks? What kind of pedagogy, practices, and communities might be capable of initiating these alternatives here, in this world of rushing currents that increasingly undermine democracy and the planetary ecosystem? We turn to these questions in the next chapter.

Action ResearchTeam

CHAPTER 2

From Mega-circulatory Power to Polyface Flows

During the first several years I was at Northern Arizona University, my second-floor office had large, south-facing windows that overlooked an alternative agricultural plot on campus called the Students for Sustainable Living and Urban Gardening (SSLUG) Garden. The permaculture garden was an often buzzing place in which I regularly saw students tending to the edible plants that grew there in a variety of microarrangements that wove together sun exposure, shade, soils, rocks, water, relationships among different plants, and compost. With great care, they explored agricultural practices appropriate to our semiarid, high-elevation region in which a very short growing season, frequent high winds, hail, and notoriously poor soils combine to pose significant challenges to those seeking to advance NAU and Flagstaff's part in the movement for alternative food systems. A burgeoning variety of related initiatives and Action Research Teams intersect with the SSLUG Garden: water harvesting from nearby roofs has been initiated by an ART called Action Group for Water Advocacy (AGWA); campus composting begun by an ART called Velocomposting, in which students excitedly haul "waste" in trailers behind bicycles from campus dining halls to compost sites, where research was conducted on the effects of moisture, composting mixtures, pile geometry, and temperature on the process; experimental cold frames and other season extenders have been deployed as part of a grant project called Local FARE; various art projects are installed there as well, and not infrequently other ARTs meet around tables and benches in the garden to discuss action research, relationships, strategies, and intersections with other initiatives. Parts of the SSLUG Garden grow native plants, and an elder in Applied Indigenous Studies, Marina Vasquez, often teaches about traditional knowledge in relation to gathering and agriculture, healing, and ecological well-being there. Sometimes, students from K–12 schools in Flagstaff where the School Gardens ARTs work come to learn and participate in the garden, as do numerous other members of the broader community. In the fall, some celebrate the modest harvest with potlucks. All the resonant movement around the garden inspires students, faculty, and key administrators to dream and initiate other plots on campus. The garden is a public space in which people and the more than human world interact in powerful ways with implications for knowledge, action, and community building that radiate across Flagstaff.

From early on, the garden began to infiltrate my thinking and conference papers, and I increasingly believe that the SSLUG Garden played a vital role in my sense of radical and ecological democracy—even bigger than I thought when I first began writing in relation with it. It was a resonant incarnation of dynamic care—as students mindfully moved seeds, small bits of soil, rocks, water channels, and themselves, and interacted with each other in ways that echoed rather palpably with a sense of possibility. Miguel Vasquez, a colleague of mine who has conducted anthropological research and collaborations with Hopi on their agricultural plots, once told me a story about a Hopi elder who said, in the face of his impatience with some young folks in the garden who were acting in somewhat frustrating ways: "Miguel, remember, we are cultivating youth every bit as much as we are cultivating the land."

I cannot say for sure what she meant, but in my ears her words speak to how the whole swirl of human bodies, plants, things, and other life around farming cultivate human beings, as much as if not more than human beings cultivate the land. We are born in and borne by all this movement. When we are attentive to it all in ways that care for the intertwinements between how this cultivates us and how it cultivates the world, we tend to engender the flourishing and resilience of ecological and human communities. When we abandon attentiveness and active engagement in the very processes of movement through which we are formed, or when such attentiveness and activities are colonized or stolen, things can go profoundly awry.

––––––––––

In the previous chapter we explored possibilities for radical democratic transformation through the lens of receptive resonance. We sought a resilient context that might engender dispositions, perceptions, imaginations, enthusiasms, relational capacities, and reflexivity that enhance the cocreative power of democratic engagement for commonwealth and ecological flourishing. Yet as we have already seen, resonance in its various modes is profoundly intertwined with *movement*. At the most elemental level, from Poincaré to Prigogine and Stengers, it is the movement of and within bodies that generates frequencies, which interact with other frequencies to disrupt Newtonian physics. At the neurological level, biochemical movements in one body enter into perceptual relationships with those of others to engender resonance. And I have suggested that—as with the movement of people in myriad other types of practices—the attentive movement of people engaged in receptive democratic practice nurtures specific fields of resonance as well, and these interact in turn with different registers of resonance, from the biochemical, to the techno-political, and beyond. The intertwining of resonance and movement is, in fact, so deep that one could say that we are less "bodies that move"—as if there were fully formed bodies prior to movement, and more "bodies that come into being through modes of movement." Our neurological development, our perceptual fields, our imaginations, dispositions, shapes, strengths and weaknesses, tastes, emotions, affinities, health and diseases, attention spans, ideological propensities, and even our capacities to move ourselves are all entangled in webs of mutually constitutive relationships with where and how we move, toward what ends, with whom and what else, in what sort of contexts, doing what, for how long, heading where else, and so forth.

This insight underscores the importance of reflecting both upon movement in relation to radical democracy and also upon the character of dominant modes of contemporary political economic power that pertain to the circulation of beings and things. A good case can be made that, along with new techno-political practices of resonance, a crucial form of power in our times operates to an unprecedented degree by moving people, nonhuman beings, and things about in ways that significantly engender, invest, and govern our bodies to enhance concentrated productivity. To counter such power and fashion a politics that might have a chance of engendering alternatives to it, we must develop a critical analysis of how it operates.

Hence, in this chapter I will focus on a mode of power that I take to be foremost in the contemporary (dis)order of things—one that at once literally sets the world in motion and flows through everything. In our times, unprecedented mega-circulations generate tremendous political economic accumulations and capacities to govern human beings. Moreover, this "governmentality" (a form of biopolitical management and control) operates through macro- and microcirculations in ways that generate resonances among bodies and things—with major impacts on our (in)capacities for attention, excitement, perception, distraction, desire, comprehension, and incomprehension—that in turn tend to enhance the circulatory powers that give birth to them. (A substantial portion of the corresponding financial flows are then invested in proliferating the corporate-megastate resonance machine that works toward similar ends.) My contention is that mega-circulations—of grains, food, goods, finance, fertilizer, waste, people, military, energy, water, pharmaceuticals, and so forth—generate unparalleled world-transformative dynamics that drive the major developments and catastrophes of our time across scales ranging from the minuscule to the monumental. Indeed, as this picture becomes clearer, it seems wise to revise our line about how "bodies come into being through modes of movement," so that it reads, "*bodies come into being through movement in relation to the juxtaposed movements of other bodies of people, nonhuman beings, and things.*"

As we begin to grasp the profundity of the operations of circulatory power in our day, we can simultaneously begin to recognize, theorize, and advance vital dimensions of counterconducts and alternative conducts that are rapidly emerging in many social movements, yet whose importance is often missed entirely or underestimated by most political theory and many who are active in other forms of grassroots organizing.[1] By cultivating theory and practice that is attentive to what is prefigured in such movements, we can enrich our political vision of radical democratic and ecologically resilient futures routed/rooted in receptive flows far more conducive to possibilities for complex dynamic commonwealth—rather than the imperatives of global corporate capital. Throughout much of this chapter, I draw on movements and organizing that are emerging in many places around the world, though the bulk of my focus is on the U.S. context. I also discuss some of the rapidly emerging efforts of the corporate mega-circulatory apparatus to stifle or assimilate these movements, and argue that those engaging in ecological political movements around alternative flows will likely need to incorporate a more agonistic political element if we are to continue flourishing and advancing our transformative power. Toward the end of this chapter, I discuss the politics of polyface flows that is emerging at the intersection of NAU's ARTs and numerous organizations in the broader community.

Mega-circulation, Governmentality, and Antidemocratic Ecocidal Megapower

The later work of Michel Foucault provides crucial insights into the emergence and character of circulatory power. Many are familiar with Foucault as the theorist of disciplinary power, of which Bentham's *Panopticon* is the infamous exemplification. Yet in his lectures from the late 1970s, Foucault shifts his analysis significantly. The panopticon now appears as "the oldest dream of the oldest sovereign," insofar as it gives expression to a central gaze that would see and control every subject "in the most homogeneous, continuous, and exhaustive way possible."[2] Insofar as the panoptic ideal is to totally enclose space and submit those within to the principle of perpetual visibility, the beings thus located were to internalize and continuously proliferate its gaze, thus enclosing the future itself within its own disciplinary logic. It would represent the consummate achievement of temporal sovereignty, in which a present configuration of spatial power would extinguish what Ernst Bloch calls the "not yet," as this present "bends an arch of closed form-contents out of Becomeness over the Unbecome."[3]

In the late 1970s, however, Foucault theorizes a dominant form of contemporary power that has a very different origin, mode, and ideal of maximization. He calls this form "security" or "governmentality" (terms I will use interchangeably), and its dominant motif is circulation rather than enclosure. Foucault traces the beginnings of security to the "suppression of city walls," which start to come down in eighteenth-century Europe in response to increasing trade, economic growth, circulation of grains, goods, and people, as well as problems of hygiene in the midst of overcrowding, and so forth. All of these developments created pressures that led to "cutting routes through the town[s]."[4] The "problem of circulation" increasingly displaces enclosure as the crucial context in which power must be exercised. Foucault does not claim that disciplinary power "goes away" with the emergence of governmentality, for disciplinary power is beginning to intensify and proliferate at roughly the same time. Yet he suggests that in the modern world disciplinary power and sovereignty tend more often than not to be deployed in ways that are subordinate to the requirements of security and the exercise of power in the context of circulation. (With Foucault, I would emphasize that these issues of relative salience and the modes of intertwinement among these powers are always historically and spatially specific—varying as well in relation to class, race, nationality, colonial legacies, and so forth. I would add that these different modes of power often provoke dissonance and conflicts at the heart of dominant regimes.)[5]

Yet circulation is not merely a *context* in and upon which the apparatus of security operates. Rather it becomes *integral to its new modes of operating and proliferating*. Indeed, Foucault argues that beginning with the Economistes in the eighteenth century, circulation becomes a *new principle of maximization* for enhancing state power in the context of interstate rivalry. In contrast to a totalizing police authority, governmentality requires a certain respect for the numerous circulations and processes upon which it depends: "a regulation based upon and in accordance with the course of things themselves"—the nature of economic activity, the stubborn properties of populations, the characteristics of scarcity, the flow of goods, and so on.[6] To this end, probabilistic sciences of government emerge to facilitate the management and intensification of circulations in different realms.[7] Governmentality may often be implicated in complex strategies that involve precise prescriptive and proscriptive exercises of disciplinary power and sovereignty. Yet its own operations seek not to block circulations of populations, goods, criminals, vagrants, grains, and so on, but rather to utilize them by *working with them—by insinuating governmentality into their flows, juxtaposing them, and facilitating their proliferation*—in order to "establish . . . [probabilistic] average[s] considered as optimal . . . and a bandwidth of the acceptable that must not be exceeded."[8] Governmentality thus works by simultaneously granting autonomy and investing in it so as "to respond . . . in such a way that this response cancels out [the worst negative effects of] the reality to which it responds—nullifies it, or limits, checks, or regulates it," while enhancing the powers to be drawn from it.[9]

Consider in this context hunger-driven circulations of people.[10] Governmentality situates circulations of the hungry poor within a market structure that generates regulated-but-not-eliminated scarcity that perpetually stimulates flows of cheap, precarious, and productive labor for "the wealth of nations" (even as a portion of the population must thus be sacrificed as "impertinent" for this to "work").[11] At the same time, governmentality begins to infiltrate hunger *as appetite* by operating on a range of factors to affect dispositions that enhance circulatory power. Indeed, in contrast to the logic of sovereignty that says "no" to desire, for security, "the problem is how to say yes . . . to this desire . . . [how to do] everything that stimulates and encourages this self-esteem, this desire, so that it can produce its necessary beneficial effects"—at least for those who are deemed "pertinent" rather than "impertinent."[12] In these ways, while disciplinary power is centripetal in character, security is centrifugal, expanding, proliferating and organizing "ever-wider circuits" and circulations (that will eventually exceed and encroach upon the powers of the sovereign states whose competitive imperatives initially stimulated the proliferation of many of these circulations).[13]

Even as governmentality facilitates developments that enable dramatic intensifications of power, Foucault argues that it paradoxically opens some possibilities for resistance. First, civil society comes to be seen as a natural sphere whose freedom must be respected precisely as a "necessary correlate of the state" whose power is to be maximized by flows that proliferate through more decentralized means.[14] Hence, "counterconducts" come to occupy spaces and employ freedoms that are created in part by the form of power that they would resist. Second, insofar as governmentality works *within* circulations in a manner that operates *not definitively but probabilistically*, it holds open some "possibility of movement[s], change[s] of place, [and] processes of circulation of both people and things" that deviate from its studied optima.[15] Governmentality rarely focuses on utterly extinguishing the possibility of unexpected future events (except at what it takes to be the intolerable "extremities" of bandwidth). Ironically, in contrast to disciplinary power, the apparatus of security and related ideologies of possibility must in principle affirm a degree of indeterminacy. Governmentality cannot *in principle* annihilate the "not yet," even as recent developments in circulatory power (discussed later) threaten to do so *in fact*. This new form of circulatory power—its dangers and its openings in political space and time—sets the stage for a series of contestations and initiatives that are crucial for understanding both the challenges and the opportunities for radical and ecological democracy in our times.

In response to the counterconducts and alternative conducts that seize these margins of possibility (Polanyi provides an insightful account of some of these movements),[16] in the middle of the nineteenth century, governmentality begins to undergo numerous transformations that facilitate hyperintensifications of power that far exceed the character and capacities associated with its original form. One way in which this intensification happens is through the development of *institutions and practices of governmentality that increasingly acquire circulatory characteristics themselves*: political and economic institutions increasingly take on liquid, shape-shifting, mobile characteristics—the "formless forms" that Sheldon Wolin critically analyzes as "inverted totalitarianism" and "Superpower."[17] Ted Nace and others compellingly illuminate some of these developments in the history of corporations in the United States and beyond.[18] The American Revolution was in large degree a response to the abuses of British corporations such as the East India Company that the colonists understood to radically encroach upon their economic and political freedoms. Hence, postrevolutionary political economic designs in nearly all the states sought to totally submit corporations to the demos by granting corporate charters only for specified and limited public purposes defined by state legislatures, placing strict time limits on charters that established democratic accountability by requiring corporations to seek legislative renewal, limiting corporate size, establishing double liability, mandating territorial attachments, prohibiting one corporation from owning stock in another, securing rights of public buyout, and so forth. This worked well for about six decades.

Yet the history of corporations from the post–Civil War period forward is one in which they gradually freed themselves from democratic accountability and then used their power to undermine democratic institutions and powers. Establishing circulatory powers that freed corporations from territorial accountability was a pivotal move in this drama, and the circulatory techno-economic apparatus called railroads played a crucial role in instigating it in order to extend the regularities and range that secured and enhanced its conditions of possibility. When the New Jersey legislature (under corporate pressure) radically loosened incorporation statutes to enable any corporation it chartered to hold stock in (and thus control) any other corporation anywhere for any purpose, this established the simple mechanism by which corporations in other states could free themselves from tighter regulations—simply by establishing a corporation in New Jersey and selling to it. Effectively, corporations acquired the power to flow beyond the bounds of legislative accountability without ever leaving wherever they were actually operating.

Once power to circulate beyond the territorial state was attained, corporations used it relentlessly to play states off against each other, as states moved to loosen all types of restrictions in order not to lose corporations to New Jersey and other early adopters. This process enabled corporations to acquire and then intensify *powers to shape-shift—increasingly transforming the powers of circulation into domains that exceed spatiality itself.* By the end of the nineteenth century, corporate identity, purpose, function, form, size, separation, and lifetime are all essentially *liquefied and set into dynamic flows* beyond the limits that had been established by the revolutionary demos concerned to protect its political and economic freedoms. Corporations gain powers of immortality (circulating through time without limit), the ability to change purposes (circulating through myriad horizons of ambition), capacities to merge with any other corporate body, powers of disguise through morphing identities, capabilities to physically move anywhere and grow to any size, and so on. Through these endlessly dynamic circulations, liability comes to be greatly limited, and corporations set in motion a process in which they have continued to gain (and usurp) myriad constitutional rights that enhance and delimit powers of corporate "personhood" at the expense of the demos and noncorporate forms of economic life and civil society. This provides an excellent example of my earlier proposition that bodies—in this case institutional bodies—are born in and become through movement.

Increasingly, as Sheldon Wolin powerfully illuminates, corporate power transforms the forms, functions, operational modalities, and purposes of the state, while previously public responsibilities such as health care, schooling, policing, prisons, and military operations are colonized and corporatized.[19] In this process, the government itself acquires corporate characteristics such as institutional fluidity, capacities for rapid downsizing, intensified imperatives to pursue narrowly defined efficiencies, and freedom from democratic accountability. Such "privatization" tends to disguise superpower in ways that allow it to circulate throughout the body politics with less resistance—thereby constituting a "system [that becomes] ever more comprehensive, pervading all spheres of life."[20]

The fluid institutions of securitized superpower function not only by infiltrating but also by producing and proliferating circulations in ways that tend to *reconstruct the world and human beings* in order to maximize megaflows of circulatory power. One could flesh out crucial aspects of this process with and well beyond Foucault's discussion of biopower,[21] but a striking analysis in relation to the journey of corn and (agri)culture may be equally or more compelling. Recall that the increased flow of grain in the eighteenth century is one of the conditions to which the circulatory power of governmentality is a response. A brief examination of circulations associated with corn production, distribution, and consumption—or what Michael Pollan refers to in *The Omnivore's Dilemma* as a global "river of corn"—illustrates the ways in which this power undergoes hyperintensifications and transformations in which *circulation becomes radically reconstitutive*—at the farthest extreme from the laissez-faire modalities of its emergence.[22] (While I focus on food here, it would be easy to extend such an analysis to other mega-circulations such as energy, finance, water, pharmaceuticals, vehicles, and weapons.)

Consider the following corn-sketch of the immensity and salience of governmentality and circulatory power: U.S. farmers cultivate a cornfield twice the size of New York State.[23] Corn constitutes three-quarters of the volume of global trade in coarse grains.[24] More than a quarter of the forty-five thousand products in the average American supermarket contain corn.[25] It is no mere accident that corn constitutes such a large component of economic circulation, but rather due to a convergence of factors that led to the bioengineering of corn as an ideal entity for commodity circulation, as well as for proliferating a host of other economic, political, cultural, bodily, and material circulations that are integral to the functioning of contemporary power.

Pollan illustrates how corn has been bioengineered to become "the protocapitalist plant."[26] It is almost indestructible and thus easy to transport through the vast arteries and capillaries of what he conceives as "this great, intricately

d stainless steel beast" through which a river of corn of sublime magnitude
lessly flows.[27] Prior to 1856, corn was a clunky commodity that circulated
in burlap bags full of distinct qualities of grain that had carefully identified
origins. Yet in response to the tremendous circulatory techno-economic powers of railroads (which we have already noted were integral to reconstituting
corporate being as a circulatory institution), corn was gradually reconceived
and reconstituted to become "less a food than an industrial raw material—
an abstraction" that is "an internationally recognized commodity grown everywhere (and nowhere in particular), fungible, traded in and speculated
upon and accepted as a form of capital all over the world." Corn has become
elevator-ready and capable of perfect circulation because it has been reduced
to "number 2 field corn": "the corn without qualities, quantity is really the only
thing that counts."[28] Each kernel is like a molecule of a homogeneous liquid
whose flow is entirely dependent upon a tremendous political, economic, and
technologically designed—and militarily secured—apparatus of circulation.
Unlike seeds in the natural world, and unlike seeds that have been cultivated,
exchanged, and passed on for thousands of years in the nature-culture nexus
of preindustrial agriculture, corn has been bioengineered into a hybrid form
that has achieved unprecedented levels of hyperproductivity.

Yet there are a number of catches. Or are they opportunities? The quantitative surge of hyperproductivity terminates with each generation of seeds,
as yields in the following generation plummet by about one-third—"making
their seeds virtually worthless" in a corn-world where quantity is the only
thing that matters.[29] Hence autonomous possibilities for circulation are effectively terminated each generation: the flow must be replenished and reinitiated
each year by the techno-corporate agri-security apparatus that, as we have
seen, itself acquires liquid characteristics enabling it to endlessly morph in
ways most conducive to an ever-increasing productivity of which it is the sole
definer. Farmers must return to the apparatus for seeds each spring, and because these seeds are genetically identical from generation to generation (unlike seeds in nature, which continually mix genetically), they are patented as
intellectual property.[30] Thus, contemporary corn is a genetic construct whose
essence embodies capitalist property and reconstitutive circulatory power
quite perfectly: it is less a thing than a power-maximizing flow that proliferates
and differentiates yet can't get away from—and remains the inalienable property of—the increasingly fluid economic, political, and technological apparatus upon which it is absolutely dependent. It should be noted, unsurprisingly,
that two megacorporations alone—Cargill and ADM—control and purchase

fully one-third of this megaflow. Moreover, "these two corporations now guide corn's path at every step of the way: They provide the pesticide and fertilizer to the farmers; operate most of America's grain elevators, broker and ship most of the exports; perform the . . . milling; feed the livestock [which consume three-fifths of all corn in spite of the fact that cows get sick and die on corn without major medical interventions] and then slaughter the corn-fattened animals; distill the ethanol; and manufacture the high-fructose corn syrup."[31]

Corn not only has been designed as the perfect circulatory substance but also has been bioengineered to stimulate and absorb the flow of that other ceaselessly morphing substance that fuels the global economy, namely, oil. In the post–World War II period, the U.S. government initiated a tremendous project to convert its munitions operations involving petrochemical ammonium nitrate into fertilizer for peacetime purposes. Corn was thus designed to consume more of this than any other plant—both to absorb ammonium nitrate and to free its productivity from the limits of naturally circulating solar energy. Each acre of corn now *consumes fifty gallons of oil per season*; each corn-fed cow, about one gallon. Because corn (and industrial agriculture as a whole) plays an integral role in increasing the flow of oil, it thereby enhances the circulation of the U.S. military apparatus that, in turn, secures these flows in the Middle East and elsewhere.

In a manner that exemplifies the transformative hybridization and fluidification of political and economic power, the corporations that manage, proliferate, and most benefit from these circulations also write the laws—price supports, tax breaks, protections, subsidies, (non)regulations, and so forth—that play a key role in ever increasing the volume of this flow. Public and private powers, players, functions, and forms circulate among each other in a manner that proliferates the volume, capillary penetration, and differentiation of the colossal river of corn. By lowering the price of corn and subsidizing each bushel, mostly big-business farmers—who have designed these rules—are incentivized to produce more and more regardless of demand.

In conjunction with all this, the agri-security apparatus also infiltrates and stimulates the demand side of this circulatory process, both by reconstituting the foods for which human beings hunger and by transforming the food-body-desire nexus so that humans can continue to absorb the ever-increasing flow. With great acuity, Pollan illustrates how the agri-security apparatus has made great strides in overcoming the biological inelasticity of demand for food. Previously this inelasticity was rooted in the body's relatively limited capacity to absorb food, feedback mechanisms through which our hunger is satiated, and our hardwired omnivorous propensity to want to eat a variety of species—not just corn. One way in which the industrial food circulation complex has increasingly overcome these limits is by pumping more and more high-fructose corn syrup into what we eat and drink—an increase of one-quarter since 1985, thereby overriding the biological mechanisms that otherwise shut down our hunger in manners more conducive to health. Thus, driven by an insatiable hunger for supersugary foods, three-fifths of Americans are now overweight and increasingly plagued by numerous associated diseases.

Our food-body-desire nexus is being reworked daily in order to transform us into "industrial eaters." As if the sugar-trickster is insufficient, a host of visceral "supersizing" marketing strategies do additional work on our hungering bodies. Simultaneously, to trick our omnivore body's propensity for culinary variety, the flow of corn is increasingly diversified into myriad rivulets across a delta of "wet milling" (which now accounts for a rapidly growing one-fifth of all corn processing), in which "the power of food science . . . break[s] foods down into their nutrient parts and then reassemble[s] them in specific ways that, in effect, push our evolutionary buttons, fooling the omnivore's inherited food selection system."[32] Ersatz novelty is added to variety, enabling the industrial food system to interface with what some evolutionary biologists believe to be a strong connection between our omnivorous character and our imaginative propensities for the new. Effectively, the radically homogenized and unchanging river of industrial corn is made to appear (and becomes) differentiated in a manner that overcomes our omnivorous predilection for multiplicitous and shifting dietary relationships and dependencies upon a manifold world. A vast network of distracted speed-eating practices—from fast-food businesses, to autos designed for food and drinks on the go, to dinners in front of the television or computer—coconspire to engender docile, satisfied-yet-insatiable industrial eaters. In all these ways, a plethora of circulatory powers associated with number 2 field corn—the common denominator of quantity without quality—rewire our bodily hungering for qualitative differences such that we thirst for the pseudodifferentiations of a single anonymous flow. Will obesity not foment widespread resistance at some point? Perhaps not: fake sugars, fake fats, and "resistant starches" have been and continue to be developed that would circulate through and pass out of the body as if nothing at all had been present. As Pollan puts it: "Meet the ultimate—utterly elastic! [read: fluid]—industrial eater." Deeply attuned to how contemporary governmentality operates through practices of circulation, revolutionary (agri) cultural Kentuckian radical democrat Wendell Berry poignantly summarizes our situation: "The ideal industrial food consumer would be strapped to a table with a tube running from the food factory directly into his or her stomach."[33] Almost. Yet we might ratchet up the dystopian ante and suggest that this image misses the ways in which the frenetic, insatiable, and highly mobile circulations of contemporary food consumers not only burn more calories and thus replenish appetites but also participate in propelling a manifold matrix of circulating materiality—from energy, to motor vehicles, to metals, to medicines, to militaries, to money, to migrant labors, and much more—just to remain with the alliterative flow of m's. It would not be hard to construct analogous critical analyses of reconstitutive mega-circulatory powers associated with each of these flows. Each, and all of them together, harbor profoundly deleterious implications for democracy and ecosystems as the atmospheric, hydrological, and biological flows of complex dynamical planetary systems begin to tip beyond the range of Holocene equilibriums.

Let me close this section, then, by offering a more fitting dystopic image of contemporary circulatory power in order to set a stage for exploring a counterimage that might illuminate meaningful radical democratic work, action, and (agri)cultural change more conducive to human and ecological flourishing. Recall that in contrast to the centripetal characteristics of disciplinary power, which enclose and seek to constitute beings according to the gravitational forces of the central tower, Foucault conceives of security as a centrifugal force. Security moves outward, insinuating itself into—and ultimately instigating and engineering—flows that circulate across space and into the future to maximize power. Imagine this form of governmentality as an enormous cancerous growth with a structure somewhat analogous to an oak tree on its side, with a massive set of branches and roots, extending and dividing into ever-smaller twigs on one side and ever-smaller rootlets on the other. This treelike structure is suspended in an increasingly liquid world and has flexibility and dynamism—more like bullwhip kelp shifting in ocean swells, in this regard. Many of these roots and branches relentlessly extend and differentiate themselves, both to absorb more and more of the world and to release growing volumes of "waste" through zillions of "nonpoint sources." Yet many other roots and branches are guided by another morphological project. Imagine that the thick trunk of the tree malignantly bends back around itself on all sides, such that the roots and branches infiltrate the same expanding spaces. These branches represent the capillary "outflows" differentiated into myriad forms. The roots represent the intake (people's engendered desires, dispositions, consumption, systemic designs, etc.) that articulates with the proximate outflow of the multitudinous branches. The entire process is governed by imperatives to maximize the diameter and flow through the trunk (megacorporations and corporatized states), whose superpower is in turn enhanced by the endless capillary proliferation of branches and roots which produce, extract, and govern through voluminous yet finely crafted circulations. This curled oak is centrifugal in the sense that, with each circulatory pulse, it proliferates the extensive capillary network to enhance further intake and outflow. Though the apparatus of mega-circulation engenders industrial eaters, the latter in turn become little operators that frequently participate in further extending, modulating, and diversifying the capillary networks through which they themselves are once again produced. Yet the logic of capillary development is governed not by receptivity to manifold requirements for the diverse flourishing of humans, nonhuman beings, and ecosystems but by the expanding volume and superpower imperatives of the main trunk that proliferate oblivion to heteronomous specificities, virtues, and goods. Governmentality increasingly seeks to maximize circulation by reconstituting the world and eliminating what it cannot incorporate and redesign. As it does, it undermines the commons and renders people incapable of democracy and ecological care.

Movements of Decentralized Receptive Circulation

I introduced this dystopian image partly in an effort to suggest ways in which the mega-circulatory apparatus is actually *worse* than Wendell Berry's depiction of industrial eaters strapped to tables with food tubes connected to factory outflows. Yet if the flows and capillary extensions of mega-circulation are partly, strangely, and indispensably coconstituted by people's appetites and movements, so too these same people can *and are beginning to* exercise growing powers to resist this apparatus and cultivate alternatives—counterconducts and alternative conducts. Hence, our dystopian image is at once worse and yet more hopeful than that of tube-infused eaters strapped to tables.

In this sense, we might think of governmentality and circulatory power in a manner that is analogous to how Gramsci theorizes hegemony. While many sloppily appropriate this term to evoke an entirely heteronomous cultural power, in Gramsci's analysis it is crucial that hegemony can never simply (re)produce itself over against passive beings from sites of powerful discursive projection—such as the state, corporate media, and schools. Rather, as Paul Apostolidis shows, hegemony must always enlist people's ongoing interpretive (and I would add affective, material, and practiced) energies in order to function:

all who are subject to hegemony "help create the systemic forms of power within which they live,"[34] through ongoing interpretive work in which both the smallest details of daily life and the larger structures we encounter and negotiate are rendered in ways that alternately confirm, perpetuate, and extend hegemonic projections, or confound, resist, and truncate these powers, or do some of both with more indeterminate effects and political possibilities. This means that each interpretive act can be a site of struggle among hegemonic, counterhegemonic, and alternative tendencies, as we variously reproduce biopower or lean toward radical democratic possibilities.

Similar insights can inform initiatives to resist and create alternatives to the governmentality of mega-circulation. The colossal rivers of grain, animals, goods, oil, labor, military, finance, medicines, water, and so forth, depend upon capillary flows that require the active engagement, uptake, reproduction, and extension of a multitude of micropractices, dispositions, perceptions, desires, bodily movements, and interpretive acts that are susceptible to alterations that harbor no small potential to transform the dominant (dis)order of things. As radical democratic and ecological Latin American activist-scholar Gustavo Esteva puts it, "Coca Cola or Marlboro have 'no real existence' or power where people ignore them; they have no more power than the power people give to them by 'believing' in what they offer."[35] By "believing," Esteva refers to practices by which we move our bodies and attach our tubes to the circulations they move our way; by disbelief, he has in mind myriad collective ways in which we might move and organize to resist these circulations, detach, and initiate alternative flows.

These powers are not mere abstract placeholders for remote political possibilities. Rather, they are being exercised daily in myriad domains and manifold ways in communities and by social movements around the world, and the creativity and rates of developing countercirculations and alternative circulations are rapidly accelerating. Indeed, in marked contrast to Ronald Inglehart's postmaterialist (or postmodern values) frame for understanding new social movements, there appears to be a growing proliferation of movements organizing around a new materialism.[36] New materialist movements focus less on formal political participation as a means of shaping governmental policy so that it reflects such values, and much more on cultivating radically democratic and ecologically sustainable relationships amid flows of goods, people, food, energy, medicine, water, finance, and so forth. The circulation of materials that articulate with basic needs becomes a primary site of engagement for these movements. While new materialist social movements often go unrecognized by scholars, in light of an analysis of mega-circulatory power, their salience immediately becomes striking.[37]

Consider, for example, the rapid growth of such initiatives related to food alone in the United States in the past fifteen years. (Again, one could easily extend this analysis to flows of energy, medicine, craft making, transportation, and so forth.) One sign of widespread interest in this new orientation is indicated by the fact that Pollan's *Omnivore's Dilemma*—a book profoundly focused on the intersection of power, circulation, and alternatives—sold a quarter of a million copies in 2008 alone.[38] Between 1996 and 2006, when *Omnivore's Dilemma* was published, the number of farmers' markets rose from 1,755 to 3,137. In the seven years following its publication, the most recent data from the U.S. Department of Agriculture website shows this figure has risen to a remarkable 8,144 farmers' markets, and the rate of acceleration continues to increase.[39] Many millions of people in the United States are drawn to these markets regularly, and growing numbers are initiating practices to make them more socially and economically inclusive.[40] Another manifestation is the growth of Food Policy Councils (FPCs). These consist of diverse constituencies in cities and states who organize grassroots democratic networks with increasing power in order to *resist* flows of junk food in schools, food insecurity, food deserts in urban areas, and unsustainable agriculture, on the one hand, and to *construct* food systems that are more economically just, good for independent farmers, more accessible, tasty, and healthy for food eaters, and better for the environment, on the other. Since the first FPC formed in 1986, one hundred have arisen in states and cities across the United States.[41] Add to the mix the rapid growth of community-supported agriculture (CSA) farms, which create an intimate and reliable relationship between specific farms and those who buy food), which now number somewhere between eighteen hundred and twenty-three hundred in the United States. Then stir into the new materialist social movement pot the more than nine thousand schools that are currently purchasing some portion of their cafeteria food from local farms.[42]

Integral to these developments is the urban agriculture movement that has taken root in thousands of vacant lots and backyard gardens in cities across the United States. One famous example of this is in Detroit, Michigan, where as a result of an evolving grassroots organizing tradition indebted to legacies of radical union, civil rights, black power, and environmental movements, people are engaged in a burgeoning array of grassroots community, food justice, and environmental initiatives that are attracting attention from around the world. Among these are the fourteen hundred (and rapidly growing) community and family gardens and small farms within the city limits supported by the grass-roots Detroit Agricultural Network,[43] which "places Detroit at the forefront of a vibrant national movement to grow more food locally and lessen the nation's dependence on Big Ag."[44] Last but by no means least are the growing number of churches and other congregations that are beginning to resist corporate mega-circulations and radically rearticulate flows of desire, consumption, markets, and relationships around food according to theological visions of reciprocity, freedom, equality, stewardship, and so forth.[45] Due to initiatives such as these and many others, the recent uptick in the number of farms in the United States (reversing a long twentieth-century trend) is now led by small farms, many of whose owners are young people, recent immigrants, and/or women.[46]

Carlo Petrini, a leader of the global "Slow Food" movement that started in Italy, shows similar trends developing across Europe, the United States, and far beyond. At the microlevel of gathering to eat, millions are beginning to *circulate away* from the impoverished homogeneity of taste discernible beneath the pseudodifferentiated products of industrial food systems. Resisting the inattentive eating, vitiated pleasures, careless haste, and ecological oblivion of fast-food (agri)culture, multitudes are seeking slower modes of producing, distributing, preparing, and eating food in ways that seek, in Petrini's words, "*to wed pleasure to awareness and responsibility*, study and knowledge, and to offer opportunities for development even to poor and depressed regions through a new model of agriculture" favoring biodiversity across several continents (my emphasis).[47] In *Grassroots Postmodernism: Remaking the Soil of Cultures*, Gustavo Esteva and Madhu Suri Prakash discuss resonant initiatives in Latin America. Vandana Shiva offers a similar account of resistance and alternatives in India.[48] Add to this the worldwide indigenous network that seeks to resist corporate genetic enclosures of traditional seeds through Western property law and patents, on the one hand, and to advance alternative practices of exchange, cultivation, and circulation, on the other. Relatedly, there is widespread grassroots resistance to the production, circulation, and consumption of genetically modified organisms (GMOs) in Europe, Africa, the United States, and beyond.[49] What we are seeing is a global explosion of new materialist social movements contesting mega-circulations and initiating (or recovering) vital, democratic, socially just, and ecologically resilient agricultural flows.

The flows of goods, people, and power upon topographies of class, race, and gender in these new movements are uneven. Sometimes they replicate—

or in some ways even intensify—these topographies, as, for example, when many farmers' markets and Slow Food initiatives are situated in wealthier sections of urban areas and develop pricey niche products for the extremely high-end and most often white consumers. The poor, people of color, women, and children remain disproportionately excluded from access to healthy food, and farmers' markets in which most food is too expensive for those who are below the upper middle class do not address this issue.[50] As late in 2012, the U.S. Department of Agriculture (USDA) database showed that only one-fifth of the farmers' markets nationwide accepted Supplemental Nutrition Assistance Program (SNAP) payments (commonly known as food stamps).[51]

Nevertheless, in the past decade food and agricultural justice initiatives have sprung up in many cities and states, as Robert Gottlieb and Anupama Joshi chronicled several years ago in relation to farmers' markets that were beginning to improve access for low-income people, farmworker–environmental justice coalitions, food-to-school initiatives in schools in low-income neighborhoods, and more.[52] Studies in the past couple of years confirm both that there is a long way to go *and* that there are many promising signs emerging in the food justice movement. For example, in 2009 the Fair Food Network in Detroit exemplified kindred efforts springing up in cities and states across the United States in response to problems of food access, food justice, and health issues in poor neighborhoods, when it pioneered Double Up Food Bucks, which enable participants using SNAP benefits to double their money when purchasing fresh food from local farmers at participating farmers' markets. Today, more than one hundred farmers' markets across Michigan participate in the program. Michigan now accounts for 10 percent of the SNAP money spent at farmers' markets across the nation, and more than 90 percent of the farmers involved report increased sales as a result of the program. Groups working in several states, including New York, Maryland, and Ohio, have begun to adopt similar programs (based on combinations of private, nonprofit, and public funding), and the federal farm bill that passed in 2014 has allocated $100 million for "food insecurity nutrition incentives" modeled on such initiatives.[53] While nationally the percentage of farmers' markets that are taking steps to be more accessible remains low, in large, progressive urban areas, myriad organizations have worked to change this, and the percentages are much higher. In New York City, for example, 93 percent of the 145 farmers' markets accepted SNAP and WIC payments as of 2013. Similarly, as a result of urban food justice groups organizing to establish markets in poor neighborhoods, 59 percent of New York City's farmers' markets were located in neighborhoods with "high" or "very high" poverty.[54] As growing numbers of farmers' markets across the country are led by and accessible to poor people, people of color, and ethnic minorities, the cultural character of these markets is changing as well—in terms of foods that are available, languages spoken, crafts, music, and visual arts.

Not surprisingly, some of the most interesting loci of alternative flows have emerged from people struggling to create new forms of life at the intersections of age-old axes of power and suffering. Typical of growing numbers of initiatives across the United States, in Austin, Texas, the Sustainable Food Center has established Happy Kitchen / La Cocina Alegre, in which mostly women (many immigrants of color) share recipes and nutritional information and incorporate fresh seasonal foods into their meals. Graduates of this program often become its future teachers (thus creating alternatives to typical "expert" flows of information) and advocates for food justice (thus disrupting dominant flows of power).[55] On the farming side, the Women, Food, and Agriculture Network has organized the women who own almost one-half of the farmland in the United States to advance more sustainable agricultural flows.[56] Where mealtime and food preparation are often associated with violence against women, backyard and community gardens, trips to farmers' markets, and healthy cooking practices are becoming integral to processes of healing and empowerment at domestic violence shelters and elsewhere.[57] Movements indebted to Chicana feminism and the United Farm Workers increasingly problematize borders and dominant circulations of food and farmworkers, while embracing new flows of people, sustainable modes of agricultural production, and alternatives to the hazardous, fast-paced movement of things in food processing plants.[58] In all these ways, those who have been subjected to the most damaging impacts of contemporary mega-circulations are among those cocreating a politics of just and sustainable material flows. While the class and race politics around new material flows is uneven, and the future by no means certain, emergent organizing in the food justice movement provides reasons to be hopeful.

Of course, questions immediately arise about whether all this activity can possibly be any match against mega-circulatory power fueled by a colossal river of corn, oil, pharmaceuticals, and capital that floods and absorbs more and more people and the earth. Wouldn't serious resistance and alternatives rather require strategies primarily focused on nation-state policy, international regulatory regimes, massive redeployments of agricultural capital, and the like? It is difficult to imagine profound and large-scale transformations that did not involve careful consideration of and movement in relation to such sites of agency. Moreover, organizing around GMOs, agricultural property rights, FPCs, access to farmers' markets, and so forth, does indeed include them among its targets. Yet new materialist social movements more often focus on local, regional, and translocal practices, flows, and networks as their primary sites of agency.

One reason for this focus is a sense that the large-scale formal institutions of power have been so thoroughly colonized, hybridized, and liquefied by corporate superpower that they are likely to be among the sites *most recalcitrant* to emerging countermovements and alternative movements. Another reason is the sense that before movements to transform the sites of superpower have any hope, there must be major shifts in desire, pleasure, vision, aspiration, practice, relational networks, and active organizing capacities—all of which are most effectively cultivated beneath, around, and beyond corporatized states and regimes. Yet another reason new materialist movements currently accent transformative initiatives beyond the formal institutions of government is related to a shift in and supplement to the paradigms of power that orient these organizing efforts. From this vantage point, politics that accents the centrality of the state may conceal more than it reveals about the current (dis)order of things and the possibilities for radical transformation. Recall that Foucault's argument is not that sovereignty and disciplinary power are *surpassed* or *unimportant* in contemporary life, but rather that they often and increasingly tend to be supplemental and subordinate to circulatory modes of governmentality. Though such governmentality emerges in relation to competing nation-states, it now exceeds and transforms the latter in ways that tend to supplant the primacy of sovereignty and incorporate it into the requirements of circulatory powers themselves.

Analogous to the ways in which mega-circulatory power modulates and repositions sovereignty and disciplinary power, I venture that growing numbers of leaders in new materialist movements are coming to understand that radical transformations of the latter powers (as well as corporate capital) will require that we develop vast practices, networks, institutions, and powers of *countercirculation* and *alternative circulation*. Shifts in state policies, in this scenario, will likely stem from powers that develop in relation to new practices, affect, vision, and political muscle associated with these alternative material flows. In sum, the recalcitrance of the megastate, a sense of the optimal sites for cultivating transformative subjects with desires, knowledge, and capacities for formulating resistance and alternatives, and the overall dominance of governmentality in relation to sovereignty have all led new materialist movements to focus on a politics of engendering radically democratic and ecologically resilient flows, more than on the state policies that are so often accented by more traditional forms of progressive politics.

That said, there are numerous signs that new materialist political movements *also* frequently engage formal structures of political power. Indeed, there is a recognition that *both* a politics of flows *and* political engagements with formal state and national institutions are necessary to catalyze transformations at a pace necessary to thwart and adapt to climate catastrophe. Food Policy Councils aim to shape policy that involves state and local governments. The movement against GMOs regularly focuses on national and transnational policies around the world. The movement 350.org and many other climate- and energy-focused movements do extensive work at national and transnational levels, both to resist the proliferation of catastrophic carbon circulations and to advocate for national and global policies that support ecologically resilient flows. Interestingly, moreover, new approaches to state and federal politics are emerging that focus on the state more as an *enabler* of citizen action rather than the primary locus of activity. Carmen Sirriani's study on "collaborative governance" identifies some emergent paths for combining formal democratic politics with grassroots politics oriented around alternative flows focusing on Seattle's neighborhood gardening project and other promising initiatives.[59] Programs emerging within the Department of Agriculture that support alternative food initiatives are suggestive of synergies between new materialist politics and national-level policy that could be expanded to proliferate an alternative circulatory politics.[60] From these vantage points, the goal is to make state and transnational regime powers subordinate to and oriented toward facilitating the development of these countercirculations and alternative circulations of radical and ecological democracy.

Imagining Ethical Communities of Receptive "Polyface" Flows

The practices, interpretations, visions, and effects of these movements are manifold, contested, and dynamic. There is more internal difference than I have accounted for thus far. Some see the locus of transformation primarily in terms of political policy at the state level. Others emphasize territorial visions of local food sovereignty. While many have strong environmental justice and radical democratic orientations, still others seek aesthetic and social pleasures that are largely apolitical, oblivious to questions of power such as class and race. Nostalgic yearnings for a return to simplicity and community belonging (to fictional agrarian or preagrarian pasts) are vital to others. While aspects of many of these frames address important issues, and some of the tensions among them are vital, they often miss or underplay dimensions that are of great significance for mounting powerful resistance to contemporary circulatory power and articulating visions of radical democratic (agri)cultures.

In this context, I offer an ethos of receptive flows that might solicit and inform an imagined community of radically democratic and ecologically resilient work and action. If we increasingly find our lives fabricated, circulating and disposed according to the requirements of a vast and malignant mega-circulatory "root clod" with enormous central arteries that lay to waste soil, rivers, oceans, atmosphere, ecosystems, and humans, how might we shift our (agri)cultural imaginations to recognize and cultivate powerful resistance and alternatives? Moreover, how might we form alternative kinds of *roots and routing* that are profoundly attentive to the human and nonhuman flourishing of specific places and attentive to the need to deterritorialize communitarian and environmental imaginaries that have often been marred by xenophobia?[61]

Near Flagstaff, the land is crisscrossed by three kinds of pathways that might illuminate these questions. Flagstaff sits at the intersection of two interstate highways—I-40 and I-17. Interstates are integral to mega-circulatory power. They move vast quantities of people, animals, and things across the land at great speeds. Increasing the rates of circulation is their logos, and hence they foster journeys that are oblivious to specific places and the roots and rooting that happen in them. They are integral to the war against the specific flourishing of places—as is exemplified by the generic corporate development around interstate exits. As large volumes of traffic speed through these arteries, they generate a resonant roar that often overwhelms the soundscapes and silences of communities, while the primary resonances to which the traffic is tuned are the audio and visual fields of corporate radio and billboards. Route 66 also runs through Flagstaff and, though now largely a nostalgic tourist destination, still evokes a very different kind of moving and dwelling. Route 66 was once the premier road for traveling across the United States and experiencing diverse communities and places. The highway went through communities, not around them, and traffic slowed and stopped. Travelers got a taste of the distinctness of each place, and communities received travelers, other perspectives—stories from beyond. Route 66 nurtured a routing connected with rooting. It enhanced the odds that the two would inform each other and check each other's weaknesses. The resonance of the traffic was punctuated, and the resonance of the communities more idiosyncratic.

A little ways to the east of Flagstaff lies Wupatki, a red-orange, multistory, thousand-year-old Pueblo ruin that includes a ceremonial ball court, a tower, and a community room amid a vast arid landscape that is at once rich and austere. For 150 years, situated at the intersection of both major east–west and north–south routes, Wupatki was a center for exchanges and encounters among ideas, people, and goods coming from vast geographic and cultural distances (from Chaco Canyon, New Mexico, to Aztecan Mesoamerica, to the Klamath in Oregon). On the one hand, they were surely intimate rooters. They had a highly textured relationship to place and were profoundly knowledgeable about the flora, fauna, seasons, and geographies of the Northern Arizona landscape. Their cultural traditions mapped onto it like a glove on a hand, and their ruins resonate with a different sensibility that is beyond most of that with which we are familiar. Yet at the same time they were intimate routers and received routers. They traveled to, and were frequently visited by, remarkably different peoples from vastly distant places. What we now consider a rigid border between the United States and Mexico, Pueblo people saw as a fluid space for journeying. And they and their neighbors traveled these vast spaces by foot. Their architecture and other traces resonate with kinships to things very far away in ways that remain plain to see yet elusive.

As discussed in the introduction, the Greek root of the word "theory," *theorein*, links it to routing—traveling, by means of which textured comparative knowledge came to be viewed as integral to living well in any specific place. It would be good to hold Route 66 and Wupatki in our mind's eye as we consider alternative modes of rooting and routing that might contribute to futures that move beyond the destructive circulations of biopolitical superpower. I think of them not as images of perfection but as windows and doorways through which we might glimpse and explore alternatives—including, perhaps, those opened by the Internet.

Consider another window, a doorway, and tarry a bit with the image of a "root clod," for it may provide a powerful metaphor of diverse flourishing and the intertwinement of roots and routes. Prior to "the Great Plow-up," the resilient prairie ecosystems were so densely rooted that special steel plows had to be invented to rip up the land. The relentless assault on root clods culminated in the Dust Bowl of the 1930s and played a pivotal role in sending soil to the sky and countless thousands routing for starvation-wage jobs on California farms. What was this root clod whose annihilation was intertwined with the development of agricultural mega-circulations?

In contrast to the malignant clods of governmentality, the root clod of the prairies was a dense entanglement of microflows of multifarious and symbiotic flourishing. A single large plant of bluestem grass, common across the preplowed prairie, has "twenty-five miles of fibrous plumbing," yet it is a *member* of an ecological community (interconnected micro and macro self-organizing systems) rather than a malignant growth that reengineers its environment in ways that destroy all other flourishing. Hence, in the ongoing process of the plant's parts dying and regenerating, they "fall into the welcoming jaws of a miniature zoo— ants, springtails, centipedes, sowbugs, worms, bacteria, and molds. There are thousands of species in a single teaspoon."[62] Through an infinitely complex and highly evolved symbiosis, the prairie species interact to form a sponge that holds water, generates fertile soil, and has tremendous resilience in the face of myriad challenges. It is dynamic and undergoes changes, but it avoids catastrophe. Each *root* is also a *route*, wherein water and nutrients circulate through a manifold and dynamic process that engenders multitudinous flourishing.

Along with the Land Institute he founded, Wes Jackson (one of the world's foremost leaders in sustainable agriculture) is seeking to emulate this process by assembling a polycultural perennial form of farming that would, on the one hand, no longer require the depletion of aquifers, endless petrochemical inputs, global warming, and a gigantic hypoxic "dead zone" in the Gulf of Mexico larger than Massachusetts, while on the other hand, solicit the movement of people and communities to the land to steward this emergent form of responsive agriculture. Jackson imagines a "homecoming" where local cultures are revitalized by many people "turning their senses to local conditions": "more eyes per acre" is a trope that becomes essential for sustainable relations with the land.[63] Janine Benyus discerns in "biomimicry" initiatives such as these the possibility of a new technological paradigm located in greater human receptivity to, respect for, and reciprocity with the nonhuman. Beyond sodbusting disasters, through an inventive attentiveness to processes and flows in the more than human world, we might begin to cultivate cultures akin to routing root clods at myriad sites of capillary output and absorption.

Let us explore this vision more fully, in order to resist nostalgic yearnings for simplicity, macro (state) or mini (local) sovereignties, comforting borders, and sedentary rootedness that sometimes poorly frames alternative food politics. Wendell Berry, friend of Wes Jackson and a pioneer in these matters, is sometimes read poorly as an exemplar of nostalgic local simplicity. In a collection entitled *The Way of Ignorance,* he anticipates this misreading when he writes about the intertwinement of farming and writing in his life. He summarizes:

This is an experience resistant to any kind of simplification. I will go ahead and call it complexification. When I am called, as to my astonishment I sometimes am, a devotee of "simplicity" . . . I am obliged to reply that I gave up the simple life when I left New York City in 1964 and came here. In New York, I lived as a passive consumer . . . whereas here I supply many of my needs from this place by my work (and Pleasure) and am responsible besides for the care of the place. My point is that when one passes from any abstract order . . . to the daily life and work of one's own farm, one passes from a relative simplicity into a complexity that is irreducible except by disaster and ultimately is incomprehensible. It is the complexity of the life of a place uncompromisingly itself, which is at the same time the life of the world, of all Creation. One meets not only . . . the wildness of the world, but also the limitations of one's knowledge, intelligence, character, and bodily strength. To do this, of course, is to accept the place as an influence . . . as a part of the informing ambience of one's imagination.[64]

Let us pass over, for now, the reductive swipe at the Big Apple. I am interested in Berry's idea of complexification, in the hopes that it may illuminate ways beyond *both* corporate recolonization of alternative initiatives through practices such as industrial organic farming *and* nostalgic simplification that sometimes accompanies alternative initiatives. Sheldon Wolin gestures to both the difficulties and the promise of complexification when he writes: "Perhaps . . . the solution to the crisis of reason, as Montesquieu suggested, is not in simplification but in complexity. But how does complexity itself avoid appearing as a simple solution? Perhaps it has to do with treating complexity as signifying diverse claims and life forms so that the marks of a solution are not simplicity or elegance or reduction, as we have been taught, but the creation of conditions which encourage complexities that live by different laws and defy Cartesian solutions."[65]

One way to begin to cultivate this possibility—common among people who gather in farmers' markets—is through the circulation of evocative stories of alternative cocreative practices. Pollan tells such a story after a week of moving around with Joel Salatin, on Salatin's Polyface Farm in Virginia.[66] Some familiar with Salatin's writing may balk at my use of him. His lurking worries about "migrants," his view that animals lack "souls," his sedimented approach to gender roles, and some elements of his libertarianism conspire in ways that would likely have him resist how he moves me along journeys toward a more transformative deterritorializing and interspecies mutualist ethics and politics. Perhaps my *transfigurative* account here will move Salatin in ways he has not yet considered? However that may be, I read many of his practices to energize movements beyond the confines of his own scripts. Many people gazing at a field see only *grass*—an abstraction born/e of the circulations of the lawn-governmentality complex that lead tens of millions to ride mowers for hours each weekend across a national lawn the size of Pennsylvania, spending billions on the flow of mowers, fossil fuels, pesticides, herbicides, fertilizers, pharmaceuticals, and associated medical bills. In marked contrast, Salatin sees—and beyond sees, *attentively circulates through on all fours, experiences with profound resonance and all his senses, is engaged by as he engages, mimetically hopes from, and hungers for*—an immense, dynamic, and fructiferous complexity of symbiotic relationships. Salatin has come to understand this "complexity not of our own making" by studying and seeking resonant emulations with the eyes and beaks of chickens, the tongues and lips of cows; by seeking mimetic relationships with their experiences of the pasture. Before he allowed Pollan to meet any of the animals on his farm, Salatin "insisted that . . . I join him down on his belly in a pasture [where], he introduced me to orchard grass and fescue, to red and white clover, to millet and blue grass, plantain and timothy and sweet grass, which he pulled a blade of for me to taste."[67] Like many "grass farmers," Salatin is "pretty evangelical about grass," and his evangelism is intertwined with the evangelism of a cow in the pasture, which sees, "out of the corner of her eye, this nice tuft of white clover, an emerald-green one over there with the heart-shaped leaves, or, up ahead, that grassy spray of bluish fescue tightly cinched at ground level. . . . The cow opens her meaty wet lips, curls her sandpaper tongue around the bunched clover like a fat rope."[68] From myriad observations like this, and from a plethora of information about pastures that is emerging from the practice called "management intensive grazing," the pasture comes to be understood as not only complex but radically dynamic, with each blade of each species seen as a photovoltaic panel—each entwined with the others; each pasture cycling through different rates of growth, grazing, and recovery; each of these and all together "constantly changing, depending on temperature, rainfall, exposure to the sun, and the time of year, as does the amount of forage any given cow requires, depending on its size, age, and stage of life." It "hurts my head to consider."[69] *This* is complexity: multiple life-forms dynamically intertwined, interpreted in myriad ways—from crawling and visceral resonance to conceptual refinement.

The moving assemblage of human beings receptively engaged with such complexity—moving about on their bellies, in their speculative imaginations and writing, symbiotically engendering interspecies knowing, hungering, and hope—is itself drawn into highly dynamic practices. Rather than a territorialized sense of the farm as a sovereign space to be statically mastered, grass farming is an art form more akin to a responsive dance with ever-shifting boundaries and practices drawn forth through profoundly receptive engagements with myriad forms of life and interconnections that "are not of one's own making." Polyface Farm does indeed have fences, but these fences—as well as much of the rest of the farm's built world—are themselves in *frequent motion*, conducting the movements of cows, chickens, pigs, as well as humans tending to them, in ways that are responsive to the diverse needs, propensities, health, and flourishing of myriad beings, and the sustainable flourishing of the pasture. *Receptive mobility is the central motif here.* Speaking of his father, Salatin says: "Moving things must be in our genes." His father invented a "walking sprinkler," a "movable electric fence, a portable veal calf barn, a portable chicken coop for the laying hens . . . a portable 'shademobile.'"[70]

One might ask: Isn't this agricultural modality very much like circulatory power on a smaller scale? Is this not a governmentality of sorts that operates by insinuating itself into the circulations of other beings in order to maximize power in relation to the more than human world? People involved in this practice offer a markedly different interpretation. Those who "practice complexity" tend to imagine what they are doing in terms of "respect"—even if it is far from Kantian in its genesis and tendencies, and far from the "respect" of power-maximizing governmentality. Pollan describes the philosophy of Sir Albert Howard, one of the founders of modern organic agriculture (who had a major influence on Wendell Berry), as one in which "*mimicking natural processes precedes the science of understanding them*" (my emphasis).[71] Similarly, when Salatin speaks both philosophically and pragmatically in terms of the way his mobile Eggmobile follows the cows so the chickens can dine on insects that would otherwise plague the herbivores, he refers to "a symbiotic relationship we're trying to imitate."

In a manner that bears remarkable affinities with the discussion of mirror neuron resonance in the previous chapter, mimetic resonance plays a fundamental role in informing, inspiring, and energizing Salatin's effort to intertwine rooting and routing. Speaking of his role in this process, he says, "I'm just the orchestra conductor, making sure everybody's in the right place at the right time." There is an intense mutualism that has developed over thousands of years, in which "depending on the point of view you take—that of the chicken, the cow, or even the grass—the relationship between subject and object, cause and effect, flips."[72] Insofar as mimetic energy and the new modes of circulation energized and oriented by this mimesis are integral conditions of such imagination, understanding, and practice, one would have to include humans in these strange "flips" too. Pollan's book *The Botany of Desire* provides a profound elaboration of this possibility, as he tells the story of the mutualistic evolution of plants and humans from the perspective of plants as the agents and beneficiaries.[73] In this light, Polyface Farm is based on a different type of efficiency, "the one found in natural systems, with their coevolutionary relationships and reciprocal loops"—one based on what Salatin calls "the pigness of the pig," or the flourishing of each constituent in a heterogeneous collaborative network.[74] It is not that there is no sacrifice in this system—forests are cleared, grass is eaten, pigs are eaten, humans work their butts off and are buried in the fields—but that in the relational network diverse beings develop interdependent thriving tuned to the predilections and flourishing of each. It is, of course, easy to romanticize this. Yet it is even easier to avoid seeing the profound alternative to which it gestures beyond the cruel, unjust, unreciprocal, and unsustainable corporate-petro-corn-security complex.

Recall again the malignant root clod that draws ever-increasing flows through the central channels of power by means of ever-extending capillary networks that infiltrate and reconstitute circulations, dispositions, and beings. In contrast to the power-maximizing imperatives of the mega-circulatory apparatus that are indifferent to heterogeneous well-being, the emergent alternative sketched by the *receptive circulations* in Salatin's pastures cultivates a more symbiotic thriving among myriad species: Salatin seeks not to be the master so much as a flourishing member of a flourishing community assemblage. This practice of responsive flows is *poly-eccentric*: Salatin moves *mimetically—with attentive resonance—to be drawn into the orbits* of cow lips, eyes, and tongues in order to approximate experiences of the pasture that enable him to tend to and flourish with more than human beings. With some of this resonant energy, he seeks to draw others into similar mimetic movements.

We might call the practice, epistemology, ethos, and power at play here "polyface," drawing a certain inspiration not only from Salatin but also from the philosopher Emmanuel Levinas. For Levinas, the "face" demands that I extend myself ethically beyond my egocentric perception, toward a singular other that can never be subsumed within it.[75] Levinas is inattentive both to how the widely varying potentials of faces are revealed and concealed in relational practices, and to how nonhumans may also call us to ethical engagements. Thus on his reading, all of nature is subsumed in the egocentric work of humans. Yet Salatin's mimetic account suggests that there are relational practices with nonhuman beings that analogously call us in ways that draw us into *eccentric*—rather than egocentric—ethical-corporeal movements.

Recall our previous discussion of intercorporeal resonances among the mirror neuron networks of different people that emerge in an infant's face-to-face encounters. These resonances enable developing selves to discover and gradually exercise significant control over their own movements—even a smile. At the deepest levels, then, our being and relationships have significant aspects of "eccentricity" that are prior to and intertwined with my very emergence. It is not a huge leap from here to suspect that we have preconscious apprehensions of otherness that are readily imbued with ethical sensibilities—both those in which we sense ourselves profoundly with and called to care for the singularity of others, and those in which we sense ourselves to be entangled with all others in a "single garment of destiny"—borrowing a phrase from the late Martin Luther King Jr. Now recall that mirror neurons were discovered accidentally when those of a *nonhuman* fired as a researcher reached for a cup. Though to my knowledge studies on these and other human mimetic neurological relationships with nonhuman beings have yet to be pursued, it seems highly likely that they happen extensively, and that this is a vital aspect of how we are drawn toward other nonhuman centers empathetically, epistemologically, and ethically. In other words, other beings likely have characteristics of what Levinas calls "face"—and I suspect these will be found even among beings without faces. Insofar as these speculations are true (and the ethical and epistemological practices of many other cultures also suggest that they are), humans would—or, rather, would have deep capacities to—inhabit a world that is "polyface," calling us to many eccentric movements with many other beings. Just as our capacities for resonance are intertwined with corporeal movements and practices involving other human beings, it also seems likely that movement and receptive resonance would be intertwined in practices with nonhuman beings. Polyface possibilities would deepen, broaden, and intensify their call in relationship with polyface practices.

Of course, Salatin eats—directly or indirectly—the faces he also "serves" in senses that far exceed the servings at the table. Yet the deep interspecies mutualism in his practices far exceeds parasitism. These patterns are not without a sacrificial dimension, yet their mimetic movements and practices repeatedly and creatively exceed sacrifice insofar as Polyface farmers hunger not only for themselves but also with, from, and for other beings. They hunger to inhabit the hungering of cows, grasses, and creeks, in spite of the impossibilities of perfect coincidence. These impossibilities repeatedly draw those thus engaged with the land into "a healthy sense of all we don't know—even a sense of mystery."[76] It is from this sensibility and wonder—knowing not to know too well—that we can imagine and act toward a future that engenders more polycentric flourishing beyond the trunks and mainstreams of a malignant power killing the future in the name of the "new." Where governmentality is driven by an imperative to maximize power, and "respects" other realms only insofar as these contribute to its ambition, a polyface ethos begins from, intertwines with, and advances *with* the diverse flourishing of a vast network of beings. Indeed, it senses and understands its own flourishing not in terms of a locus of power (e.g., corporate, state) that enters into flows in order to maximize itself, but rather as an intensification whose modes, sensibilities, and orientations are transformed by, as well as transformative of, the vaster network. A polyface ethos is qualitatively decentered in its sense of (its) good and vitality. The evidence of this appears as much in *how* Salatin *draws others into relationship with* his farm as it does in *what* he does that engenders its healthy yield. And it appears in a temporal vision of reciprocal ecological and human flourishing that—far beyond the rapidly discounted futures of governmentality—enters into geological time.

This sensibility is circulating not only on farms and in stories circulating in farmers' markets. It is also circulating at the tables around which people gather in new ways in the translocal movement known as "Slow Food" mentioned earlier. Slow Food, as Petrini says, intentionally crafts complexities of taste—the sensuousness of the tongue and the nose, and love of convivial gathering at the table—to local ecologies in ways that engender visceral flows of "responsibility for the future, the salvation of a heritage of memory, biodiversity, and creative capacity; and the affirmation of a pleasure principle that is the indispensable foundation for the strategies that we are working out as we go along."[77] The movement seeks to join ecological tending with each region's "patrimony of flavors," in a way that connects the diversities and complexities of "gastronomic legacies everywhere" to ecological, agricultural, and cultural heritages of places in a manner that links territory not to sovereignty, nor terror (*terrere*), but to something akin to the French *terroir*, which indicates a far more symbiotic commingling of human and more-than-human differences conceived of as "polycentric."[78] While *slow* is, of course, an important aspect of Slow Food, Petrini emphasizes that the depth of the movement is missed when framed in dichotomies such as slow versus fast: most basically, the issue at stake is "attentiveness" and "carefulness."[79] The ethos of Slow Food is one that calls us to movements upon different "terroirs" that are receptive to the unique complexities of (agri)cultures of tending to specific places. This solidaristic cultivation of receptive tastes, flows, and practices around the world is evoked in the 1989 "Slow Food Manifesto's" call to "turn this (slow) motion into an international movement with a little snail as the symbol."[80] It calls us toward a fully sensuous and convivial attentiveness to polyfaced circulations.

What counterimages might we juxtapose to the malignant root clod of megacirculatory power? We undoubtedly require many, and the images of Salatin moving mimetically on his belly and orchestrating a symphony of moving fences are richly suggestive. Yet let me offer another, inspired by the bluestem grass root clod and those who are drawn toward it in resonant relationships of biomimetic eros. Picture an enormous clod consisting of many different roots and root clods with abundant flows and many associated species. If you are still, you can sense that it is full of motion. Imagine a wildly diverse community of human beings gathered amid and around this and other clods, enthusiastic and attentive. Let us make visible what you can't quite actually see: resonant energies animating the humans (and other beings) through fields of vision, smell, sound, touch, and taste when different parts of the clod are sensuously encountered. Awash in these energized fields, the humans feel themselves moved by uncanny sympathies beneath their flesh—a twisting sensation here, an intertwinement there, a feeling of extension in the toes, a strange sense of abundance in the torso in response to the rich smells of earthy loam, a haunt of death in the moving jaws of an insect. The primary effect of these resonant fields of perception is to further intensify an attentiveness from which new forms of understanding and practice begin to emerge that are more finely tuned to qualities of relationality, dynamics, interpenetration, complexity, fragility, reciprocity, and care than most of those that are dominant today. Sometimes people are drawn to emulate the clod of roots in ways that are quite literal— replicating and caring for relationships they find there. Other times we are inspired to create relationships with the clod that manifest certain semblances but are largely new. At other times still, we are creatively inspired to modulate many human-human relationships in inventive response to sensations, practices, and reflections that occur in relation to the clod. All of these times and modes begin to interpenetrate and multiply their effects in ways that exceed predictability yet more often than not tend to enhance polyface vitality—and also resilience for when things go awry. *Clods are beginning to form among humans and among the humans and the nonhuman beings and things amid the roots.*

Everywhere in these energized fields, resonance is drawing out new movements. Every root is a route, a flow, and thus every rooting is a routing, even at the most micrological levels. And every movement has a frequency, and among the frequencies there are resonances. Every sinking into the dynamic specificities of place is also a micrological exploration, extending and inter-twining and inventing in countless ways.

All these movements are forming routes and roots between the humans and the more than human world, and through a complex process of resonance, rooting, and routing, a doubled-back root clod is emerging. Mimetic energies inspire and inform the doubling back. Yet the two sides are not mirror images, for forming on the human side are increasingly creative patterns of receptive tending to the polyface flourishing betwixt and between. As was the case with the malignant root clod, there are proliferating capillaries, flows, and ener-gies exchanged in many directions. But there is no trunk; there are few large arteries even as many capillaries venture great distances; and the flows and forms modulate in relation to questions of complex and manifold well-being of which natality and resilience are constitutive elements.

Immersed in these relationships, humans begin to invent and reinvolve themselves in new and old modes of vast yet attentive movement across re-gions, continents, and oceans. The specificities of each place begin to acquire information, energy, and some characteristics from distant places, even as most places remain profoundly unique. Suddenly, we realize the clod is mov-ing not just geographically but also in time, (re)working pasts and futures with dynamic receptivity. We realize that it is entangled with another clod—the mega-circulatory clod that is ravaging the globe. Yet from the smallest cells through multifarious levels that reach planetary scope, we begin to see that the polyfaced rooting/routing is undoing the destructive clod: it is detaching from the malignant capillaries, forming rich alternatives, blocking the destructive clod here, cutting it back there, all the while cultivating a habitat—a habitus— that is increasingly generative of perceptions, dispositions, energies, imagin-ings, relationships, and practices that are accelerating the defeat of the govern-mentality of mega-circulations, and proliferating the flourishing of polyface flows. Radical localisms and radical cosmopolitanisms become increasingly indistinguishable, as "Behold, we are doing a new thing."[81]

Polyface Routing and Rooting at NAU and in Northern Arizona

During the past several years, many students, faculty, and staff at NAU have joined with Flagstaff community members in campus gardens, K–12 school gardens, neighborhood community gardens, tables of conviviality, campus and community composting, a domestic violence shelter, a food center, a CSA, an initiative to catalyze an alternative food system based on cooperative economics, and more. The visceral experiences formed in these countercultural receptive flows of bodies, beings, and things that constitute these alternative (agri) cultural practices—as well as the circulation of countless stories in relation to them—have inspired the vision of polyface flourishing sketched in the previous section. At odds with superpower mega-circulations, we are generating a complex rooting/routing that resonates with kindred initiatives around energy, education, economy, health, immigration, art, and much more in the new materialist movement emerging at the ARTs intersections between the NAU campus and the broader community. These flows and modes of moving are cultivating perceptions, dispositions, sensibilities, tastes, relationships among humans and the more than human world, ways of knowing, things known, reflective capacities, hopes, and powers that are crucial for counterconducts and alter-conducts upon which the future of people, democracy, and the planet likely depends.

As I walk through the garden, I am enthused by the *resonance* of these fields of creative interaction between the people and the land. This resonance of roots and moving bodies has a contagious and proliferative quality if you linger with it for even a little while. You can taste it in the food that the garden provides—the sharing. Some top administrators on campus, who were less enthusiastic earlier on, are beginning to sense this too, and they have begun to offer support and make more spaces available for other alternative gardens on campus. Many faculty members are finding that our sense of teaching, learning, and political engagement are being profoundly influenced by our involvement in these resonant clods of interaction.

An alternative habitus is emerging—rooting and routing—on campus, across Flagstaff, and beyond. Intertwined with these new flows with the more than human world, we are intentionally cultivating new flows and webs of relationships among disparate human communities with long histories of conflict, subjugation, and indifference. Hence, the (agri)cultural ARTs are often engaged in collaborative work with people in poorer neighborhoods where many are new immigrants, Native Americans, or Hispanics who have been here much longer than most whites. Many have a great deal of agricultural knowledge.

Consider from this vantage point the work we are doing in elementary schools such as Killip (discussed in chapter 1), where NAU students mentor children in the arts of gardening, cooperation, and ecological knowledge. Beginning in their first year, growing numbers of students find themselves on community buses, or carpooling, or bicycling across town through decidedly poorer neighborhoods, walking through the front doors of an elementary school where they are greeted by excited children, and then venturing out behind the school, where a thriving and expanding garden is growing. Soon they find themselves with a group of several kids carefully planting seeds, pointing out how a butterfly seems drawn to a particular plant species, watering new shoots, sharing in the excitement about pepper blossoms that have just given way to tiny peppers, walking over to a bare patch of the garden and attentively engaging the enthusiastic speech, animated gestures, and pensive reflections through which the kids imagine what might grow there. Some of the children are talking about their grandparents' amazing gardens out on the Navajo reservation; others are talking about their parents' backyard gardens and have heard stories about farms left behind in Mexico. Many talk about dishes they love that are made from some of the plants growing in the garden. Several remember that last year their moms gathered hundreds of peppers, tomatoes, onions, and carrots and made a gigantic chili in the school cafeteria that everyone thought was delicious. Someone mentions that one of those moms was picked up by Immigration and Customs Enforcement and has not been heard from again. Quite a few are proud of the fact that they took some of this chili and a lot of vegetables to the nearby food center. Some kids know the center from the inside, as clients. Some know other folks who are clients. Quite a few kids who are typically quiet and reserved in school come alive in the garden. They begin to talk a lot, listen to others more attentively, imagine great things for the garden, become visibly blown away by the beauty of new growth and very curious about how plants develop, manifest growing excitement to work together digging, designing, planting, weeding, picking—they are beginning to make connections to science, math, writing, and grassroots community building. Symbiotic intercropping in the garden and the interweaving of cultures and experiences share much in common.

The NAU students coaching and mentoring in the garden discover that beyond feelings of powerlessness, fear, indifference, or demonization that may have constituted their sense of neighborhoods like this, there are lives full of capacities, intelligence, enthusiasms, relationships, narratives, love, friendships, dreams, discipline, growth, suffering, anger, and fears of their own. As they find themselves working side by side with the children, their own attention spans and intensities are growing right along with those of the kids with whom they are increasingly entangled in a complex garment of mutual growth. They find themselves thinking differently about power, democracy, difference, and gardens. In giving and receiving stories and by moving together in the garden, school, and neighborhoods, a complex epistemological process is under way in which filaments of different lives are intertwining, becoming aware of each other, cocreating extensive new shoots, and forming a clod of roots and routes for more just, democratic, and sustainable communities. In modest but important ways we are rebuilding a broken world, and it is becoming beautiful.

Soon the NAU students find that the elementary students are curious about them, curious about the university. Talk emerges of unexpected circulations in the other direction too: the children want to visit NAU, crossing lines they may have hitherto taken to be impossible. Soon they will be in the SSLUG garden outside my office window. As a group of us brainstorm about a garden at the center of campus in front of a platinum LEED-certified building that is among the most visible sites visitors encounter as they come to NAU, our conversation turns to how the design might give expression to these reciprocally generative flows to and from campus and across our region. We are engaged in a conversation about what might become a central symbolic and literal root that our campus sinks into the ground of a place to which it has often been oblivious in the past. Yet the character of this rooting we are imagining is a routing.

This moving is *moving—soulful.* The resonant fields of sensibility, interaction, and public work are generating enthusiasms that are proliferating other movements, and the cycles appear to be acquiring a certain self-generative quality. Analogous to how the movements of bodies discussed by Prigogine and Stengers generate frequencies that then resonate in ways that disrupt Newtonian paths and engender new movements—new futures—these movements amid the emergent rooting/routing clod of polyface flourishing are opening futures that were less possible before they began. For example, the NAU administration has begun to contribute a modest but significant stream of funding to support the ARTS, new instructorships, and even a couple of tenure-track lines. They have funded a campus organic gardener position to help facilitate the development of and activity around campus gardens. The Flagstaff school district has also begun to support alternative gardening initiatives, and bigger possibilities are under discussion. More and more undergraduates are being drawn to courses and campus organizations linked to action research, and many are beginning to explore more expansive questions and possibilities. All of this is part of a larger constellation of initiatives that are increasingly linking ecologically responsive agriculture with receptive movement among different communities: the Flagstaff Farmers Market opened a second market a couple years ago in the Sunnyside neighborhood we have been discussing; the CSA has initiated an experimental "mini-CSA" in Killip Elementary; numerous people in these initiatives have joined with the Sunnyside Neighborhood Association to explore expanding community gardens in the neighborhood, developing a "backyard growers cooperative," and seek funding to launch a youth cooperative enterprise called "SunnyCider," which would harvest and process the abundant apples that grow on scores of trees across the neighborhood. A solidarity economy project called the Mercado de los Sueños (Market of Dreams) has been organizing powerfully for more than a year and in January opened a large center in the heart of the neighborhood that will catalyze cooperative economics, microentrepreneurship and lending, local economic circulations, a vibrant multicultural market, grassroots democracy, sustainable products, youth leadership development, and beautification of a run-down traffic corridor. Many students, community members, and faculty who have been involved in the NAU ARTs have played important roles in organizing the Mercado as well as several of the other initiatives. These projects and processes are young, but they are an indication that many are beginning to work and act with a renewed sense of expanding possibilities.[82]

Those involved in these initiatives are on the cutting edge of inventing an art that is indispensable for radical democracy and ecological sustainability. We are learning how to cocreate *roots* in a place not by creating new modes of exclusive territoriality (e.g., mini-sovereignties, nostalgic enclaves, xenophobic localisms, communities of depoliticized withdrawal) but by *routing*. We are learning to move with receptive generosity and collaborative practice beyond familiar places and faces, comfort zones, prescribed highways of "success," proscribed lines not to be crossed. We are going to places and people with whom we must relearn how to see, think, imagine, work, and act to cocreate democracy and an ecologically resilient commonwealth. We are attentively immersing ourselves in ecosystems at numerous scales—participating with the movements of other beings and things that generate deep sustainability and resilience. And akin to orchestral conductors, we are moving ourselves, things, and beings into relationships that tend—in permacultural modes—to cultivate their flourishing as well as our own perceptual, cognitive, and relational capacities to deepen our tending practices themselves. In so doing, we are becoming confusing to the powers that be because no one knows what to think when disparate people begin to move about together and collaborate in unwonted ways. The resonance machine scripts of dismissal become less and less plausible, as many are beginning to see that we are doing a new thing, and growing numbers are becoming interested in this unwonted politics where "hope is a verb with its sleeves rolled up."[83]

As we have discussed, resonant receptivity and movement are different faces of a single process that is usefully illuminated through discussions that accent each. Yet this chapter illuminates an additional element that is indispensable for cultivating a radical and ecological democratic habitus. We are beings who are cultivated/cultivate ourselves not only through our own movements but in relation to the world of beings and things that circulate around us—the world in which we are immersed. Many of these beings and things are moving according to agentic processes and systems dynamics that are largely nonhuman, and perhaps the wisest thing we can do in many cases is to move ourselves in relation to their movements in ways that are highly attentive and careful. In this sense, practices of letting beings and things be—letting them circulate around us and attuning ourselves to their flows—are the most profound ways of becoming human in relation to the movements of the nonhuman. Yet our becoming human and our capacities for ecological resilience and radical democracy are also cultivated in relation to the things that we set into motion around us—seeds, waters, plants, animals, compost, trash, vehicles, medicines, the rise and fall of buildings, and much more. As we stimulate, facilitate, and guide such motions, we variously intensify and diminish our powers. Those who seek to cultivate a radical and ecological democratic habitus would thus do well to cultivate a world of moving things in a manner that is highly attentive to their public effects; highly attentive to how the things we cultivate, in turn cultivate us and our public powers to facilitate communities of reciprocal flourishing. New materialist movements would do well to put "ownership and control of the means of production" back on the political table in relation to institutional practices and relationships around property. Yet in regard to the most prominent themes on the politics of circulation we have discussed in this chapter (and in some tension with certain renderings of "ownership and control"), perhaps the language of cofacilitative relationships that cultivate flows that empower beings to engender reciprocal forms of complex commonwealth would be more on the mark. We don't own this place.

Contentious Circulations: Struggles in the Roots/Routes

Of course, these practices are not nearly enough. They must be gathered into larger configurations of power, given multiple kinds of inventive institutional support, linked with networks of similar initiatives across the country and around the world, and make inroads that resist and supplant the gargantuan circulations of contemporary superpower. Even during the brief life span of the initiatives we have just discussed, we have seen how small steps are being taken in these directions, at NAU, in schools, CSAs, and emerging FPCs, as well as in growing cooperative initiatives. Yet there is a very long way to go, and the contestations are likely to get more (not less) intense, more (not less) complicated. To paraphrase Mark Winne's response to a comment in a discussion at NAU about the nationwide alternative food movement: for all the great work we are doing, if you step back, it is like we've organized a bunch of fast bicycles heading in really promising directions. Yet coming down the road in the opposite direction is a huge fleet of semitrucks.[84] Even as the alternative circulations are developing at an impressive rate, the circulations that are devastating people and the planet continue to intensify at an even quicker rate.

The character of the emerging dynamics and contestations among mega-circulations of superpower and new materialist "polyface" flows is far from clear and raises many questions. Two potentially interactive factors are particularly salient in this regard. First, dominant modes of circulation are assimilating alternative visions and practices in ways that draw new materialist flows and desires back into mega-circulations of power. Whole Foods Market, for example, has pioneered corporate organic in ways that are often greatly at odds with the democratic flows of sustainable materialism.[85] As I write this chapter, an article in the *New York Times* details the ways in which "giant agri-food corporations [like PepsiCo, Fritos, Heinz] and others—Coca-Cola, Cargill, ConAgra, General Mills, Kraft, and M&M Mars among them—have gobbled up most of the nation's organic food industry." Predictably, these corporate firms in the (often semi- and pseudo-) organic industry have moved aggressively to colonize regulatory boards that set the standards regarding what is considered organic. They have displaced smaller independent firms, colonized seats that were designated for consumer representatives, placed corporate staff who are not farmers in the seats designated for organic farmers, filled other seats with representatives of corporations that are only partly organic—and advocated for genetically modified organisms, myriad synthetic substances, and practices that are considered anathema by most in the new materialism movement.[86] Second, and simultaneously, some articulations of the movement for sustainable materialism present it primarily as a new "yes" that avoids more conflict-laden aspects of change (e.g., protests, civil disobedience, politics of disturbance, the long, hard slog through formal institutions of governance to establish supportive contexts for emergent developments). Such articulations may emphasize nostalgic forms of solace that tend to diminish the critical vision and sense of injustice, as well as the energies and will to engage in agonistic political actions that are *also* necessary to supplant catastrophic circulations and institutions. In celebrating the emergence of alternative farming, they may tend to look away from growing evidence of the difficulties and unsustainability of this movement in the context of a political economic context that remains profoundly inhospitable and requires radical change.[87]

Yet in spite of widespread yearnings for struggle-free radical reformation, on the one hand, and soothing assimilative corporate strategies, on the other, the profoundly discrepant circulatory characteristics of superpower and polyface flows make it likely that they will collide—with varying levels of frequency, intensity, and significance—in ways that invite and engender political contestations, as well as creative intermingling. As with many earlier social movements, increasing new materialist movement success will likely draw flows of investment, people, and institutions with very different ambitions that may often threaten the viability of many of the movement's most profound practices and objectives—even as these new flows may sometimes be redirected to provide opportunities for advancing these objectives.

The Detroit food justice movement provides an illuminating case in this regard. The growing success, visibility, and promise of the movement have begun to draw corporate interest and potential investment in Detroit's urban agriculture—in ways that may undermine its grassroots polyface promise. In the eyes of many in Detroit's grassroots urban agriculture movement, the symbol of this corporate strategy to assimilate, capitalize on, and undermine community-based initiatives is Hantz Group, founded by one of the richest men in Detroit, who lives in a 14,500-square-foot mansion filled with Tiffany lamps and first-edition volumes of Ayn Rand, in the city's richest neighborhood. Community leaders of urban agricultural initiatives across the city are critical of Hantz Group, contending that they have been excluded as the company formulated its designs and negotiated a substantial incentives package with the mayor behind closed doors (including free tax-delinquent land and reduced tax rates for land newly zoned agricultural). As a result, they claimed, Hantz Group was now poised to make a "land grab" that would generate wealth for a few white men, return most of the African Americans (82 percent of the city's population) who would work on the Hantz farms to something analogous to sharecropping status, create gentrification on the edge of farms, and threaten the viability of the delicate social, ecological, and solidarity economy systems that are beginning to reemerge from the bottom up. Grassroots leaders, inheriting Detroit's legacy of political struggle, have begun to organize significant opposition to the corporate model—holding meetings, speaking at city council hearings, protesting, favoring instead a vision of a community-based land commons.[88]

When I wrote the first draft of this section in 2013, the outcome of this conflict was uncertain. Yet a couple months later Detroit declared bankruptcy and was placed by the state of Michigan under "emergency management." Thus the game began to transform in ways that greatly favored corporations and weakened the position of grassroots groups. Soon after the state of emergency, Hantz Group "purchased" the first 150 acres for three hundred dollars per lot, and the path is now clear for the far greater acquisitions Hantz has planned. Within months, an impossibly ironic scene of astroturfed civic engagement took place as an army of about a thousand white suburbanites (mostly workers in Hantz's many subsidiaries and the project's corporate sponsors) were bused in to plant thousands of trees that will likely enhance gentrification dynamics from which Hantz Group will reap profits but not benefit the community.[89]

Simultaneously, the grassroots solidarity economy continues to grow, and how Detroit's community-based and corporate-driven agriculture initiatives may develop, radically contest one another, or coexist uneasily as part of a complex polyculture is still unclear. New materialist futures will depend in no small part on the capacity of grassroots organizers to generate creative power in relation to a corporate-municipal complex that is stacking the deck in ways that will likely pose tremendous challenges to the radical possibilities of Detroit's grassroots movements. Those in movements that are insufficiently attentive to power and allergic to intense contestations may be ill prepared for challenges that will almost certainly emerge. So too may be those too uncreative to seize new and unorthodox alliances. (I am not suggesting this is a strategy to pursue with Hantz.)

This tangle of problems also appears in the context of a rather stark picture of the potential stakes, risks, and contending logics of superpower mega-circulations and polyface flows when we shift our analysis to wind. Wind power has often been touted as integral to what Amory Lovins in the mid-1970s famously coined the "soft energy path." Bearing kinship with key motifs in the new materialism, soft energy employs diverse renewables that are designed for particular circumstances, frequently located in close proximity to the facilities they supply, and highly sensitive to both local and global issues of ecological sustainability and resilience.[90] Because wind (and solar) are widely dispersed, they have often been taken to be particularly amenable to highly decentralized production and distribution, in ways that could release contemporary economies from the megapowers that proliferate circulations of fossil fuels. With power (in many senses) thus dispersed, designs could be developed and deployed that are finely tuned to specificities of wind flows, capacities of local ecological and cultural terrains, community needs and aesthetics, and so forth. Wind power easily infuses the imagination with possibilities akin to those stimulated by polyface agriculture.

Indeed, this is precisely how authors deeply steeped in the tradition of wind energy in the Sydthy district of Denmark—an area that has the richest tradition of wind power on the planet—seem to imagine it. Evoking a responsive and collaborative relationship with wind, they write: "Renewable energy is, by nature, decentralized, and in Thy it has been possible to organize things in a way that makes new technology a part of ordinary people's everyday life. Not only has this served local development and the environment, but it is also a manifest instance of how individuals and households may play an active part in changing the social system and create a model reaching out far beyond the borders of the local area and the country."[91] Responding to these suggestive possibilities for relative decentralization and flexibility provided by flows of wind across the land, the people of Sydthy created an energy-rich network of dispersed windmills "that complement the landscape and the location of the farm buildings," creating a "well-balanced economical and ecological structure in the landscape."[92]

If the claim that wind is "by nature decentralized" oversimplifies things significantly (recall that colonialism and capitalism were significantly fueled by wind power),[93] nevertheless the people of Sydthy and the Danes responsively created a set of socioeconomic practices that *mirrored and amplified the decentralized flexible possibilities and resonant suggestiveness* of widely circulating winds. In the 1970s they legislated "that windmills should be owned by people living in the mill's neighborhood, and that private individuals could only own shares in them corresponding to their household private consumption. . . . The intention was to create broad popular involvement and local ownership in the development of Danish wind energy"—intentionally carrying on a century-long folk tradition.[94] They created conditions for developing functional and efficient windmills that were similarly decentralized, involved local windmill cooperatives and do-it-yourself technologies, and were highly experimental—based on "a broad exchange of experiences and open access to information" among the people engaged in the emergent wind industry.[95] The result was a widely dispersed yet well-integrated production of windmill components by numerous firms. The result of this responsive network of people and things was "massive good will toward wind energy" on the part of localities, and a

Danish wind energy sector that grew quickly and steadily until it produced 20 percent of the nation's electricity by the turn of the twenty-first century and involved 150,000 households in co-ownership of local windmills. In 2001, 86 percent of Denmark's wind energy was produced by cooperatives.

Yet the growth rates in decentralized and decentered flows of people, money, enterprise, wind energy development, and enthusiasm dropped off precipitously at the beginning of the twenty-first century, when the Danish state moved aggressively to liberalize the energy sector. As restrictions on ownership were abolished, large flows of private investment moved in to buy out and capitalize on the success that had been created. Many cooperatives were taken over, wind energy wealth was greatly concentrated and "result[ed] in a dramatic decrease in public involvement," and the wind energy industry was reengineered to develop standardized wind farms with far larger turbines more conducive to the concentrated mega-circulations of capital, energy, and finance. Within a few years, the share of cooperatively produced wind energy dropped to 75 percent, and today it is a small fraction of that. However suggestive wind may be of more decentralized and responsive energy possibilities, liberalization proved that initiatives for contrary developments based on megaflows are also possible.

However, while the process of diminishing the earlier networked system of flows took place with considerable dispatch, the new system of circulation met with considerable contestation and often stalled: "The attitude towards wind power has suffered a reversal—now the erection of every single windmill becomes a local problem, and results in bitter conflicts that lead to long delays or cancellations."[96] As a result, net wind energy development came to a standstill in Denmark from 2003 to 2008.[97] For a time, circulatory paralysis seemed to be the outcome of the effort to displace polyface wind flows with mega-circulation. Nevertheless, by 2009, Denmark's wind energy production began to soar again, as a combination of huge corporate investments and state research led to tremendous increases in offshore wind energy developments, and the state took steps to reduce local resistance by ensuring that local persons could purchase at least 20 percent of the ownership of new installations, establishing a compensation plan for decreases in property value resulting from wind turbines, and promoting a scenic compensation scheme as well.[98] Presently, Denmark is the world's leader in wind energy production, and the cooperative element—though now dwarfed by large corporations like Vestas and Siemens Wind Power—is still touted as key to the rapid rise in production (and has been emulated by other countries such as Germany). While the more radical character of cooperative and decentralized developments in the 1980s and 1990s has been greatly curtailed, both Denmark's leadership in renewable energy and the fact that some of the cooperative legacy remains appear to have greatly diminished criticism and resistance.

In places where long histories of mega-circulation (colonialism, imperialism, neoliberalism, and so forth) have been especially severe on communities and ecosystems, the topographies upon which circulatory contestations take place are much steeper and favor gargantuan flows over those that seek poly-face alternatives. In this situation, some of the darkest possibilities of mega-circulatory conquest of possibilities for alternative ecological and human flows can emerge.

As large and likely insurmountable problems concerning climate change and peak oil threaten to curtail dominant circulations of fossil fuels, growing corporate speculation, political activity, and investment are beginning to flow toward the creation of conditions that can modulate the shift toward renewables in ways that maintain the hegemony and governmentality of mega-circulatory power. One particularly intense zone of conflict is located on the coast of the Isthmus of Tehuantepec in Oaxaca, Mexico, a region inhabited by indigenous communities that are seeking greater autonomy. Like Denmark, this region has some of the greatest potential for wind energy in the world. Drawn by already lucrative and cost-effective opportunities, global corporations are moving into the region with a gusty swiftness that has been called a "wind rush." At the cutting edge of their effort is one of the latest in many waves of capitalist enclosure, which seeks to concentrate and privatize the wind commons by establishing exclusive rights to exploit its circulation. According to this public-private scheme, the region has been divided up into territories "marked with the name of the foreign corporation in charge of energy generation," in conjunction with consortia of large corporate consumers. This avoids competition among the corporations and gives them monopolistic negotiating powers with local communities (never consulted about the broader enclosure scheme), which are left to either accept a contract that offers them 1.5 percent of the gross wind income generated on their land (and is biased toward the corporations in other ways as well) in return for major restrictions on land use—"or reject the use of their wind."[99] Because the communities involved are extremely poor, approximately fifteen hundred farmers have thus far signed the contracts. Thus, as state sovereignty is deployed to facilitate corporate megaflows of circulatory power, something as wild as the wind is being constricted into the channels of superpower in the name of a transition to renewable and regional development.

In this context, many indigenous communities are beginning to initiate resistance and alternatives, contending that the enclosure process was undemocratic, lacked transparency, violated communal landownership principles, and so on. Increasingly there are calls for community ownership and participation in the development of wind energy, and one of the most interesting initiatives in this regard is being developed by the Yansa Group, which seeks a commons-based energy system that promotes community and ecological resilience. Yansa, fittingly in the context of our discussion of receptive resonance and movement, is the "Brazilian name of the Yoruba goddess of wind, lightning, and passionate change."[100] The Yansa Group aims to generate financial flows that enable commons-based energy, as well as a do-it-yourself paradigm that promotes local communities' access to, training for, and participation in the technological developments of renewable energy production. With a vision of radically dialogical and voluntary relationships, it seeks to organize technological, economic, ecological, and policy changes that have a significant resemblance with what we have been calling polyface flows. Its capacity to contest, skirt, and supplant rapidly developing powers of mega-circulation is still emerging and remains unclear.

What is clear, however, is that myriad new materialist movements will have to take very seriously questions of political power, disruption, and contestation. The very success of these movements will draw the investment of superpower and mega-circulation in ways that will make that nearly certain. "Power," because it is so often rendered in instrumental technocratic terms, is a word that frequently has a dissonant ring for many who are cultivating polyfaced sensibilities and practices. However, without serious considerations of how power functions, as well as new radical democratic political arts that can generate alternative powers and contestations, radical and ecological democracy movements may be overwhelmed in the midst of increasingly fast and turbulent currents that intensify circulatory superpower and spell disaster for the communities and ecosystems through which they surge.

In the next chapter, we explore some of the theoretical and practical lessons that may be gleaned from complexity theory in order to better negotiate radical paths by generating dynamics that are self-intensifying—or autocatalytic—and resilient. In chapter 4, we explore the need and potential pathways for interweaving quotidian democratic practices, on the one hand, and a politics of disruption, on the other. Combined, these suggest ways in which the politics discussed thus far in this book might be supplemented to dramatically amplify the potential power of radical and ecological democratic movements.

CHAPTER 3

System Dynamics and a Radical Politics
of Transformative Co-optation

The modes of receptive organizing and scholarship to which I aspire frequently draw me into relationships, conversations, and unexpected radical democratic collaborations with a wider range of people than many scholars and activists may typically cultivate. This is a source of both substantial political pleasure and significant frustration. Leaving aside my relationships with people along a much broader portion of the political spectrum for now, I often find myself circulating with people in different locations along what most would take to be "the left" (whether those thus positioned wish to be placed there or not). Frequently many of these folks have a visceral disdain for each other, and they sometimes are suspicious of me for crossing lines and having, as Ani DiFranco puts it, "more than one membership to more than one club."[1] Of course, the left is famous for its finely honed sectarianisms—the antagonisms among the many different tendencies within anarchism and Marxism provide endless case studies. Yet many of my experiences of left hostilities find articulation at a more general level, namely, those between radicals who pursue visions and modes of organizing that lean toward "reform," on the one hand, and those whose politics are explicitly "revolutionary," on the other.[2] People on either side of this antagonism often define their own position by articulating their distance from and disdain for people on the other side.

I cannot tell you how many times I've been in one-on-one conversations and large meetings with organizers and leaders in reform-oriented community organizing initiatives where proponents repeatedly rehearse their identity and legitimacy through performances of dismissal and disdain for radicals who profess more revolutionary visions: "We deal with issues—specific winnable challenges like streetlights, safety, or job training programs that meet the needs of both an industry and individuals who want to be able to support their families," says an organizer several times in a training session in a school gymnasium. "We don't deal with problems—like 'racism,' or 'poverty,' or 'capitalism.' All you can do around problems is crazy revolutionary posturing that doesn't achieve anything, can't build power, and is just the regular old flash-on-the-screen then it is gone. We want to be in relationship to folks in power, collaborate, sometimes apply pressure, and hold each other accountable. We're not trying to dress in black and run around like a bunch of nuts trying to 'overthrow the system.'"

When several people repeatedly press questions about possibilities that may have potentially more transformative horizons, modes of engagement, or sites for organizing that the broad-based organizing frame appears to preclude, they are met with rehearsals of the paradigm and effectively marginalized rather than offered a real argument. The possibility that connecting issues and problems might be at the heart of more powerful organizing is rarely taken seriously.[3]

Yet the situation is just as bad on the other side, as when I was discussing the advantages of simultaneously using several strategies for transformative organizing around immigration at an anarchist meeting and began to sense—from rolling eyes, dismissive body postures, and grimaces—that for many in the room what I was trying to say and do was indistinguishable from the Koch brothers. As the engagement went on, it became clear that for many, those of us who cultivate collaborative political relationships with, for example, some in city government seeking less than 100 percent of our political ideal are viewed as pathetic dupes inadvertently working for the system by assimilating radical energies into containers of meaningless activity. Critical conversation in these contexts is extremely difficult, as many seem ensconced in a politics of posturing more akin to identity politics than to the radical organizing they profess. If many of the more reformist broad-based democratic community organizers I've known tend to build comparatively substantial and enduring organizations that nevertheless often hold fast to cramped optics with modest impacts, those embracing a politics of revolutionary posturing tend to have an exceedingly narrow range of people with whom they are able to work, rarely move beyond short-lived mobilizing around hot issues, often scorch each other and splinter internally, and tend to organize in ways that are rather inconsequential. The radicalness of posture is matched by a vagueness of strategic vision.

When the philosopher in me whispers in the ear of the organizer, he observes something like what Immanuel Kant called an antinomy. Antinomies are conflicting positions that are irresolvable because they are rooted in a misunderstanding ironically shared by both sides that prevents reflection. Each side is energized and sustained by its compelling insights into errors on the other side.

Each side is absolutely defenseless against the other side's criticism of its own weakness, yet assumes that the transparent fallaciousness of the other side is sufficient evidence for the truth of its own claims. For Kant, philosophical arguments about whether the universe had an end or was endless were of this character. Those who affirmed that it was endless pointed out how the assertion of an end could easily be refuted by advancing to the next point in space and asking "What's that? Not the universe?!" Those who affirmed that it had an end pointed out the absurd impossibility of conceiving of a thing that was boundless—an empty thought. For Kant, in this case what sustained this opposition was that neither side critically examined their shared assumption that the universe was a given fixed thing (somehow either infinite or finite), rather than, as Kant argued, a world dynamically synthesized by transcendental subjectivity.

Stepping back from the specificities of these philosophical debates, my organizing self sees an analogous political problem. Both sides of the political divide sketched here share the assumption that systems are given as nearly immutable totalities. One side works in the margins in an effort to rectify the worst, yet it cannot imagine an order of things beyond its current basic structures. The other seeks to provoke an "event" that has an unimaginable or nearly unimaginable eschatological quality—breaking the order from seemingly nowhere (even when this nowhere is named "immanence"), because the world as it is seems to offer no textured possibilities for forming such a break. Each is energized by its compelling dissatisfaction with the other side: The revolutionaries see the painful insufficiency of reforms that have for decades addressed problems like streetlights, as inequality grows more severe, democracy is being destroyed, and we rush toward planetary catastrophe. The reformers see the weakness of a politics that is empty and inconceivable and has a track record of now-predictable rebellions with little capacity to endure, shift dynamics of power, and organize alternatives.

Perhaps we are all more implicated in this dilemma than we think. I have often experienced it running through me as I struggle with how we might organize in specific ways that enable powerful and transformative action in dark times. Nevertheless, the longer I theorize and organize, the more I have come to believe that the widely shared understanding of systems that undergirds so many positions today is deeply flawed and undermines the possibilities of cultivating radical democratic power and transformation. It does so in at least three ways. First, insofar as we understand the driving locus of system dynamics to be "out there" in subjugative corporate markets and state bureaucracies (even as each of us is marked by and perpetuates these dynamics), we have tended to view system dynamics as such as bad and essentially heteronomous things. Thus we have not carefully considered the possibility that there may be generative relationships between systems dynamics and radical democratic receptivity. We have avoided asking whether and how we might unleash specifically receptive radical democratic system dynamics, and whether such dynamics might be indispensable for cultivating the power of receptive radical democratic movements. Second, and relatedly, because we have reified system dynamics as fixed totalities rather than contingent dynamics, we have too often avoided asking how we might create interfaces between radical democratic dynamics and neoliberal dynamics in ways that enable us to co-opt some of the latter in ways that enhance the former in potentially transformative ways. Though we have often and rightly criticized the politics of capitalist co-optation, we have failed to ask whether and how we might generate a politics of radically democratic co-optation that moves in very different directions. Third, as a result, the flawed systems theory that undergirds the antimony between reformers and revolutionaries not only sustains their weakness in relation to the critiques each presents to the other but also maintains their incapacity to generate genuinely transformative power. Currently this fuels a politics of entrenchment that tends to block the sorts of receptive inquiry and experimentation that I think might enable us to move beyond the current stalemate. The exploration of complex dynamic systems theory that follows suggests that there are more hopeful possibilities for theory and practice.

In the previous two chapters we explored receptive forms of resonance and circulation emerging in radical democratic movements and suggested that the two are profoundly intertwined. From one side, in the register of physics, resonance disrupts Newtonian trajectories and generates new and significantly unpredictable movements. In neurological registers, intercorporeal resonances among mirror neurons are intertwined with the generation of new processes, structures, affect, and bodily capacities for perception, mobility, and interaction. In ethical-political registers, practices of receptive democratic resonance across differences are integral to the emergence of new forms of perception, unwonted relationships, interrogative capacities, capacious sensibilities in relation to game-transformative actions of others, and a sense of the future as more open to our own powers to radically change the world. We can look at the intertwinement of resonance and movement from the other side: the frequencies that resonate among objects are themselves born in movements. Our bodies' biocultural neurological capacities for resonant receptivity are cultivated and suppressed by myriad modes of movement associated with our engagement in the relationships and practices of our lifeworlds. The ethical and political circulations of our bodies and the bodies of other humans, non-human beings, and things greatly influence our (in)capacities for resonant receptivity and mimetic relationships.

In an important sense, resonance and movement are different dimensions of a single phenomenon, perhaps especially so in ethical-political life. Ultimately, there are no movements without profound orientations of resonance and dampening, and cultivating receptive resonance always involves attention to bodily movement—even if this may take the form of practices of stillness, as when John Paul Lederach counsels an ethics of peacemaking receptivity inspired by what he calls "the Zen of going nowhere."[4] Nevertheless, these different lenses call our attention to these different aspects of ethical-political life in ways that may facilitate a refinement of our capacities to sense, reflect upon, and cultivate more receptive and powerful modes of game-transformative democratic practice.

Yet, what Wolin calls the "inverted totalitarian" powers of our time are themselves highly adept at intertwining resonance machines and mega-circulations in ways that generate amplificatory game-transformative dynamics of their own that are antidemocratic, extremely inegalitarian, and ecologically catastrophic. Even if we can generate powerfully transformative dynamics for radical and ecological democracy, are there reasons to have any hope in the face of this enormous apparatus of destruction? I think that there are. Though the challenges are great, they are not insurmountable, and there are possibilities for movements to do far better in their struggles to change the world than we have mustered in the past several decades.

To perceive and seek to enact such possibilities, however, requires that we develop a far sharper analysis of complex system dynamics than most movements have employed in the past. As I have suggested, too often radical democrats of various stripes argue or assume that systems are essentially closed totalities whose goals, actors, sectors, components, political contestations, and so forth are thoroughly integrated in ways that are essentially uniform, homogeneous, and functional. Yet I suggest this understanding is *itself* a consequence of one of the foremost effects of contemporary neoliberal power—let us call it the "Wizard of Oz effect"—whereby the order projects an ideological mirage of its omnipotence. Like all hegemony, the power of this projection and the power of the order itself hinge very significantly on the myriad ways those subject to it continue to consume and proliferate the projection. Our uptake and dissemination of the imaginary omnipotence of "the system" vitiate our capacities to contest the order in radically game-transformative ways. By assuming the "Wizard of Oz effect" as the foundation of our analyses and strategies, a large portion of today's "left" too often unwittingly plays a vital role in perpetuating the order.

This imaginary basically discloses three vantage points that largely frame debates within "the left." One is a despairing version of Margaret Thatcher's celebratory proclamation that "there is no alternative" to contemporary ever-deregulating capitalism. There is no possibility that radical agency might make significant changes in the seamless system—which leads proponents of this view to political withdrawal and exclusively critical work. A second version also reifies the basic order but perceives some elasticity in the margins that matter for the future of democracy and, in turn, how the system works. The "three-sector" model that is employed by many Habermasian scholars and broad-based organizing initiatives conforms to this perspective: there are two major systems in our world whose orientations and modes are fundamentally immutable (state bureaucracies and corporate markets) and a third sector called civil society where democratic life-forms are located.[5] While civil society can do nothing to radically transform the larger systems, it can "hold them accountable" when people are powerfully organized, such that states and market powers may do a better job in relation to people's interests. The systems themselves have little plasticity in terms of their core tendencies, modes of operating, and predominant outcomes, but as noted in the preceding vignette, there are margins that really matter in terms of neighborhood infrastructure, schools, living wages, job training, housing, safety, and so forth, and the job of radical democrats is to cultivate democratic relationships, knowledge, and power so ordinary people can avoid the worst—and sometimes do better than that. A third angle within this basic topography is to agree that the current system is totally closed but to view our addiction to pointless work in the margins as futile in relation to democracy, inequality, and planetary catastrophe. Hope rises in some form of revolutionary rupture or event that would radically alter the course of things (call it the "Toto effect," whereby a highly unexpected event pulls the curtain in a way that discloses the illusory and vulnerable nature of the "Wizard of Oz effect")—though revolutionary pathways, modes of organizing, theories of radical transition, and goals are typically left extremely vague. "New Leninism" and some forms of anarchism often position themselves here.

Yet I want to question the paradigm of systems as closed totalities that often underpins such positions, and instead explore themes in complex dynamical systems theory that disclose indispensable directions for radical and ecological democracy. In this way, I too seek something like a "Toto effect," yet one that involves thinking and acting in ways that are at once novel and involve specific, textured, and resilient practices and pathways. It should be clear by now that I am aware of the powerful tendencies in neoliberalism that undermine democracy, generate intolerable inequalities, and have taken us to the edge of planetary ecological catastrophe. Nevertheless, if we analyze these in terms of specifiable feedback loops that are powerful yet not immune from potential disturbance and transformation, on the one hand, and if we employ a much suppler sense of system dynamics as we cultivate movements for radical and ecological democracy, on the other, possibilities emerge that have significant promise particularly in relation to the politics of resonant receptivity and poly-face flows discussed in previous chapters.

Others have written insightfully on how totalizing systems theory can conceal flexibilities, contingencies, and transformative possibilities that are far from having been exhausted by radical democratic movements. For example, Roberto Unger and William Connolly have convincingly shown (albeit in different ways) how totalizing approaches to systems can conjure up images of seamless developmental logics that diminish our sense of the *contingency* through which different elements have come to be articulated and assembled in ways that could have been—and could become—significantly different.[6] Moreover, the language of system tends to project a uniform totality in ways that occlude the vast coexistence of what J. K. Gibson-Graham calls the noncapitalist "community economy"—from domestic practices, to cooperatives, to informal exchanges, to nonprofit activities, to fair trade relationships, and so forth.[7] When radical critique becomes totalizing, it conceals this plethora of alternative practices and thereby diminishes their potential transformative powers. These implications converge in ways that nurture a sense of powerlessness, what Wendy Brown has called "wounded attachments," and a culture of *ressentiment*.[8]

In response to these pitfalls, I explore key themes in the complex dynamic systems theory of Stuart Kauffman that have made important contributions to the democracy movement at Northern Arizona University. I begin with a discussion of autocatalysis, or the way in which entities (like molecules, cells, or democratic actors) form relationships, patterns, and positive feedback loops that can catalyze—speed up and proliferate—the production and reproduction of new formations. With greater attentiveness to the formation of autocatalytic relationships, a democratic and ecological culture might create patterns and powers that increasingly acquire self-organizing characteristics that generate complex, dynamic, and powerful systems with greater capacities to challenge, co-opt, and supplant the dominant regime. In this context, I argue that receptive generosity is not only an ethical virtue but also a political virtù (Machiavelli's term for a sharp strategic sense and virtuosity around power) integral to the emergence of powerful radical democratic autocatalytic dynamics.

Next I develop this argument by examining the conditions in which systems tend to become fecund with emergence *as such*—prone to stimulate transformative learning, experimentation, and patterns of becoming. We can discern a great deal about the potential power of radical democratic systems through the lens of Boolean networks (depicting the characteristics of different types of regimes) that help us theorize a politics that approximates what Kauffman articulates as an ordered regime just this side of "the edge of chaos." Kauffman argues that such regimes combine flexibility, surprise, and resilient order in ways that are generative of the most complex and creative behaviors. His discussion of evolution in the midst of extremely challenging conditions— or what he calls "rugged fitness landscapes"—illuminates why and how organizational practices near the edge of chaos are crucial, especially, I contend, in the context of the pervasive precariousness created by neoliberal systems dynamics. His experiments around problem-solving processes in the face of complex and challenging conditions suggest a theory of organization in which redundancy is integral to emergence (contrary to the tyrannical parsimony and technocratic logics of "efficiency" that currently hold sway, including in the activities of many progressive and environmental organizations) and diversity becomes key to "an explosion of creativity" rather than the innocuous feature of a multicultural smorgasbord.

Yet in the context of this book on game-transformative practices, Kauffman's discussion of extremely rugged and risky fitness landscapes begs a question he does not really explore: How might a self-organizing system such as radical democracy transform the basic political economic terrain upon which it struggles, in ways that create conditions less rugged and more conducive to our flourishing? Placing this question in the foreground of our discussion calls us to develop a theory of radically democratic co-optative power. By this I gesture toward the ways in which autocatalytic dynamics of democratic movements can be selectively connected with particular dynamics in neoliberal systems in order to co-opt their powers for the purpose of supporting and intensifying dynamics of radical democracy. Radical democrats often alert us to powers of co-optation in order to enjoin us to keep a distance from an ever-corrupting system. While by no means oblivious to this concern, here I am interested in exploring ways in which co-opting a politics of co-optation may be an indispensable *aspect of* radical and ecological politics in our times.

Working through these details of complexity theory in chemistry and biology requires some patience on the part of readers who share little intrinsic love of science. Yet I will show how each theme provides a highly provocative lens for understanding and advancing democratic theory and action, using our work at NAU and in Northern Arizona to exemplify this claim. Our wild patience, in other words, opens up wild and hopeful possibilities.

Autocatalysis and Self-Organizing Dynamics of Radical Democracy

Many believe that radical democratic initiatives are doomed to be short-lived—or what Wolin called "fugitive." Yet the history of events that make this idea compelling may stem as much from the contingent characteristics and strategies of many of these initiatives as it does from dominant antidemocratic powers. For example, mainstream U.S. environmental organizations have often opted to embrace "professionalization" and market logics in order to fight legal battles, lobby for legislation, and partner with large corporations. Yet Robert Gottlieb compellingly shows how these strategies have cut them off from community organizing (beyond canvassing to raise funds) and people's everyday experiences in ways that have undermined the grassroots power that is crucial to environmental movements' capacity to radically challenge the powers that continue to devastate the planet.[9] A similar story could be told about the labor movement and many other democratic initiatives of recent decades.

How might we theorize and initiate political dynamics that harbor more potential to engender other kinds of stories? I think the theory of autocatalytic emergence can provide important insights and serve as a luminous heuristic metaphor for transformative and resilient political thought and action. For some complexity theorists, the difference between "metaphor" (loose and imaginative) and "real theory" (disclosing probabilistic laws) is rather sharply defined.[10] However, I am not looking to theories of complexity for such laws, nor for the next reductive political appropriation of insights from the natural sciences. Rather, in the metaphoric light of the interactive relationships, patterns of emergence, transitions, and intensifications that appear in complexity theories of physics, chemistry, and biology, we might discern new and more potent dynamics and possibilities for radical democratic transformation. As we do so, we may enhance the *power* of these disclosed possibilities by shifting them into the animating foreground of our imaginations, aspirations, and actions. In times when many radical democrats find ourselves gravely doubting the possibility of transformation—even as we repeat the World Social Forum's insistence that "another world is possible"—I read complexity theory in order to *intensify the plausibility* of such *possibilities* in ways that *enhance the probability* that we might smartly *engage in actions* that help *actualize them.*[11] In the present discussion, complexity theory is used to amplify—not merely analyze—the phenomena under discussion.

Stuart Kauffman, one of the foremost theorists of complexity and evolutionary biology, argues that self-organization is (in combination with chance and selection) integral to the evolution of life. The theory of autocatalytic systems—systems that generate conditions of their own reproduction and sometimes development—is integral to his thinking on these matters. Catalysts are entities (whether molecules or people or organizations) that enhance the probability of relationships and reactions that may otherwise have difficulty forming. Many molecules (say those of A and those of B) may have the capacity to form chemical reactions (that produce, say, C), but do so only rarely and with great difficulty, after which the products may break apart as readily as they formed and thus never accumulate. Catalysts (e.g., molecule D) can play a role in enhancing the probability and speed of these reactions and accumulations. In the simplest metaphor, they do so as both A and B attach to D in ways that hold A and B together so they are much more likely to join and create C. If C has catalytic properties for A and B, the dynamic may be still further intensified.

Erase the board and let us use these letters in a different way. Autocatalytic systems, Kauffman writes, are those "in which the molecules speed up the very reactions by which they themselves are formed."[12] Let's picture this dynamic in terms of two basic molecules, A and B. Imagine that A combines with B in two different ways, to form either AB or BA. Now imagine that BA turns out to be a catalyst for joining A and B to form AB, and AB is a catalyst for joining A and B to form BA. Such a system would "feed itself" in a way that is self-sustaining (provided it has an energy supply). If in this example we represent AB as C, and BA as D, the autocatalytic equation here is A + B makes either C or D, while C in turn catalyzes A and B to produce D, and D in turn catalyzes A and B to produce C. Here we have two reaction strands linked in an autocatalytic network in which C and D are at once products and catalysts in a process of self-propelling loops. Systems that are self-organizing abound in such molecules, or other entities such as species, institutions, organizations, or economic goods, with analogous characteristics.

Yet what is the actual likelihood that molecules that are products will simultaneously play a catalytic role in the chain of reactions that produced them? Kauffman argues not only that there is an overwhelming probability that molecules will self-organize in this manner, but that this probability is built into the nature of the universe (or, in this case, chemistry). Far more than being a product of uncanny chance, the probability of the emergence of autocatalytic sets at the molecular level tends to increase until it is nearly inevitable—"rooted in mathematics itself."[13]

Kauffman supports this claim with the following account, backed by numerous computer simulations. Return to our model of A and B, which react to make AB and BA. However, now remove our previous heuristic supposition that each product catalyzes the reaction that produces the other. How does the probability of autocatalysis increase according to the nature of things? The crux of Kauffman's answer lies in the way proliferating reactions tend to enhance the complexity and diversity of molecules in the soup, thus enhancing the probability that catalytic agents will be produced. Once AB and BA are produced, they can react with each other to form ABBA or BAAB; and AB and BA can react with A to form ABA or AAB; and they can react with B to form ABB or BAB—and these latter products can react in a similar manner with each other and their subcomponents to produce more new compounds. The complexity and diversity of the next round of possible reactions grow many times again, and so on and so forth—thus producing an exponentially growing diversity and complexity of molecular products. As the diversity and complexity increase explosively (because complex molecules can react with other molecules not only by joining as wholes but also by cleaving into a variety of parts), the number of reaction potentials increases even more quickly than the number and diversity of molecules themselves. (For example, consider the enormous number of reaction potentials of a single polymer in this mix, such as BAABABBBAB, which can break at many points to form subset molecules that can react with others.) Here is how Kauffman puts it: "This increasing ratio [of reaction possibilities to molecules] means that as more complex and diverse sets of molecules are considered, the reaction graph among them becomes ever denser with paths by which they can change from one into another. The ratio of reaction 'lines' [connective possibilities] to dots [molecules] becomes denser, a black forest of possibilities. The chemical system becomes ever more fecund with reactions by which molecules transform into other molecules."[14]

If, say, a computer simulation is run with "random catalyst rules," such as "each polymer has a fixed chance, say one in a million, of being able . . . to catalyze any given reaction," then as the diversity and complexity of the molecules increase, a threshold (in this case when the ratio of reaction possibilities to molecules becomes in turn greater than a million to one) is crossed after which catalyzed reactions become highly probable and a vast web of autocatalytic reaction loops arises.[15] This, Kauffman claims, is how complex dynamic self-organizing molecular systems—and life itself—emerged. Of course, energy is required to fuel the reactions that form complex polymers. Yet dehydration (in terms of nonliving chemical systems) and the linking of "exergonic" reactions (energy releasing, such as the degradation of food molecules) with "endergonic" reactions (energy consuming, such as those we have been discussing) are common ways in which this challenge is met in the real world.

There is another mathematically guided characteristic of things that Kauffman says is crucial to the formation of autocatalytic systems, namely, the formation of *connected webs*. Imagine an array of buttons on a table, gradually being connected by threads, which stand for relationships or reactions. At first, the number of threads is relatively small in proportion to the number of buttons, so the threads simply form separate strands between particular buttons. Yet as the relationality or reactivity of the situation is increased, and the ratio of threads to buttons passes 0.5, an amazing thing happens in graphic depictions and computer simulations: "Most points become connected in one giant component."[16] Kauffman calls this a "phase transition," evoking something analogous to the transition that happens when water turns from gas to liquid, or liquid to ice. In the present case, the transition is from relatively isolated and disconnected phenomena to an interconnected system with emergent properties. Though made of the reactions and products of myriad entities, the system itself represents a newly emergent *type* of thing that is irreducible to its component parts and their relationships. It will have characteristics that manifest *differences in kind and interact with the surrounding environment in novel ways*. Add autocatalysis, and this new system tends to become self-organizing, self-reparative, and reproductive.

Let us put Kauffman "on hold" now so that we may begin to explore some of the political implications of his analysis thus far. Clearly the lesson we might learn here is *not* that there are, in some essentialist way, both positive feedback loops and phase transitions that tend—for reasons "rooted in mathematics itself"—to emerge automatically in radical democratic movements. Human relationships, reactions, combinations, and formations are intuitively and empirically far too complicated to be rendered in such a simple formulation. Moreover, myriad dynamics within and among many human individuals, groups, and systems tend to preempt, homogenize, disorganize, undermine, disintegrate, and disempower interactions among individuals and groups that would lead to emergent dynamics. So how could we learn about human ethical and political life from the comparatively simple relational dynamics of molecules?

Given Kauffman's analysis, we would expect that the formation of a new democratic assemblage with emergent properties would involve proliferating resilient public relationships (threads) among myriad selves (buttons). Yet numerous antidemocratic tendencies decrease the political relationality of selves. Isolation and anomy inhibit interactions: civic privatism tends to diminish the public potential of relationships that do occur; power hierarchies establish myriad walls and steeply sloped interactions that prevent democratic commingling; the hypermobility of people repeatedly forced to exit one place for another to survive economically regularly tears people from relationships and relocates us where we must start from scratch; and postures of ideological dismissal tend to suppress unexpected political relationships and pathways. Such political landscapes tend to have many buttons and few democratic threads. They are terrains that are easy to colonize and govern with antidemocratic connections, resonances, and circulations. Strategies that seek to advance democratic aspirations yet fail to change the challenging character of this terrain—such as the "professionalized," legalistic, bureaucratic paradigms of many "Big Ten" environmental groups, unions, consumer protection groups, and so forth—may win battles here and there but are likely to "lose the war."

To change this terrain, then, would require generating movement cultures of radical receptivity that can catalyze and cultivate connections beyond the limits of our isolation, walls, hierarchies, and quick-draw dismissals. Otherwise we remain profoundly unrelational and ungenerative "As," "Bs," and "Cs"—with weak capacities at best to engage each other, produce new combinations, become catalytic, and generate growing and transformative configurations with emergent properties and powers. In this sense, then, receptive generosity, an *ethical* virtue to be sure, would also be a supreme *political* virtue for generating radical democratic power. At the most basic level—and here the attentive one-on-one relational meetings that good community organizing cultures cultivate across myriad differences are exemplary—practices of relational receptivity generate political qualities analogous to "compounds" (e.g., "ABs" or "BCs"). I do not use the term "compounds" here to suggest that we join to become one thing but rather to evoke registers of connection and assembling that are far more powerful and resilient politically. Consider the manifold generative capacities and relational qualities that are enhanced by movement cultures of receptivity: the *supportive powers of solidarities* and civic friendships, as we attentively tend to each other to discern and forge intersections of interest; the *sharp powers of subtlety*, as very different peoples' experiences, affects, and perspectives come to deeply inform your more textured sense of the world; the *mobile powers of suppleness* we acquire as we have our sense of things repeatedly reworked by others in empathetic—if intense—contexts; the *expansive powers of access and engagement* that emerge as people share and move along each other's networks and generate new public relationships across wider ranges of difference; the *assembling powers of alliance* as each becomes more capable of helping to generate diverse organizations and coalitions for public work and political action. In all these ways, movement cultures of receptivity enhance our capacities for generative relationality and bonding, thus rendering us more richly complex in ways that increase potentials for generating political power.

As our amalgamative and receptive characteristics grow, our political capacities may be further enhanced by two phenomena that are also illuminated by the discussion of Kauffman. First, as we become beings increasingly complex and extended in a variety of ways, so too there is an exponential increase in our possibilities for "subdividing" into many different segments and bringing various partial strands of ourselves (of our interests, political visions, passions, experiential perspectives, etc.) into relationships with segments of others to form new assemblages. Needless to say, we are finite and can realize only a small portion of these possibilities, but their growth involves a tremendous intensification of our democratic potential and power for relationships—including the power to cultivate a keener sense for which ones will best enhance receptive democracy itself. Good democratic organizing will thus tenaciously seek to hold open these possibilities for subdividing by eschewing doctrinaire uniformity, total allegiance, purity, quick-draw dismissiveness, and so forth.

Second, our catalytic capacities would appear to increase. Recall that catalysts enhance the probability and speed of reactions by holding together other entities in ways that enhance their capacities to interact and form bonds. The probability that an entity will manifest catalytic capacities in relation to other entities increases with the growing complexity, diversity, and receptivity of its composition (making it more likely that there will be configurations within its overall structure that can break off and catalyze relationships between and among other entities). Politically, as we ourselves become more complex and diverse in myriad ways—*and more attentive to these qualities in ourselves and others*, our potentials for facilitating relationships and amalgamations among different people and organizations increase in a similar manner, as we can more readily connect with a wider array of people and in turn facilitate their connecting with each other.

As indicated earlier, these are real potentials, but not probabilities or necessities that simply unfold on their own. They require organizing cultures focused on nurturing receptive relationality to actualize their political potential. Hence, we might think of such cultures as "metacatalysts," insofar as they cultivate amalgamating and catalyzing characteristics among the individuals and organizations with whom they interact. They call us repeatedly to recognize and deepen our relationships to practices of becoming receptive and relational. One political implication of this insight for broad-based organizing cultures is to continually radicalize their receptivity—to nudge each other beyond the bounds of emergent dogmas in ways that revivify curiosity, tarry with ambiguity, and know not to know too well how and where our politics is heading. This is a lesson we repeatedly forget, but it is indispensable for cultivating radical democratic power as well as ethics.

When organizing goes well, as threads of connection multiply, we begin to witness a "phase transition" in which people and organizations generate a web that forms a configuration with new system dynamics and emergent properties. Whether these amplify in ways that acquire increasing power and resilience hinges in large part on the new configuration's capacity to generate autocatalytic dynamics. Once again, the theory and practice of broad-based organizing have much to offer in relation to this question.

Recall the most basic representation of an autocatalytic reaction is A produces B which produces C which catalyzes A. Consider a very basic model of community organizing along these lines. Thoughtful practitioners of grassroots community organizing theorize the positive feedback loops in their work roughly as shown in figure 3.1.

Community organizations, such as Northern Arizona Institutions for Community Leadership, begin a "cycle of organizing" (whose arrows and order are often more complex and intertwined than the heuristic simplification in the diagram in figure 3.1), with a certain amount of talent, energy, and democratic power. They then host dozens of small meetings and one-on-one relational conversations among members of congregations, associations, neighborhood organizations, schools, unions, and so forth, in a process through which people discern (and forge) interests, issues, and intersections they deem to be important to their community. They begin a series of training sessions on ethical, practical, and strategic aspects of organizing. Having chosen a few key issues,

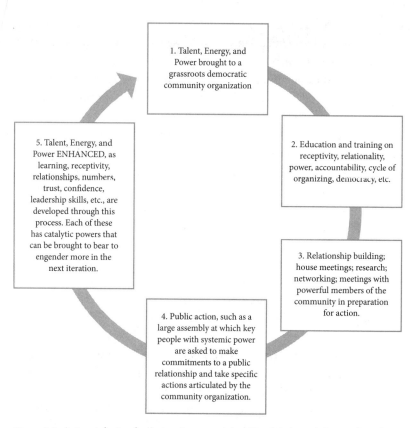

Figure 3.1. Autocatalysis of community organizing. Freely adapted from Edward Chambers's discussion in *Roots for Radicals*.

they organize action teams to conduct research through which they craft an agenda for change, meet with myriad community leaders with whom they desire to collaborate or pressure, and repeatedly seek to expand their network to include other organizations and individuals who are interested in this public work and action. Throughout this process, citizenship education takes place on how to facilitate house meetings, engage in attentive and meaningful one-on-one public dialogues, identify and gather pertinent information on an issue, frame political action at a level that is significant yet winnable, generate power and networking maps that are key for crafting strategic action plans, creatively engage people in various positions of public and private power, become proficient in the arts of political drama, build core teams in each member institution so that each institution builds leadership internally and in relation to the broad-based organization, and so forth. Typically, then, all this work culminates in a large public action at which hundreds of people gather at an assembly in which there are dramatic celebrations of the work that has been done, feisty oratory on the centrality of grassroots democratic leadership, and intense engagements with public officials aimed at securing commitments to specific measures that advance the agenda of the community organization along with their pledges to continue a public relationship for further work on issues that advance common goods. A successful assembly leads to a set of victories and commitments that confirm the importance (and raise the visibility) of the organization's work and the substantial possibilities for transformative grassroots leadership. People leave highly energized to do more public work and political action, further enhance their education and skills for active citizenship, and broaden the conversation to involve more people in the next round of activity. Moreover, figures in the official institutions of power and the media gain a sense of the growing importance, credible capacities, and substantive aspirations of the organization. When it goes well, this entire cycle results in more people acquiring greater leadership skills, receptivity, relationships, political knowledge, democratic sensibilities, and confident enthusiasm, as well as expanding their taste, visions, and aspirations for grassroots power—all of which they bring to the next cycle of organizing that will further enhance power and draw more people and institutions into the organizing process. *When it goes well*, there is a certain magnification of energy, talent, and power each step of the way—in one-on-one meetings, house meetings, creative research, small and large actions, organizing trainings, and so on—that propels and hastens the process, and generates a contagious enthusiasm.[17]

Though "autocatalysis" is not a term that is typically used by grassroots organizers, it well-describes important aspects of the approach to organizing employed by the best of them. While issues are important, the deeper action and focus is on creating autocatalytic dynamics that enhance democracy's own conditions of ethical-political power and possibility with each round. The cultivation of relationships brings people together in ways that catalyze the development of political knowledge, energy, and power. Political knowledge and imagination involve capacities for sensing, synthesizing, and strategizing that further enhance relationship building and power. The successful movement of an organization enhances its magnetic capacity to draw more people into receptive relational organizing processes, maintain their involvement in public work, and so forth. As the relationships develop, they become analogous to the "threads" in Kauffman's discussion of Boolean networks: as the density

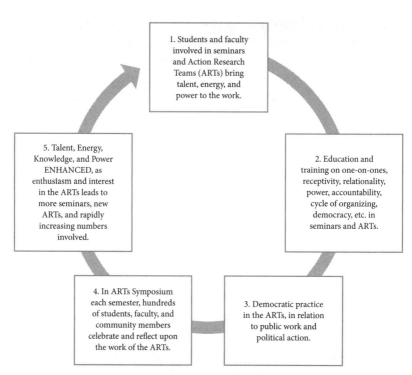

Figure 3.2. Autocatalytic dynamics in Northern Arizona University's ARTs democracy movement

of connections increases, emergent configurations, processes, properties, and dynamics continue to appear. All of this may enhance a movement's capacities to exceed the narrow ruts, prescribed resonances, and suffocating dynamics of the present order of things.

In the radical and ecological democracy movement at NAU, we have cultivated a similar autocatalytic dynamic indebted to the community organizing tradition (figure 3.2). Yet it is easy for emergent self-organizing systems with autocatalytic dynamics to generate characteristics that tend to shut down possibilities for further emergence and, relatedly, erode many of the more promising conditions for autocatalysis to which they have given rise—perhaps especially those we have just discussed involving generative receptive relationality. The fructiferous zone that Kauffman calls the "phase transition" is demanding, and it is easy to slip away from and destroy it by becoming overly ordered or overly chaotic. To gain insight into this problem, consider how Kauffman develops his account of this self-organizing sweet spot.

Kauffman argues that the concept of "phase transition" is incredibly important for evolutionary theory because it describes the rich qualitative and quantitative relational characteristics of *systems whose dynamic capacities for ongoing emergence and resilience are great*.[18] One might say that the zone called phase transition is fecund not only with (and for) whatever the system presently generates, but actually *fecund with fecundity*, rich with evolutionary potential for birthing newness. Drawing the ghost of Hannah Arendt into this discussion, we could say that phase transition is a condition that is particularly stimulating for natality. Let us explore this claim with some care.

Kauffman offers a "mental movie" consisting of a Boolean lightbulb network to portray how both chaotic and highly ordered situations on either side of phase transition suppress the emergence of complex dynamical systems with emergent characteristics.[19] Imagine a square matrix of lightbulbs—say one hundred bulbs wide and one hundred bulbs high. A chaotic regime is one where most lightbulbs randomly twinkle off and on, and each is directly connected to a vast number of others doing so as well. Imagine these twinkling bulbs are represented as green. Within this vast sea of green bulbs, there are some islands of bulbs that are frozen on or off—color them red. Chaotic regimes are extremely vulnerable to—and perpetually undergo—wild changes, as each shift in any bulb "cascades" through the vast undulating sea of twinkling bulbs to which it is directly connected through myriad back-and-forth relationships. Such "chaotic systems show massive sensitivity to small perturbations . . . the butterfly effect," in which the air stirred by wings thousands of miles away may provoke major changes in the winds on the other side of the planet.[20] In chaotic systems, each minor alteration sends cascading waves of massive change upon waves of massive change, rapidly and repeatedly undoing any coordinated relational patterns, and thus preventing emergence of phenomena with temporal duration. Newness is born and disappears instantaneously in the flashing seas of chaos.

Highly ordered regimes, on the other hand, are exactly the opposite. They tend to form vast seas of bulbs that are frozen off or on in some persistent pattern (thus red), each of which gives and receives inputs with a relatively small number of other bulbs. Within this vast frozen sea are little islands of twinkling (thus green) bulbs. Within these islands, small changes can cascade about in more or less chaotic fashion, but they can only rarely if ever penetrate the frozen sea of red bulbs, which acts like a wall of constancy. The islands of activity are isolated from each other in ways that pose tremendous barriers to emergent relationships among them, thereby inhibiting complex interactions and coordinated behaviors. Highly ordered systems thus share with chaotic systems the property of being highly recalcitrant to emergent phenomena—albeit in radically different ways.

Phase transition names a sweet spot slightly on the orderly side of the edge between order and chaos, where emergent phenomena are most likely to occur. It is the zone in which interactions tend to combine significant stability with dynamic flexibility in ways that are pregnant with evolutionary potential. Kauffman depicts this edge of chaos in the following manner: "At the edge of chaos, the twinkling unfrozen islands are in tendrils of contact. Flipping any single lightbulb may send signals in small or large cascades of changes across the system to distant sites, so the behaviors in time and across the webbed network might become coordinated. Yet since the system is at the edge of chaos, but not actually chaotic, the system will not veer into uncoordinated twitching."[21] At this point, because changes are communicated far and wide, there is a high probability that emergent behaviors linked to communication and coordination will repeatedly occur. Yet because there are only *tendrils* of connectivity and communication between different islands of dynamic interactions, rather than a situation where every part is directly connected to and communicating with so many others, emergent interactions happen that allow for the coordination of new complex behaviors in the system, rather than launch it into perpetual floods in which newness instantaneously extinguishes itself.[22] At the edge of chaos, then, each island with dynamic yet significantly persistent patterns receives and gives pulses of communication with the other islands, yet each is protected from being flooded at every moment by so much surprise that new coordinative patterns are prevented from emerging and enduring.

You might ask, what is the probability of complex dynamic systems enduring near this edge of chaos? Kauffman argues that it is quite high and hypothesizes that "evolution takes them there."[23] In essence, the interaction of autocatalytic explosions of diversity and complexity, on the one hand, and pressures of selection, on the other, nudges systems into close proximity with this edge. We have already seen an example of the explosive tendency, in the case of molecular reactions where diversity and complexity quickly begin to feed on themselves to generate an exponential growth of the ratio of reaction possibilities to molecules. Kauffman argues that similar explosions of diversity and complexity—where autocatalysis feeds unfathomably expansive fields of emergence—occur in relation to other phenomena such as cells, species, and much more. Left to themselves, such "supracritical" explosive tendencies would generate situations that would become so chaotic they would actually inhibit the emergence and stability of complex dynamical systems by generating toxicity—*there would simply be too much newness.* Yet pressures of selection push back on this tendency because systems that tend toward overly explosive novelty are outcompeted by those that do not. Thus, selection favors "subcritical" systems that are relatively stable, even as they are capable of flexibility and generating surprise. Indeed, when Kauffman and his colleagues have run computer simulations in which different systems play competitive games against each other, they find that the evolutionary pressure of this situation tends to select systems that evolve toward the edge of chaos—"not exactly on this edge, but toward an ordered region near it."[24]

If Kauffman's hypothesis and the initial insights from this computer simulation hold up, it would imply that the twin pressures of explosive proliferation and selection continually act on systems such that those which are significantly subcritical creep upward (due to the way diversity and complexity tend to feed on themselves in exponential patterns of growth, and due to the competitive evolutionary advantage of systems that are dynamic and flexible), and those which are significantly supracritical either go extinct or shift backward toward more stable and less toxic configurations of emergence. Among the most amazing conclusions suggested here is that *selection pressures and self-organization tend to coconspire to favor the emergence of conditions that are fecund with emergence itself!* Combining relative stability and dynamic flexibility, subcritical systems not far from the edge of chaos are most capable of evolving in the context of a universe of continual change. Yet another way of putting this is that these twin pressures tend toward the evolution of evolvability itself, the zone where newness and durability combine in highly flexible, dynamic yet persistent patterns. Kauffman notes: "Evolvability itself is a triumph."[25] This hypothesis is consonant with the observation of Santa Fe Institute's John Holland (discussed in chapter 1) that there is a discernible overall tendency toward greater responsiveness as things combine to form new emergent patterns.

Kauffman's discussion helps shed light on how the closed aspects of *both* some community organizing reformers *and* some revolutionaries likely engender conditions that freeze the sea of possibility and isolate deviant tendencies in ways that suppress emergence and thus vitiate democratic power. By creating cultures that are readily dismissive of receptive dialogue and experimentation with alternative modes of organizing, alternative ways of engaging different political, economic, and social sectors, as well as different visions of transformative pathways and aspirations, they generate cultures of "frozen bulbs" that tend to isolate and vitiate new ideas and practices within and among their organizations. Yet pure "horizontalism"—striving toward a "radical openness" in which everyone can have an equal voice in everything at every moment—is equally problematic insofar as it resembles Kauffman's sea of chaos wherein each difference overwhelms and is overwhelmed by every other, such that newness is repeatedly stillborn.[26] How might we organize in ways more conducive to evolutionary learning at the "sweet spot" that enables powerful new patterns to persist while avoiding their reification and entrenchment?

Kauffman's discussion suggests that a radical democratic habitus more conducive to natality and evolvability should cultivate an *ecology of different modes of democratic engagement* in a manner that is akin to the fecund zone a bit this side of the edge of chaos. The different modes are like "islands" with distinctive patterns of interaction, but rather than being walled off from each other, or seeking to become the entire "sea," they are joined by tendrils of connectivity and communication. They are significantly insulated in ways that buffer them from overwhelming floods of change that far exceed their mediating capacities; yet each receives and sends signals with others in ways that enhance learning, experimentation, and selective collaborations.

In our efforts to engender a radical democratic habitus at NAU and Flagstaff, we have tried to cultivate conditions very similar to Kauffman's image of a Boolean network near the edge of chaos. While many campuses across the United States that are doing good work in the democracy education movement have focused heavily on one or two modes of democratic engagement (e.g., civic deliberation, public work, service learning), our approach has been to cocreate a movement that is profoundly heterogeneous in its modalities, sites of engagement, thematics, and horizons of aspiration. Thus, we have cultivated an environment that is capacious enough not only for vital initiatives of civic deliberation, public work, and engaged service learning but also for those that focus on broad-based community organizing, more insurrectionary modes that employ street protests, modes focused on aesthetic interventions of various kinds, modes engaged in more traditional forms of advocacy, humanitarian modes, and more. For example, the Immigration ART engages in humanitarian and witness work on border issues with No More Deaths (an advocacy group that provides humanitarian aid to immigrants and deportees on both sides of the U.S.-Mexico border); broad-based community organizing strategies with Northern Arizona Interfaith Council (an organization that pursues a more moderate approach and focuses on building working relationships among immigrants, nonimmigrant residents, police, schools, businesses, and so forth, that enhance democratic capacities and relationships for addressing community issues); abolitionist democracy visions and strategies with Repeal Coalition (a radical social movement that affirms the "right to live, love, and work wherever you please"; resists all legislation, policy, and practice that discriminate against undocumented people; and engages in political protest); educational events with a variety of campus and community partners; and broad-spectrum civic discourse with another ART called Hot Topics. With many different teams and subteams working in different ways across myriad problems and locations, a wide range of people can become engaged in modes with which they find resonance. Just as importantly, through regular processes of communication among the various initiatives, we can all learn from, hybridize, and cocreatively modulate our initiatives as we witness the achievements and shortcomings of different approaches in different contexts. This not only provides a rich setting for liberal arts political inquiry but also engenders reflective understandings of and dynamic involvement with a vast toolbox that enhances radical and ecological forms of democratic power.

Often this process is full of tension, as people negotiate very different dispositions and tendencies. Yet what makes it resilient and fecund is something analogous to the seemingly viscous sea in Kauffman's image that both provides some insulation from storms of self-extinguishing novelty and facilitates generative connectivity. Just as I tried to show how the discussion of catalysts and autocatalysis discloses the metacatalytic character of receptive relationality, I think the image of the Boolean network near the edge of chaos discloses how a capacious ethos of receptive generosity is analogous to the sea-in-between, as it both affirms a capaciousness that insulates myriad semiautonomous modes and opens to, supports, and solicits attentive dialogues and collaborations among them. It as an ethical medium that enables us to interact generatively and powerfully, just this side of the edge of chaos.

Kauffman further crafts organizational insights that are of value to radical democracy in his discussion of experimental processes that tend to best enable self-organizing systems to learn and evolve in the midst of conditions—or "fitness landscapes"—that are complex, precipitous, and ever-shifting. His discussion of rugged fitness landscapes both underscores why creative processes are so crucial for self-organizing systems and has important implications for specifically political systems. At the same time, however, his discussion begs questions about the character of such landscapes themselves, in political

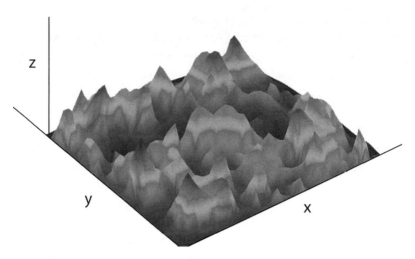

Figure 3.3. Rugged multipeaked fitness landscape

economic contexts: Are such landscapes immutable? How might transforming them itself become elemental to the aspirations and practices or radical
democratic self-organizing systems? First we will explore his organizational
insights, after which we will draw everything presented thus far into a theory
of terrain-transformative radical democratic co-optation.

The situation to be negotiated (by entities, species, individuals, organizations, movements, etc.) obviously far surpasses questions of internal relationships that we have discussed and centrally concerns the character of the
surrounding condition. Kauffman conceives of this environment through the
analogy of a topographical "fitness landscape" in which well-being increases
on higher terrain and vice versa. In its most basic form, a fitness landscape will
show the relative well-being (on vertical axis z) that is achieved by combining
two variables (on horizontal axes x and y). Fitness almost always involves far
more than two dimensions, but nevertheless this image has heuristic value.
Darwin imagined the evolution of species as a gradual step-by-step upward
movement on fitness landscapes that were relatively smooth, single peaked,
and stable. Yet Kauffman argues that often fitness landscapes on which evolutionary processes occur are better portrayed as multipeaked, rugged, and
shifting.[27]

Insofar as a fitness landscape is multipeaked and precipitous, as in figure
3.3, entities may ascend a relatively low peak that is a great distance from much
higher peaks of fitness. Peaks of varying heights may be separated by cliffs and

steep valleys, such that gradual movement might well involve getting devoured by extremely unfavorable conditions on one's way to a different (presumably higher) peak. In such not-uncommon contexts, it would be easy to become trapped on a low fitness peak (e.g., in a mode of being or paradigm that is better than the worst, but far from realizable possibilities that are much better), such that minor cumulative mutations (or step-by-step gradual behavior shifts) would rarely provide a means of escape precisely because minor changes might induce radical reductions in fitness. Similarly, if an individual or organization becomes nearsighted from focusing on narrow frames and tasks, it may have little idea that there are much better possibilities (fitness locations) that may require a bit of a leap but are not that far off.

For heuristic purposes, take an oversimplified example in which the power of an organization is related to access to people in elite positions in corporations or government (y-axis) and the grassroots vitality of its member institutions and leaders (x-axis). An organization that had achieved a modest but not insignificant fitness peak (e.g., some political influence on environmental legislation, or the ability to work with corporations for conservation land swaps) might sense it could gain power by developing greater grassroots organizing capacities. Let's assume for a moment that this is true. Nevertheless, if it pulled, say, 20 percent of its resources away from its investment in relationships with elites and redirected them toward grassroots organizing, it is possible that it would significantly damage its capacities in the former area (e.g., by tending less well to elites, alienating them with prospects of grassroots pressures) while not increasing them sufficiently in the latter to compensate for this loss. It might then discover itself tumbling into a very unfavorable area in the fitness landscape. It would thus be the case that evolving its power would require a "leap" of some sort—far more resources to organizing, rethinking its mode of engagement—that would also have its risks. The upshot is that evolution on such landscapes is very complex, uneven, tricky, and often not amenable to gradualist approaches.

This difficulty is compounded again by the fact that because many species (and other complex systems) are coevolving, fitness landscapes may change markedly as changes in one species or system alter the conditions for others. A species on a rapidly shifting landscape will likely be served poorly if it can only make minor adjustments during highly dynamic periods. Finally, in human systems, the difficulty is compounded insofar as problems are frequently misspecified and misinterpreted, such that our learning processes send us in useless or deleterious directions or conceal possibilities for beneficial movement.

Kauffman argues that systems that are streamlined to maximize efficiency in relation to a specific set of objectives are highly problematic, insofar as they privilege the present "fitness landscapes." Genuine fitness in such contexts requires high levels of evolvability, or a propensity for generating emergent phenomena in ways that foster more radical modes of responsiveness that are more analogous to (or actually are) paradigm shifts than to gradual step-by-step improvements. For all these reasons, Kauffman claims, as we have seen, that "evolvability itself is a triumph," which exceeds any specific evolutionary manifestation. What characteristics might enhance entities' capacities to experiment, learn, and change in ways that enable them to escape the trap of low fitness peaks, supplely track and shift to moving peaks amid deep valleys, and thus maintain or improve their well-being—or in our case the power and receptivity of a democratic movement?

Kauffman takes a hint from certain molecular systems that escape "bad local minima" (i.e., configurations that represent a mediocre low-energy location arrived at through minimal reconfiguration from a previous state, yet one that is far from more desirable configurations that require much lower energy to maintain and are thus more stable) through thermal vibration. For heuristic purposes, as this example aims at *lower* energy conditions, let us reverse the fitness valences of our topographical imagery, so that better fitness is represented by deeper basins rather than by peaks. As increasing heating causes increasing thermal vibration, molecules increasingly collide with each other and tend to push one another in random directions such that some move downward on the fitness slope, some jump to different (and perhaps lower energy) basins, and some are jostled upward to poorer locations where they disintegrate in chaos.[28] Under conditions of great heat, the molecules jostle each other so intensely that they leap every which way chaotically, rather than shifting toward an overall condition of low-energy stability. Under conditions of too much cold, the molecules move little and are unable to evolve toward low-energy stability configurations in multibasin contexts. Yet the solution is not a happy medium because this leads to the trap of gradualism we discussed earlier.

Metallurgists solve this problem through a process called "annealing" that employs cycles of heating and cooling a metal. The aim is to create conditions of sufficiently intense thermal vibration during the heating cycle so that molecules achieve more than gradualist movements, and many are enabled to jump ridges to other deeper basins (yet the overall condition remains this side of chaos). This is followed by a cooling cycle where the benefits are consolidated as the molecules in deeper basins adjust to each other in stabilized low-energy configurations. The process is then repeated with slightly less heat intensity so that molecules in more unstable (poor fitness) locations can once again jostle each other toward deeper basins, consolidate during the cool phase, and so forth, to facilitate minimally stressed and maximally stable molecular configurations—or very hard metals. By attentively working these cycles that oscillate between thermal intensification to a point this side of chaos and cooling that consolidates stable configurations, metalworkers (and metals) learn how to evolve the metal toward the desired goal of maximal hardness.

Analogously, Kauffman argues that systems whose internal interactions occur in ways far more complex than these physical-chemical processes might maximize evolvability through processes of "simulated annealing." In simulated annealing, systems become highly animated (yet this side of chaos), as various parts experiment with changes. Some of these changes are interesting and helpful, while others are not. Those that are most creatively useful metaphorically "jostle" other parts in the system into innovating and coevolving with them. If we imagine the deeper basins of inventive learning as those locations that represent changes that tend—like a comparatively better paradigm—both to *better* solve problems and to solve *more* problems better, then processes with comparatively greater evolvability will be those in which the animated parts tend probabilistically to shift toward those basins over time.

Yet here the analogy breaks down because, unlike metals, which have well-defined and static conditions of maximal stability and hardness, we have seen that human processes coevolve on landscapes that are frequently very dynamic, while goals and strategies are frequently misinterpreted as well. Hence, radically democratic dynamics require a type of "simulated annealing" that must frequently resume "reheating" insofar as we seek to enhance ongoing processes of receptivity and transformation in relation to a complex dynamic commonwealth (and catastrophic possibilities) that repeatedly calls for reassessment, contestation, and reimagination.

Kauffman names these processes for ongoing evolution inspired by simulated annealing "patch procedures," and they work like this: "Take a hard, conflict-laden task in which many parts interact, and divide it into a quilt of nonoverlapping patches. Try to optimize [problem solve] within each patch. As this occurs, the couplings between parts in two patches across patch boundaries will mean that finding a 'good' solution in one patch will change the problem to be solved by the parts in the adjacent patches."[29] This creates a dynamically coevolutionary situation in which each patch functions in a manner somewhat analogous to a thermally vibrating molecule or a species undergoing adaptation. Innovations in each patch generate what amounts to deformations and reformations in the fitness landscapes of surrounding patches. Each of the latter is agitated to adapt to the former with "a new burst of rapid learning," which in turn alters the landscape in ways that provoke further adaptations in other patches.

The key to generating a coevolutionary situation that maximizes evolvability—or learning—is to divide the problem space properly, which means finding the number and kinds of nonoverlapping patches that maximize innovative moves just short of the point where such moves create so many inputs in every direction that the system devolves into chaos. This hypothesis is confirmed by computer simulations showing that patch procedures maximize learning when they move to a position near the edge of chaos. Increasing the number of semiautonomous patches effectively heats up the process so that many semiautonomously learning parts push each other into coevolutionary learning—short of provoking chaotic cascades that destroy the process. Such patching systems turn out to be able to attain good compromise solutions (when there are multiple conflicting variables) and track moving peaks in a changing landscape with great dexterity. In light of our discussion of resonance in chapter 1, I would emphasize that in addition to the number of patches, cultivating qualitative intensities of receptivity and transfigurative enthusiasm within and among the patches is integral to the "thermal vibrations" that enable selves and action research teams to sense, initiate, and provoke new possibilities for thought, work, and action.

All this suggests that political sensibilities and processes that create fairly high levels of decentralized dynamism somewhat this side of chaos are extremely important for democratic flourishing and power. Kauffman suggests that designs that have "analogues of patches, systems having various kinds of local autonomy, may be a fundamental mechanism underlying adaptive evolution in ecosystems, economic systems, and cultural systems."[30] He wonders if U.S. federalism is in this sense "utterly natural" insofar as it allows experimentation and innovation that can then be copied in other places if it proves to be an improvement. Even so, he wisely reflects: "One is always in danger of deducing the optimality of the familiar. Let's call this a Mill-mistake. God knows, we all suffer the danger."[31] I suspect that reducing his insight to U.S. federalism does indeed risk "deducing the optimality of the familiar," even as I think that his analysis harbors important insights for innovations in democratic theory and practice, as I suggest later.

Let us return to the earlier discussion of our efforts in Northern Arizona to cultivate a movement that remains proximate to a politically dynamic and fecund location a bit this side of chaos. I suggested that one dimension of this effort is connected with an ethos of receptive generosity that is capacious, hospitable, and engaging with respect to extant and emerging difference. Yet, as the image of the Boolean network already suggested, the organizational characteristics of the movement are crucial here as well. My thinking and participant leadership (along with that of several others) on these matters have been importantly influenced by systems analyses of simulated annealing and patchwork.

As noted earlier, our Action Research Team initiative has a patchwork structure, with each ART having substantial autonomy to modulate its processes, goals, strategies, and tactics in relation to the specific issues, problems, community partners, locations, challenges, and opportunities that constitute a terrain of engagement. Moreover several ARTs (like the Immigration ART) are organized into subteams, each of which has significant autonomy in relation to the ART of which it is a part, even as we also seek to create good structures of communication and collaboration within and among the ARTs movement as a whole. Subteams have patch relationships with each other, as the successes and failures of new initiatives in each subteam solicit coevolutionary shifts with the others. Hence, the grassroots democracy education ART called Public Achievement works in semiautonomous subteams to cocreate durable collaborations with three schools. Each PA site works with the administration, students, teachers, parent organizations, and dynamic conditions at each school, and this requires a receptivity that modulates the work significantly in each case. At Kinlani Bordertown Dormitory, significant reflection revolves around crafting modes of cultural translation back and forth between indigenous traditional knowledge and practices of leadership, community, and relationships with the Earth, on the one hand, and PA themes and practices of grassroots democracy, on the other. Dense histories of colonialism as well as rich possibilities for recovering and cocreating emergent pedagogical, ecological, and political practices are questions at the forefront of this evolving initiative, in which students from NAU's Department of Applied Indigenous Studies are very active. Public Achievement's work at Killip Elementary also must address particular challenges (such as extremely high levels of transience brought on by harsh policing and employment challenges faced by the many immigrant families) and opportunities (such as the richly multicultural character of the school and neighborhood). Working at Kinsey Elementary involves many of these challenges and many others as well. Both an ethos of responsiveness and semiautonomous organizational structures geared to the specificities of each place have ensured that PA is a living and diversely evolving process rather than a dogmatic practice we seek to impose. At the same time, innovations at a particular school around cultural context, transience, working in unstable after-school programs, organizing with parents, and so forth, tend to "jostle" the work at other sites in a coevolutionary learning process.

"Patch procedures," "coupling" relationships among patches, and "tendrils of connectivity" are extremely important in exercising judgment in this process. Hence, in the case of Public Achievement just discussed, each PA subteam in the patchwork of the ARTs quilt has closest coevolutionary relations with the other PA subteams—each learning from the successes and challenges of the others. Similarly, thematically proximate ARTs form coevolutionary patch relations as well, as, for example, when the alternative agriculture ARTs (around campus gardens, elementary school gardens, community gardens, composting, etc.) tend to be in closer communicative learning processes with each other than they are with most other ARTs. Broader coevolutionary relationships of patch relationships are built into the structure of the ARTs insofar as all the ARTs facilitators gather every couple weeks to share and discuss the specific challenges, creative initiatives, questions, potential modulations, synergistic possibilities emerging around the work and action of their particular ART, important interfaces among specific ARTs, and so forth. In this way, each ART informs, is informed by, and cultivates a network of dynamic learning, mutual support, and provocation in which the overall movement reflects and develops.

It is important to emphasize that systems theory in the context of democracy remains a heuristic lens that informs judgments about processes in a manner that is far more akin to art than to common understandings of science, and we endlessly negotiate and rearticulate responses to questions concerning desirable degrees and modes of integration and autonomy, types of connections, rates of modulation, processes of learning, and so on. If we are organizing well, the edge of this dialectic generally moves too quickly to be caught at rest—but not so fast as to knock us all off our feet. What we seek is a vantage point and organizing process that avoid *both* the disintegrative tendencies of many forms of pure horizontalist anarchism *and* the tendencies toward stifling closure we have discussed earlier.

I think it is useful to consider the interactions in this zone of organizing as analogous to what Kauffman calls "simulated annealing." When the broad movement is organizing well, the different modules, or patches, are jostling each other provocatively in ways that keep us moving on our toes and changing our practice as we are compelled to repeatedly modulate in relation to impulses from evolving initiatives with which we are in relationships of communication, collaboration, and degrees of interdependence. Perhaps the vast majority of this jostling and these modulations involve making modest shifts—midsize steps. Yet equally important—if less frequent—are the processes of more intense jostling that move us to change in response to another ART that has experimented with what seems to be a better way of doing things, or has surfaced hitherto unrecognized problems, or gives rise to disagreements the outcome of which remains in question. The shifts and learning that occur in these instances are more akin to the "leaping" that is required on terrains that are rugged, multipeaked, dynamic, and frequently misspecified. However they are resolved, they force us to leap up and away from the patterns we have come to take for granted—even if this merely means to defend them in new ways. They call us to consider other modes of relationship; exclusions or power dynamics of which we had not been aware; possibilities for doing promising work in sectors many thought were totally dead, or with people many had dismissed; newly recognized problems that open astonishing and unexpected collaborative possibilities; a tremendous surge in outrageous ambition that several seize out of a great sense of urgency in ways that force others to pose questions about how they themselves will respond. Variously, these events create enthusiastically generative passions, friction, and heat, all of which are akin to "thermal vibrations" that enhance capacities within the group to leap into new reflection, relationships, work, and action in response to a challenging shifting landscape of dangers and opportunities. They facilitate our capacities to see distant possibilities—peaks, basins—that may be far more desirable than those more proximate ones we took to be exhaustive of the real. They provoke us to imagine and cocreate paths across difficult terrain upon which straight lines and modest steps are often not sufficient for traveling.

The key, I think, is cultivating a culture of organizing sensibilities that are also frequently able to step back a bit and calm down at points when it seems like everything may begin to leap in ways that generate disintegrative chaos. Simulated annealing provides an excellent heuristic here, too: for processes of cooling are integral to the cycle in which heating is employed. The key is to learn how to cycle and oscillate between the two. We are learning not to underestimate the arts of detecting well when to take some rest, relax righteousness, and gather ourselves—and yet grow wary of extended periods of time that remain unvisited by bouts of leaping.

Yet for all the virtues of episodic leaping and honing our capacity to evolve on fitness landscapes whose characteristics are rugged, complex, and frequently shifting, we might ask: How well do these characteristics describe the fitness challenges and conditions that learning processes must address? Even within evolutionary biology there are differences of opinion on this matter—and it is probable that the conditions to which beings strive to adapt may vary significantly across different times and places in their degrees of steepness, multipeakedness, and volatility. However that may be resolved in biology, these differences in degree are clearly evident across different locations and times when it comes to the human-created political, economic, and social topographies upon which people seek to survive and thrive. This raises another vital question: If human-created fitness landscapes vary dramatically (as, for example, between the comparatively stable conditions of the social contract that emerged with the New Deal and the crisis-laden precariousness that is increasingly pervasive in contexts submitted to neoliberal "shock doctrine"), shouldn't radical democratic learning processes seek to hone capacities to survive and thrive not only in relation to neoliberal terrains but also by transforming such terrains? This, at any rate, is the aspiration of radical democracy as a game-transformative practice. Insofar as such topographies of fitness (and catastrophe) are heaped high, dug deep, and wrought by regular earthquakes and volcanoes, these features are largely created by dynamical processes of political and economic systems. Might there be ways to co-opt some of these dynamics in order to enlist them for purposes of transforming landscapes in manners more conducive to radical democratic and ecological flourishing? If this were possible, it might facilitate the development of radical democratic movements by enabling them to gain some traction on terrain designed to destroy the demos.

The Dynamics of Radical Democratic Co-opting

Rather than understand contemporary political and economic powers as uniform, seamless, and immutable, with Unger, Connolly, Gibson-Graham, and others, I think it is far more illuminating to view them as a set of complex systems dynamics that are remarkably powerful, yet are nevertheless assembled of heterogeneous entities and autocatalytic processes. For all their power, they are made and unmade by processes very much like those we discussed earlier in this chapter. They are not exhaustive of political and economic practice and possibility. They interface with myriad ecological, geological, and social systems in increasingly disruptive and catastrophic relations. They have strung themselves together in ways that are significantly contingent and episodically rearranged, and some elements and dynamics can be drawn into radically new dynamics with other self-organizing systems in ways that foster very different processes, vectors, and visions.

Contemporary political economic systems combine increasingly narrow oligarchical tendencies with stunningly flexible relationships and oscillating patterns near the edge of chaos that subject the world in ways that sometimes resemble images of overly ordered Boolean networks that tend to dampen and isolate pockets of emergent resistance and alternatives, and at other times resemble chaotic Boolean regimes in which waves of chaos erode pockets of alternative life-forms and arrangements that resist the oligarchy. As I discuss in the next chapter, the alternation of chaos and totalizing order is integral to the tyrannical operation of these power dynamics. It is a formidable concoction, to be sure.

Yet, as I suggested earlier, there is something like a "Wizard of Oz effect" that also plays an indispensable role in perpetuating these power dynamics. For, in no small degree, the "frozen sea" that renders alternatives impotent in the Boolean image itself becomes thus frozen when and only when we overwhelmingly accept and proliferate the frozen image of a totally implacable order and thereby seal hegemony's deal. The sea is cold and hostile, to be sure, but we have a power to prevent it from freezing solid, and this thawing power begins when we refuse the image of total, unified, immutable solidity and begin to organize resonant receptivity, responsive flows, and radical democratic systems dynamics that move in other ways and directions to generate amplificatory connections among multiple modes of resistance.

In this regard, the discussion of complex dynamical systems theory conjures something like a "Toto effect" that unveils systems not as totalities but as assemblages of autocatalytic dynamics amid diverse ecologies of other autocatalytic assemblages, many operating across diverse registers and spatial scales, and according to different and often asynchronous temporalities.[32] As beings proliferate relationships and undergo a phase transition, many of them begin to form an aggregate component that develops emergent characteristics. Yet this latter consists of entities (e.g., atoms, molecules, species, ecosystems, human individuals, institutions, geosystems, cultures) that continue to have self-organizing systemic properties and potentials of their own that are irreducible to the whole. These entities and tendencies may be intertwined with, destabilized by, and undergo shifts in relation to a variety of other micro- and macrosystems in which they are or may become involved—especially when these latter relationships are amplified. Each system is entangled with others in relationships of symbiosis, parasitism, and conflict, and these relationships are dynamic, phasing in and out of resonance and dissonance according to myriad factors. In other words, though there are numerous macrosystems with powerful autocatalytic processes, these processes are not closed uniform totalities but coexist in significantly contingent and complex relationships (e.g., coexistent relationships that might be characterized variously as internal, external, nested, crosscutting, mixed, oscillating, or episodic) with many other processes and may undergo transformations toward remarkably different settlements and equilibria. Repeating these ideas in several ways in order to dislodge reifying tendencies in our affect, perception, and cognition is an important part of the Toto effect—*along with careful action research* that begins to explore potent alternatives. It animates a political ethos that is more hopeful, attentive to opportunities, relational, experimental.

Because these ideas have informed the radical and ecological democracy movement at NAU and in Northern Arizona, we can explore some of their implications by examining how they are playing out there.[33] Yet, first, consider key elements of the broader political and institutional context. During the six-year period under discussion, Arizona's long-standing antipathy toward education and public things, one of the worst budget crises in the nation, and arguably the most vitriolic assault in the U.S. culture war to date all sadly converged to create a set of mutually amplifying neoliberal dynamics that provided a highly challenging setting for this experiment. Undocumented immigrants were ground zero for this assault, but the LGBTQ community, proponents of sustainability, ethnic studies, public education, and even moderate Republicans were all kneaded into the targeted mix. Budget crises and hostility toward higher education led to large cuts in the number of tenure lines, a rapid increase in adjunct hiring, growing class sizes, increasing workloads, and daily news that sent shocks through the university, in Flagstaff, and across the state. The affective ambience was largely one of great anxiety, cynicism, despair, defensiveness, and powerlessness. The Arizona Board of Regents (ABOR) quickly advanced neoliberal transformations by implementing "outcome-based funding" schemes that linked public spending on higher education not to enrollment numbers but to "student success" narrowly conceived in terms of metrics such as retention and graduation rates. In response to ABOR, the NAU administration rapidly proliferated a neoliberal culture of "assessment," "results-based planning," "best practices," "outcome-based metrics," "uniform branding," and so forth, that all absorbed tremendous amounts of time, disciplined (in the Foucauldian sense) faculty, and increased our sense of being under regular surveillance.[34] For many, this suppressed creativity as we felt overburdened, pressured toward narrower objectives, and worried about the punitive possibilities associated with more frequent interventions. Similar dynamics were felt throughout the broader community. As student debt continued to rise, many felt pressured to adopt more narrowly career-oriented educational paths and often approached those objectives with a consumer mentality. Increasingly, the imperatives of corporate business culture were becoming integral to the discourse of how we should refashion ourselves. The university launched a hiring strategy that focused on "research-active faculty"—defined as those who brought in at least $800,000 in external funding annually. If our radical and ecological democracy movement could quickly begin to make significant shifts in the hyperintensified neoliberal dynamics of the university—cynically viewed by many as a hopelessly totalizing system—then the approach would likely have transformative implications for radical and ecological democracy in many other contexts.[35]

We have discussed NAU's radical and ecological democracy movement from a variety of angles and shown how alternative practices of resonance, circulation, and autocatalytic system dynamics have developed in quite promising ways. Integral to launching, sustaining, and amplifying these developments, however, were questions concerning how these dynamics might powerfully interface—in trickster ways—with the dynamics of a neoliberalizing university in an extremely right-wing state. In other words, in what ways might a movement for democratic education develop inventive practices, purposes, processes, interests, visions, and cultures that not only initiate their own powerful democratizing dynamics but also, and relatedly, *co-opt* dynamics that are non- or antidemocratic in order to enhance our hand and increasingly tilt the table in favor of democracy in each round? Co-optation is something we are rightly taught to fear. Yet it is also an indispensable and fine art that we should learn how to employ. Complexity theory suggests that we need to put some skin in this game. How might we craft radical democratic initiatives that advance a clever and increasingly powerful game-transformative-practice with some chance of outmaneuvering and co-opting dynamic forces of neoliberal corporatization?

At NAU we are framing our work around democratic education and sustainability in two key ways. On the one hand, we argue that it is crucial for the future well-being of our city, the region, the nation, and the globe. In myriad ways and in relation to a growing range of challenges upon which we are working, we are developing the case that a flourishing, complex, democratic commonwealth hinges upon educating people capable of critically, creatively, and powerfully engaging in collaborative public work and political action. In this regard, the initiative at NAU is involved in a nationwide (and global) movement for democracy education that is taking form in the United States in association with networks such as the Civic Agency Initiative of the American Democracy Project, the American Commonwealth Partnership, Imagining America, Public Achievement, and so forth. Increasing numbers of faculty, students, staff, administrators, and community members are finding these arguments and the associated practices discussed throughout this book to be compelling alternatives to political cultures of cynicism, disengagement, and myopic reaction that are frequently pervasive on many campuses and in many communities.

Yet as we have advanced this movement "on its own terms," from the outset we have also actively cultivated a second frame in order to pursue a parallel strategy. We have somewhat paradoxically sought to co-opt some neoliberal dynamics into radical democratic dynamics, for the purposes of generating autocatalysis and game-transformative shifts at NAU that build resistance and alternatives to neoliberalism. In this context we employ a second frame, in which we argue that democracy education is a highly effective means by which the university can increase its efficiency (thus saving money); boost retention and graduation rates (thus gaining state funding); enhance student interest, achievement, and success in coursework (thereby reducing failing grades, for which the university and ultimately the faculty are penalized under the new regime); recruit high-quality students from within and out of state (thus drawing revenue to the university and increasing our stature, which positively impacts the first two objectives); and retain faculty through an exciting set of initiatives that engenders a growing space for creative collaboration in an otherwise shrinking and poorly remunerated shock-box.

In these ways, the NAU ARTS movement has always played a delicate "trickster game" with respect to neoliberal governance, accessing pockets of funding and institutional support by hypothesizing that engaged pedagogy would have a major positive influence on the specified rates to which state funding is pegged. By using the trope "trickster game," I am not implying that we are behaving dishonestly but rather that we are playing one (neoliberal) game very well, primarily in order to institute a transformative counterpractice and alternative practice that is much more important to us. It is not, for example, that we do not care about retention and graduation rates—far from it—but that we care about student civic agency, radical democracy, sustainability, social justice, and liberal arts education far more, and primarily value these rates within this transformative frame.

Initial funding for faculty and graduate student involvement in this initiative came from the Program for Community, Culture and Environment, the First Year Seminars (FYS) Program, and the Masters of Sustainability Program, which formed the core leadership group. Almost immediately, faculty began to see many students getting excited, becoming intellectually animated by the connections between theory and practice, and acquiring a taste for the arts of active citizenship in which they were becoming change agents in relation to the diverse and complex commonwealth of broader communities. Soon after, we began to see how these results could become part of a powerful strategy for engaging and retaining students; enhancing academic performance and graduation rates; cultivating maturity, collaborative agency, purpose, and so forth. We gathered these ideas into a proposal to NAU's President's Innovation Fund (aimed at enhancing "student success" in what ended up being a largely unimaginative response to ABOR's neoliberal pressures) and secured a modest but significant pot of money to further develop our project, as well as to generate some provisional interest and buy-in for our strategy from several higher-ups in the administration. The following year we secured another modest pot of money for faculty development around engaged pedagogy from a supportive dean. As we acquired a growing track record that included positive student performance, public work with community organizations that increasingly garnered good press, a trip to the White House where our initiative was featured at the launch of a Department of Education civic education initiative, visible signs of a more vibrant and engaging campus, and so forth, institutional support was increasingly forthcoming. Moreover, variously employing neoliberal and democratic frames in different ways at different times, we have since gained substantial funding from the National Science Foundation (for a pedagogical research and practice initiative combining climate change science, regional and cultural contextualization, and civic engagement across the Colorado Plateau); the Arizona Technological Research Investment Fund (for cooperative and alternative food economy research and organizing); the J. P. Morgan–Chase Foundation and the United Way (for a center called the Mercado de los Sueños that promotes microentrepreneurship and lending, community-based and cooperative economics, a multicultural market, and grassroots leadership); the Kettering Foundation (for sponsored research and collaboration around civic engagement and democratic education), and more.

The strange heterogeneity of our funding sources reflects an emergent organizing philosophy that seeks to assemble a vast array of tools for transformation, as well as supple trickster dexterity in our use of some of them. J. P. Morgan–Chase is an absolutely corrupt institution that should be abolished (even as several in the foundation are well-intentioned, good people with whom we can work), yet we were able to draw a crucial pool of start-up funds from its foundation to support excellent work with economic autocatalytic dynamics suggestive of a future (far down the road) without corrupt corporate banking. Through this overall process we are gaining substantial resources for promoting radically democratically engaged publics around myriad issues and modes discussed earlier.

Yet our ability to do so is significantly related to how we have engendered trickster connections with neoliberal dynamics to successfully initiate game-transformative pedagogy and politics. Students at NAU have very high dropout rates, with roughly 27 percent of first-year students leaving the university before their second year. This is extremely "inefficient" for the university because a great deal of funding is spent (far exceeding their tuition dollars) on students who will fail to generate state revenues because they will not graduate. Using neoliberal rhetoric and rationales, we were initially able to pull modest but significant funding our way from the administration (in which there are some excellent individuals with whom to collaborate, as well as many who have no business anywhere near leadership positions in higher education—again, systems are nonuniform and complex). A recent assessment study of the FYS-ARTs found significant increases in retention rates from the first to the second year among students who take one such seminar. Minority students who took a FYS-ARTs course showed increased retention rates of 17 percent; women's rates increased 9 percent; overall rates were up 7 percent.[36] These findings strongly suggest that students who connect their education with resonant public engagement, alternative flows, commonwealth purposes, and democratic agency not only "turn on" to education but also are not as likely to "turn off." It appears that radical democratic practice is proving to be more successful at addressing these neoliberal goals than anything else at the university, even as our modes and visions work toward very different— and even antagonistic—ends.

As the assessment studies confirm our initial wager, very substantial funding is rolling in, including steadily growing allotments for graduate student assistantships, scores of undergraduate peer-teaching assistantships, support staff who are also catalytic organizers, numerous full-time faculty lecturers teaching

ARTS seminars (long-term positions with benefits, yet paid significantly less than tenure-track faculty), and (this year) two tenure-track positions shaped by our work (one focusing on community-based sustainable economics, and the other on community-based sustainable water and agriculture). More and more faculty and units from around the university are getting involved in collaborative democratic pedagogy and community engagement initiatives.

One way to look at these allocations of funding and commitment is that they are mostly utilizing underpaid precarious labor—undergraduates, graduate students, and non-tenure-track lecturers. There is significant and profoundly frustrating truth to this. At the same time, all of these people are self-consciously inhabiting these significantly exploitative spaces in order to transform the structures of power that have created them, in classrooms, the broader campus, the community, and far beyond. And there are significant and growing spaces for creative freedom and democratic agency that far exceed exploitation. Undergraduates can pursue a newly established civic engagement minor while getting paid to work ten hours a week as peer-teaching assistants facilitating ARTS about which they are passionate, so by the end of their time at NAU they acquire a rich body of theory, empirical scholarship, and organizing experience pertaining to engaged democracy—and quite a bit less debt. The organizing acumen of faculty (several of whom are recent graduates from the Masters of Sustainable Communities Program) has manifested in a successful initiative to reduce teaching loads for FYS-ARTS faculty from 4/4 to 3/3, to allow time for the organizing work of civic engagement. Recently FYS-ARTS faculty constituted themselves as a (now recognized) Faculty Steering Committee to gain more power in relation to the conditions of their work. Similarly, graduate and undergraduate leaders in this movement meet once every two weeks to discuss, debate, dream, challenge, expand, and modulate the practices and directions of the ARTS initiative.

In effect, in this example, we have initiated an intensifying movement by developing and interrelating three autocatalytic dynamics. The first is the dynamic around NAU's democratizing pedagogy movement, depicted in figure 3.2. Here, the autocatalytic dynamics resemble those discussed earlier in the context of community organizing, though we are pursuing increasingly profound changes in no small part from *within* a system that is often taken to be immutable by many organizers and revolutionaries.

The second is a metadynamic at the interface between this first set of dynamics and the dynamics of educational success more narrowly defined, as depicted in the cycle on the right side of figure 3.4. As students become engaged in democratic pedagogy, they tend to become more interested in the course material in related seminars, and their performance improves as measured by grades, retention rates, and graduation rates. To some extent this happens automatically, but this interface involves ongoing work to create and fine-tune generative interactions between the seminars and the ARTS, between theory and practice, between students' and faculty members' senses of themselves as civic beings and as scholars, and so forth. One outcome of this dynamic is institutional cost savings (e.g., by increasing passing, retention, and graduation rates) and potentially increased funding (e.g., as public funding to the university linked to these outcomes increases and as out-of-state tuition dollars grow). These outcomes, in turn, are key to co-optative interfacing with the third dynamic, namely those of neoliberal corporatization, in order to draw funds for the other two dynamics in ways that seek to subvert it. As we master the arts of this interface, the aim is to diminish neoliberal autocatalysis and intensify democratic pedagogy dynamics in a game-transformative movement. Figure 3.4 summarizes this.

Of course, democratic dynamics involving holistic education and holistic efficiency address only some of our challenges, for "efficiency" is only one dimension of the assault on higher education and commonwealth. Many who lead attacks on the "inefficiency" and "wastefulness" of higher education simultaneously attack K–20 institutions for teaching "political correctness," "ethnic hostility," and "critical thinking"; assaulting "the moral fiber of America" and "our Christian heritage"; producing knowledge that is absolutely useless to "everyday Americans," and doing nothing to promote economic competitiveness in the global market. In Arizona this takes the form of legislation outlawing ethnic studies and teaching Paulo Friere, increasingly explicit attacks on democracy in the name of an elite-accented republicanism, bills to allow guns on campus, and so forth. Similar culture war processes are receiving resonant articulation in many other states, as the Texas 2012 State Republican Party Platform makes clear in no uncertain terms in the section called "Educating Our Children": "We believe the current teaching of a multicultural curriculum is divisive. We favor strengthening our common American identity and loyalty instead of political correctness that nurtures alienation among racial ethnic groups. . . . We oppose the teaching of Higher Order Thinking Skills (HOTS) (values clarification), critical thinking skills and similar programs . . . which focus on behavior modification and have the purpose of challenging the student's fixed beliefs and undermining parental authority."

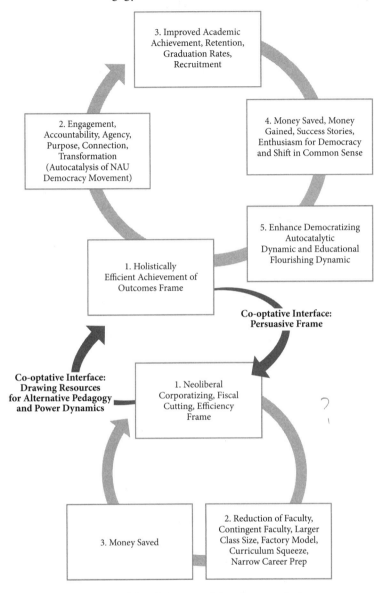

B. Democratic Pedagogy-Neoliberal Educational Outcomes Autocatalysis

3. Improved Academic Achievement, Retention, Graduation Rates, Recruitment

2. Engagement, Accountability, Agency, Purpose, Connection, Transformation (Autocatalysis of NAU Democracy Movement)

4. Money Saved, Money Gained, Success Stories, Enthusiasm for Democracy and Shift in Common Sense

5. Enhance Democratizing Autocatalytic Dynamic and Educational Flourishing Dynamic

1. Holistically Efficient Achievement of Outcomes Frame

Co-optative Interface: Persuasive Frame

Co-optative Interface: Drawing Resources for Alternative Pedagogy and Power Dynamics

1. Neoliberal Corporatizing, Fiscal Cutting, Efficiency Frame

3. Money Saved

2. Reduction of Faculty, Contingent Faculty, Larger Class Size, Factory Model, Curriculum Squeeze, Narrow Career Prep

A. Neoliberal Corporatizing Autocatalysis

Figure 3.4. Co-optational democracy autocatalysis

The platform singles out "SEIU or other community organizers" as those who should be prohibited from turning schools into instruments "to promote political agenda."[37] Given that the rhetoric of "efficiency" is often intertwined with a far-right-wing economic-cultural resonance machine that ceaselessly assaults commonwealth and democracy, and might at any time target initiatives such as those we are discussing, it is evident that radical democracy education must cultivate a game-transformative practice that reaches far beyond the academy in ways that address both dimensions.

This involves focusing on what is perhaps the most important autocatalytic dynamic in the mix: cocatalyzing new publics, as well as new senses and modes of publicness, at the intersections between higher education and broader communities, so that a new "we" comes to *own* higher education in a manner that far exceeds paying taxes that support it.[38] Rather, and most elementally, new publics become involved as cogenerators and collaborators in public work and political action in ways that increasingly co-guide myriad processes of action research, teaching, and scholarship. In this way the university ceases to be an aloof and remote place that is relatively easily tarred and destroyed by the far-right resonance machine and instead becomes the following: *these* people who have with us cocreatively generated wonderfully imaginative new pedagogies that are engaging and empowering our children; *this* mix of folks who are part of a new collaborative of people thinking and acting together in hopeful ways across what had been absolutely discouraging and despairing divides; *these* students and faculty who, in responsive dialogue with us, are researching cocreating new modes of hospitable community practice with migrants; *these* folks who have collaborated with us to create new community gardens and farm-to-school flows that are healthy, increase food justice, and start to address food security problems in our community; *these* faculty and students who have formed seminars, research projects, and collaborative community study groups around alternative economic, educational, and civic engagement possibilities, partly in response to aspirations in the broader community; *these* individuals who approached us with the beginnings of a vision for proliferating energy efficiency retrofits in homes across our city and invited our imaginative engagement, which is all now leading to no-cost financing, lower utility bills, more comfortable homes, and an emerging green energy sector where some of our youth are beginning to find good jobs; *this* team of people with whom we worked as we generated a community-based economic center that is revitalizing our community; *these* students and faculty who sometimes seem wild-eyed with crazy ideas and impossible ambitions for justice, democracy, and the environment when they come our way but who have managed to spark many new dreams among us, too, and, more important, listen carefully to *our* dreams and knowledge, and collaborate with us in response to them in ways that are powerful and effective. *The most important and powerful public work and political action anyone ever does is the work of cocreating new publics.* The new resonances, flows, and dynamics of such publics promise to generate their own capacities for judgment, action, and cocreative public work far beyond the incapacitating effects of hierarchical technocratic resonance machines. We are finding that those about whom many faculty tended to be cynical and dismissive are becoming integral to autocatalytic dynamics without which the future of higher education, democracy, and the planet is extremely bleak.

Does this require becoming narrowly pragmatic in ways that kill the rich possibilities of knowledge creation toward which the academy aspires? Far from it. Rather, it expands the circles of knowledge and culture that may participate in these productions. If we rerun the preceding paragraph with an accent on affirming highly imaginative knowledge, it might sound like this: tarred knowledge "over there in ivory towers behind walls that protect the narrow interests of alien elites" becomes "*this* knowledge we are involved in creating and utilizing to generate new and promising grassroots democratic community power and change; *this* knowledge through which we are learning to work cooperatively *and* agonistically across differences long fraught with hostility and oblivion; *this* theory of receptive relationship building that has drawn students, parents, teachers, and community organizations into regular action to improve our schools, neighborhoods, and communities; *this* new way of thinking about "wasted" people and things that generates new networks and practices of tending to one another and a municipal-scale composting cooperative that is generating rich soil for urban agriculture, jobs, and a lower carbon footprint; *this* theory of cooperative economics that is not "anti-American" but instead has deep roots in numerous diverse age-old traditions and movements across the United States, and is at work in our region to generate a resilient economy that experimentally produces equitable wealth, resists and provides alternatives to global corporations, and generates opportunities for creative and meaningful work; *this* new conceptual approach to the border and migration that has generated more responsive solidarities, safety, and collaborations that are far more hopeful than the descending cycles of vilification; *this* theory of the relationships among the human and more-than-human world that is leading to different horizons of witness and ecological action in the U.S.

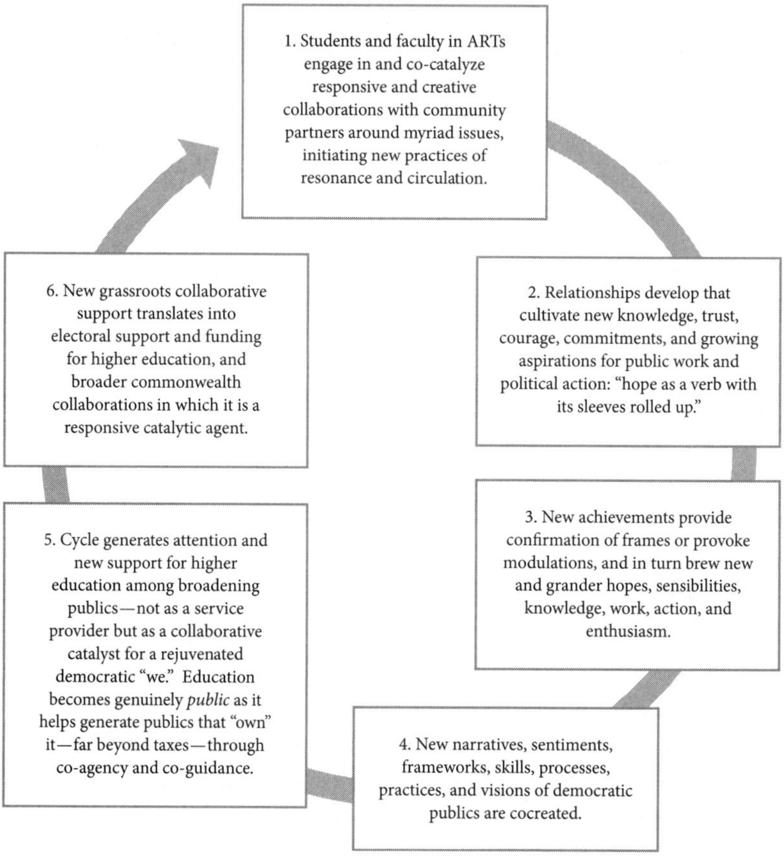

Figure 3.5. Autocatalytic dynamics of democracy education *becoming public*

Southwest. We might diagram key elements of this autocatalytic cycle as shown in figure 3.5.

From this brief account, it becomes plausible that a democratizing movement may generate numerous and entwined autocatalytic loops and interface these with autocatalytic dynamics in other complex systems that it seeks to transform in ways that enhance game-transformative practices. While institutions of higher education are part of the state apparatus, that apparatus is not totally uniform, seamless, and closed. Moreover, the dynamics of these institutions of higher education are irreducible to that system of power, even as they are profoundly shaped by it. Faculty, students, staff, administrators, and members of the broader community have significant opportunities to initiate actions that—if fashioned with attention to autocatalytic dynamics—have substantial transformative powers. Indeed, the democracy movement I have been discussing is indebted to previous efforts—around race, gender, sustainability, social justice, civic engagement, and so forth—that opened cracks in the order, fed transformative practices and aspirations, and fostered emergent possibilities in relation to which our work has been able to grow. Radical and ecological democratic movements might, then, engender game-transformative practices in relation to myriad institutional locations and their associated publics: K–12 schools, health care organizations, job-training institutes, agricultural programs, community colleges, crisis centers, community-based sustainable economic development centers, and so on. Yet these doors open only if the "Toto effect" counters the "Wizard of Oz effect" to reveal—and solicit experimentation toward—possibilities for transformative autocatalysis. Theory matters.

CHAPTER 4

Shock Democracy and Wormhole Hope in Catastrophic Times

The Philistines and the Israelites have gathered their forces, have assembled for war, and face each other from two hilltops separated by a valley. Early in the introduction, I discussed this scene of battle and read the story of David and Goliath as an allegory, in which David illuminates possibilities for game-transformative practices and visionary pragmatism. Yet reconsider this story in order to linger for a moment with *Goliath*, for he exemplifies pivotal challenges we face in relation to contemporary modes of power and planetary crisis, whose measure we have not yet fully taken. We live in a time when shocking Goliaths are (yet again) integral to the functioning of power and increasingly emblematic of our experience on Earth for the foreseeable future.

The account of Goliath begins with a series of measurements: he stands just a few inches shy of ten feet tall; he wears a coat of armor that weighs 125 pounds; the iron tip of his spear alone weighs 15. Yet these measurements do not begin to take the measure of Goliath, for there really is no measure. When Goliath stands and bellows his challenge, he performs a *sublime* event that can only be registered in Saul and the Israelites' response: they are "dismayed and terrified" (1 Samuel 17:11). For forty days, twice each day, Goliath stands forth and shouts his challenge, and each time the Israelites "all fled from him in great fear" (1 Samuel 17:24). The king of Israel has offered the man who can kill Goliath great wealth and his daughter in marriage, but it makes no difference. There is no earthly measure that can overcome the trembling terror and hopelessness each soldier feels in the depths of his being.

As we have seen, David draws confidence, passion, and freedom from God and shifts the frame of the encounter so that Goliath becomes little more than a stupid, overconfident, easily beaten giant. In the language of chapter 3, we might call this "the Toto effect." Yet what if the contemporary scene is much worse than this biblical epic encounter or my discussion in this book captures thus far? What happens when Goliaths themselves become ever larger, shape-shifters, rapidly reproducible, able to morph their armor in the midst of battle according to their needs, and strategically much smarter? What happens as they become creatively attentive to ways in which they can utilize the ever-more-frequent (and themselves shocking) disasters of a climate-changed planet to increase their power and demolish the collective bodies of the demos? What happens, too, when Goliaths invent combinatory modes of power in which gargantuan and shocking incursions oscillate with insidious quotidian micropowers of resonance, circulation, and autocatalytic dynamics (as well as surveillance, discipline, and punishment)? *What happens, in other words, when Goliaths learn how to become Davids, such that they are virtuosos at creating game-transformative practices—perpetually reinventing "five smooth stones" in places, times, and ways the demos least expects?*

I think a vital response to this question is that *Davids must carefully study and learn from the Goliaths who have learned from David.* In one sense this book can be read as such a study and effort to learn. In each of the previous three chapters, I have traced how contemporary power deploys resonance, mega-circulation, and complex system dynamics to undermine democracy, equality, and ecosystems. In each case, by sketching the characteristics of neoliberal modes, we have sought to disclose registers of life—how we resonate with others, how we move, how we might organize active assemblages with autocatalytic dynamics that can transform systems—in which we must cocreate counterpractices and alternative practices. I have worked back and forth between theory and practice to suggest that such alternatives, though often beyond the radar of many scholarly and political perspectives, are emerging in radical and ecological democracy movements—paying close attention to the NAU ARTS movement in which I have been a catalytic leader. By working in and interweaving these different dimensions, we are at once learning powerful ways to counter some of the most salient operations of neoliberalism and at the same time engendering the textured beginnings of a radical and ecological democratic habitus with very substantial capacities for receptivity and resilience.

But of course there is much more we must learn from Goliath. For though I alluded to how shock politics is folded into neoliberalization, and have also emphasized the need for shocking radical political modalities such as street protests, outrageous aesthetic interventions, and civil disobedience, because my focus has been on generating alternative quotidian practices and strategies for a durable radical habitus, I have not yet tended sufficiently to the more ephemeral yet utterly crucial aspects of a politics of shock resistance. The Goliaths of our time are masters at this game-transformative practice. They protect and proliferate their powers of resonance, mega-circulation, and system dynamics by intertwining them with shocks that surge through the body politic with increasing frequency and obliterate alternatives. If we do not tend to this characteristic of contemporary power, we will fail to fully grasp its operation and will continue to be blindsided and unnecessarily vulnerable to these devastating impacts. Moreover, if we do not invent our own politics of countershock in response, radical and ecological democratic movements will likely be far less dynamic than they might otherwise become.

I believe this is the case for numerous reasons I discuss at length in this chapter. One is that if we fail to cultivate a radical democratic politics of countershock, we will lack certain crucial tools for *blocking* the malignant advance of neoliberalism that reduces our communities and institutions to the imperatives of corporate technocratic capitalism. Moreover, we will all miss crucial opportunities to dramatically prefigure alternatives that *open and reconfigure* the hegemonic common sense of our times. Like night lightning, shock politics harbors powerful potentials for disclosure. However, another reason a politics of evanescent countershock is indispensable concerns not simply its own qualities but also the vital ways in which it can—and I believe must—be *interwoven* and *oscillate* with quotidian practices and dynamics. On the one hand, no matter how receptive and generative it may be, all quotidian politics takes place in the context of neoliberal capillary and shock politics that continually threaten and often tend to dampen, truncate, and overwhelm its transformative tendencies. In this context, quotidian organizing can very easily become diminished, stale, colonized, and compromised in deleterious ways; complacent about limits that seem implacable and modes that are hollowed out by neoliberal pressures; and dulled in its sense of creative possibilities. Alternatively, interweaving practices of more dramatic evanescent shocks with quotidian practice can re-enliven and expand our own senses of possibility, transformative aspirations, and energies for more imaginative quotidian work and action. Yet the beneficial implications move in the other direction too. Radical democratic countershock politics, when separated from the lively energies and agencies of quotidian political practice done well, tends to fall in love with itself in ways that can quickly leave it clueless about how to organize to generate more transformative waves, broader and more durable assemblages, and radical effects. It can become narrowly sectarian, unimaginative, and unresponsive to other struggles—complacent with what readily become routinized protests that barely make a ripple in the order of things. In contrast, when it is interwoven with the best of quotidian democracy, we can be jostled out of the dogmatic slumbers of what can otherwise devolve into an "identity politics of the radical posture." In the alternating currents and oscillations between the quotidian and the evanescent, I shall argue, we find far more promising possibilities than either may harbor on its own. These oscillations are among Goliath's most important powers—Davids would do well to develop analogous capacities. Reading Naomi Klein's account of power in *The Shock Doctrine: The Rise of Disaster Capitalism* in relation to our discussions of circulation, resonance, and complex dynamic systems begins to illuminate the plausibility of these claims, from which we explore pathways beyond.[1]

The Indispensable Alternating Currents of Shock Politics

In *The Shock Doctrine*, Klein considers "shock" through a variety of lenses, drawing highly provocative and illuminating parallels among the electric shocks once regularly deployed in psychiatric therapies (beginning with CIA experiments); those deployed in war ("shock and awe"); neoliberal shocks to the economy that surge through circuits linking "debt crises," dramatic cuts in spending, deregulation, and so on; stunning military coups (exemplified by Chile's simultaneous deployment of shock-and-awe military violence, electroshock torture for thousands, and neoliberal shocks to the economy); "disaster capitalism's" utilization of "natural" environmental shocks to further privatize regions (such as New Orleans in the aftermath of Hurricane Katrina); and the security state's response to terrorist shocks such as 9/11, which it uses to extend its police powers in "states of exception." With psychiatric shock treatment, the aim was to deploy large and repeated doses of electroshocks to a person's brain (along with drugs, extreme isolation, etc.) in order to totally "unmake and erase faulty minds."[2] The idea was to radically dismantle all neurological connections, relationships, patterns, and dispositions in the brain that might resist the psychiatrist's reconstruction, in order to build from the cleared ground on up. The pioneer of this treatment, Ewen Cameron, "believed he could reach [a tabula rasa] by attacking the brain with everything known to interfere with its normal functioning—all at once."[3]

Klein argues that this intensively destructive-reconstructive operation is the metaphoric and operational heart(lessness) of the contemporary modes of political power mentioned earlier: Quickly seize the flooded city to rebuild it in a purely capitalist image without recalcitrance from now stunned and dispersed former occupants. Annihilate, with shocking military force and torture, the associational and party life that would resist economic restructuring according to the hegemony of "laissez-faire." Dismantle public institutions and goods through repeated cuts to government in order to create shocked anxiety, precariousness, chaos, and diaspora that render resistance to the initiatives of the neoliberal corporate state increasingly difficult. Strategically deploy resonant shock waves in the virtual sphere that amplify the terror of an event like 9/11, so that a shocked population offers minimal resistance to extraordinary expansions of the police state. "Shock and awe" takes these motifs to infinity and needs no commentary here. The idea is always the same: catastrophic leveling and scrambling of recalcitrant relationships, social topographies, and associational powers, followed by the relatively unhampered development of antidemocratic relationships, institutions, and powers. "Shock" acts as a kind of "preemptive repression" that clears the field for new circulations, resonant energies, and electric flows of political, economic, and social power that would otherwise face resistance from those previously in place or emerging.[4]

In this context, Klein interprets many movements—from the resurgent left in Latin America, to the Occupy movement in the United States, to climate warriors of an increasingly global "Blockadia"—as emergent forms of "shock resistance."[5] Especially in the context of Latin America, she argues that there has been an increasingly reflective effort to build "shock-resistant" forms of politics, economics, and associational life that are less prone to the types of shocks for which Latin America was historically ground zero. At the heart of what is new in shock-resistant politics, she argues, are more decentralized, grassroots, and broadly networked forms of politics that can better withstand the toppling of a single leader; new flows of energy that are resistant to the shocks of global corporate oil markets; new financial institutions that create alternatives beyond the International Monetary Fund; and the emergence of vast cooperative economic networks in places like Brazil, Argentina, and Venezuela that increasingly democratize power and control in dispersed and poorer populations.[6]

While Occupy was much less developed in its political and economic directions, Klein sees a similar "spirit" at play in people coming together to rebuild decentered networks of democratic enactment and initiative. In an interview shortly after the Occupy movement began, she spoke of a palpable "hunger for connection" and alternatives to corporate capitalism. One of the striking aspects she experienced was that it was "such a joyful space, such a joyful movement, people get addicted to it." Yet, even as she articulates a capaciousness with respect to the amorphous character of the movement, she worries that without organizing alternative political, economic, social, and media institutions, the movement could quickly be captured by reformist articulations that greatly truncate its capacity to "unleash a much more radical imagination."[7]

Klein's account of shock resistance is important in many ways. As one would expect from an astute student of shock, she is deeply attuned to the "energetics" of antineoliberal protest gatherings such as Occupy and fossil fuel blockades (e.g., hunger for, joy in, and addiction to relationships beyond corporate capitalist patterns, circulations of biopower, dominant resonance machines, debilitation systems dynamics), manifestations of natality—or miraculous unexpected forms of new political speech and action—that are intrinsically related to such energetics (e.g., unleashing radical imagination), and the need to create radical practices and institutional forms for these openings in order to nurture their enthusiastic development, endurance, and transformative power. This analysis is consonant with themes I have been developing in earlier chapters and elsewhere.

Yet in the context of Klein's analysis of how shock politics is deployed both to short-circuit resistant social and political configurations and to intensify neoliberal dynamics, I want to tarry more closely with questions concerning how we might learn political arts of wisely and powerfully *oscillating* between evanescent radical democratic shocks and resilient quotidian currents in order to short-circuit neoliberalism and advance commonwealth and ecological resilience. If dramatic and overwhelming macrosurges play an integral role in decimating the thickets of connection in our brains as well as in our political, economic, and social bodies, perhaps radical democrats ought to reconsider and reinvent modes of dramatic and overwhelming electricity-like surges for very different ends. In the struggle with today's Goliath, it is likely that David's capacities to *interweave* more durable quotidian democratic practices with episodic dramatic surges will be integral to creating both the spaces and the necessary speed for revitalizing and reinventing myriad registers, practices, institutions, and powers of radical and ecological democracy. The operative words here are "reconsider" and "reinvent," because the deeply worn ruts of many dramatic modes have little resilience and have been framed (by both proponents and opponents) in ways that often drain them of most of their potential power—indeed, *most of their shock.*

To explore both the destructive operations and the democratically and ecologically generative potentials of oscillating energetic political currents, consider a too-brief sketch of how macropowers of shock and quotidian powers of circulation and resonance are interwoven in the advance of neoliberalism.

For every decimating shock, as I have noted, there are surges of microcharges, steadier resonances, and capillary circulations that move in to reconstruct the circulations, resonances, and system dynamics of our political, economic, and social being. Thus, a more complete account of shock politics would have to carefully trace the pivotal and intricate intertwinements among the micro and the macro, the dramatic and the insidiously subtle, and the deconstructive and reconstructive energies and actions that are indispensable to the development of neoliberalism in our time. Shock opens possibilities for new flows, resonances, and dynamics, which reconstitute the (individual and collective) brains and bodies that have been decimated, in ways that in turn render them less recalcitrant and more exposed and vulnerable to the next set of shocks. This cycle, if unimpeded, intensifies patterns of docility, compliance, dependency, and intensified exploitation.

In this context, I suspect that radically democratic and ecological counterconducts and alternative conducts will require that we carefully craft political work and action capable of engaging all these levels, registers, and modes simultaneously. More important, we will need to transform *how* we do this, so that our dramatic macroactions and our quotidian political organizing develop *immanent relationships* with one another, and a *transfigurative dexterity* that is even greater than what global capitalism and the megastate have created in our times. This is a tall order because the powers engendered by neoliberalism are nothing short of spectacular, and because within the array of common radical democratic approaches to politics, I think there are theoretical lenses, dispositions, political modalities, and identity attachments that impede developing more promising possibilities for a multidimensional politics.

To explore these possibilities, consider some of the characteristics of radical democratic shocks more carefully, for there are two dimensions in particular that offer indispensable articulations with the quotidian politics of resonance, circulation, and dynamics. The first dimension is akin to what Walter Benjamin referred to as an "emergency brake," when he wrote, "Marx says that revolutions are the locomotives of world history. But the situation may be quite different. Perhaps revolutions are not the train ride, but the human race grabbing for the emergency brake."[8] At other times, closer to the metaphor of shock, he wrote of "blasts" that stop the progress of catastrophe.[9] This aspect of a radical democratic politics of countershock has certain affinities with the shock politics of neoliberalism, insofar as it seeks to stop or derail neoliberalism's assault on democracy, people, and the planet in ways that are dramatic, outrageous, disruptive, and confrontational.[10] As neoliberalism seeks to level radical democracy, Benjamin's emergency brake would level neoliberalism if it could. Nonviolent forms of grabbing for the emergency brake in ways that send shocks through a polity may include widespread and dramatic forms of street protests, occupations, general strikes, sit-ins, freedom rides, blockades, cyberattacks, forms of monkey-wrenching that do not endanger human beings, and so forth. Their efforts to impede neoliberal power typically target not only immediate institutions and operations—for example, a World Trade Organization meeting, Wall Street banks, Shell Oil, Monsanto—but also, and more important, the hegemonic common sense that accepts these operations and the shocks they employ as the "new normal." They seek to blast open the continuum of historical consciousness, affect, and practice that resonate with and move to neoliberal tunes with a discordant "no!"

Yet along with (and related to) this dimension of blocking, shutting down, and derailing, there is typically another characteristic of radical democratic shock that is very different from neoliberal shocks insofar as it opens, prefigures, performs, and extends possibilities for receptive relationships and outrageous powers.[11] Christina Beltrán insightfully illuminates this evanescent dimension of what I am calling radical democratic shock politics in relation to counterpublics (those that flaunt the common norms of speech, relationships, and action) indebted to forms of Latino politics that have sought power through pluralizing mass participation in dramatic performances. Beltrán shows how evanescent political events can send shocks that transfigure senses and tastes, and engender energetic aspirations for possibilities far beyond the limits of the dominant order. Her argument is particularly vivid in relation to the 2006 National Immigration Rally that featured the unwonted commingling of different bodies and signs, transgressive movements of a bus full of "illegals" exercising citizenship beyond borders, and the creation of a strange translocal polity that actively involved millions as the bus rolled into different places.[12] She argues that beyond the limits of more quotidian practices that remain significantly tied to consequentialist forms of democratic work and action, the carnivalesque characteristics of such outrageously performative events unleash bursts of natality that are indispensable to democratic flourishing, insofar as they not only short-circuit but also *redistribute and refigure* common sense. A rich and diverse affective ecology of "civic emotions" is unleashed in such events, "including indignation, determination, irony, outrage, . . . joy," and humor—reenergizing political life.[13]

Paradoxically, Beltrán argues that an ethos that often relaxes consequentialist metrics and aspirations in order to "recognize the value and consequentiality of the democratic *moment*" of shocking politics itself is more conducive to political flourishing in which the recurrence of natality becomes *more possible and more powerful*.[14] On the one hand, this is because we thereby decrease the *stifling pressures* of action imperatives that otherwise inhibit irruptive and disclosive political actions by overburdening us with questions concerning immediate effects and sustainability. On the other hand, diminishing pressures associated with a singular focus on immediate consequences enables us to simultaneously increase our *responsiveness* to and *recollection* of shocking moments, which are both integral to their reinauguration *and* becoming.

Beltrán articulates a radical notion of what Sheldon Wolin calls "fugitive democracy" that helps us think supply and creatively about shock politics. Formulating a vision that I think resonates with no small number of the sharpest activists today, such politics is necessarily evanescent yet somehow strangely less so than many common readings of Wolin would have it.[15] A shock politics animated by Beltrán's fugitive democracy, if it were to become a more wisely and widely cultivated political art, would have a more pervasive and powerful impact on our cultural ethos than it currently does—"a special standing in our consciousness."[16] On the one hand, because we would *both* enact and experience evanescent politics more frequently *and* become more responsive to it, these shocking fugitive moments would tend to become "a critical element of how subjects come to cultivate a more enduring ethos of democratic openness."[17] On the other hand, a political culture that was more populated with recollections of such moments would inspire us in ways that would help "sustain political actors through the tedious, frustrating, and disillusioning aspects of ongoing, worldly, political work."[18] In such a political culture, shocking dramatic performances would become more frequent and widespread, even as they enact an evanescent temporality.

Working with rich senses of possibility for radical democratic shock politics drawn from Benjamin and Beltrán, we can now begin to respond to the questions I raised earlier concerning how we might cultivate the fine arts of interweaving and oscillating between evanescent shock politics and quotidian practices of radical democracy to generate something like an alternating current that vivifies the demos. At this point, I think Beltrán is less helpful, *precisely* insofar as her writing tends to reduce quotidian organizing to "the tedious, frustrating, and disillusioning aspects of ongoing, worldly, political work." Surely there is a good deal of this. Yet throughout this book I have repeatedly tried to disclose how everyday radical and ecological democracy done well is teeming with miraculous relationships and action—emergent modes of intercorporeal resonance, mimetic movement, autocatalytic dynamics, new capacities, organizing achievements, and modest movement victories that seemed impossible a short time ago. *Everyday democracy when it is attentive to these multidimensional qualities has dense circuits charged with the electrical currents of agentic energy. It is so often a poetic experience—an improvisational form of intense political musicality—a theme Cornel West has riffed on in countless ways.*

With and beyond, and reinforced by the crucial consequentialist aspects of everyday politics, there are one-on-one meetings in which listening to and sharing profound narratives about our sources of inspiration and aspiration begins to generate powerful new connections, senses, and possibilities. We circulate questions in a gathering that may significantly open us toward different yet indeterminate horizons—and even more questions. Expressive intensities of ecstatic joy, sorrow, empathy, humor, and energized yearning pass among us in an assembly and ignite flames. A thawing demos is stimulated and begins to move. We find ourselves swept up in a sense of receptive solidarity across lines of difference that comes upon us unexpectedly and powerfully like a zephyr that washes down from a ridge. We experience a breakthrough of imagination that seems to emerge from a cacophony of voices in a gathering; the rumblings of broad critical awakening that radiate out from a narrower inquiry; powerful recollections of a past moment that erupt into the present, offering hope or wisdom or the perception of a hitherto concealed strategy; a heightening of receptivity that shifts the axis of our being as we walk, greet, listen, talk, and collaborate in a neighborhood we have hitherto avoided; an unanticipated movement of our feeling for the scope of the possible that occurs in an "impossible" conversation across lines of faith; a feeling of expansive energy, heightened courage, and a sense of vision that emerges from a relatively small achievement or victory; a sense of shifting power that grows from a comparatively modest action such as occupying the official chairs where the city council or school board typically stare down at people who attend the meetings; a sense that we can change a world with trillions of dollars invested in ecocidal energy systems, after a day of working in a heterogeneous group to advance energy efficiency and renewable energy projects in our city; a realignment of one's sense of self as a political event dredges up long-forgotten moments that now press forth a most unwonted story line of agentic power. In all these instances, we feel involved in world-transformative microsurges and shifts. Often these are subtle, extraordinary-ordinary events, in which the hegemonic automaticity of the world blinks, begins to tremble and crack, and we sense democracy moving—as well as our capacities for moving democracy—in ourselves, others, and the world.

I think it is this politics, teeming with natality, that is among the most profound aspects of everyday democracy.[19] In both receptive and initiatory dimensions, our capacities for radical democratic engagement begin to engender a game-transformative practice in which the world becomes pregnant with "possibility." Our receptivity to and involvement in *potentia*, the emergent becoming quality of the world, are heightened.

In Hannah Arendt's account of natality, the miracle of action—our capacity to "interrupt" and "interfere" with otherwise "automatic processes" with an "infinite improbability that occurs regularly"—accents the *performance* of speech and deed that discloses a unique being and new possibilities in the world, as a person begins "to take initiative, to begin (as the Greek word *archein*, 'to begin,' 'to lead' and eventually 'to rule' indicates), to set something in motion."[20] My understanding of natality very much includes these dimensions but accents receptivity. From the moment we are born, we are not most primordially responding to the fact of our own birth as a beginning, as Arendt suggests. Rather, as the discussion of mirror neurons suggests, we would do better to understand our uniqueness initially as our singular responsiveness or receptivity to the world and others, which is stimulated and nurtured by and entangled with the responsiveness of others in their actions with us. Our initiatory capacities are born in these responsive relationships, and throughout our life our natality is cultivated in this interplay of receptivity and initiative. Each time we sense or speak or act in a unique manner awake to possibilities beyond the "automatic processes," there is an affective charge. These charges circulate among us and stimulate more—if we tend to them through radical democratic practices.

If *both* quotidian democratic politics and evanescent shock politics are teeming with natality, and if this natality is itself stimulated by circulating affective charges that accompany the birth of our own and others' perceiving, saying, and acting anew, then the potential relationships between quotidian and evanescent politics shift significantly. Simply put, they become potentially *interanimative*.

As we begin to grasp and cultivate quotidian politics in a manner that is attuned to how it is coursing with agentic energies—millisecond resonances, minishocks, capillary surges, charged dynamics, reconfiguring fields—on the one hand, and cultivate sophisticated modes of shock politics coursing with analogous yet more dramatic and outrageous macroagentic energies, on the other hand, new and promising possibilities emerge for crafting a politics that interweaves and oscillates between the quotidian and the evanescent. Such a politics would carefully tend to the alternating currents and electrical relays between the evanescent and the quotidian in ways that reciprocally stimulate the agency, natality, and power of each. Indeed, each is immanent in the other.

Consider a few ways in which the quotidian and the evanescent may interanimate one another. *First,* they enhance each other's possibilities for becoming vital (living, dynamic, responsive, powerful), insofar as they reciprocally stimulate, amplify, and proliferate disclosures, senses, and capacities for opening the world beyond the limits and practices of the hegemonic order. These intensities circulate between the best quotidian organizing and more sharply hewn dramatic situations, in a call-and-response fashion. Within the agentic fabric of everyday politics there are nurtured calls (energies, aspirations, visions, voices, enactments) for more dramatic and transformative natality, to which more evanescent political actions are frequently amplificatory and transfigurative responses (consider the visceral relays of emergent disclosure and agency that run through Rosa Parks in her journey between Highlander Folk School and the Montgomery Bus Boycott).[21] In turn, more evanescent political actions resound with energetic calls. Creative quotidian politics serves as a resonant sound chamber that carries echoes and overtones that imbue the wildly patient labors of daily political life with new energies, intensities, visions, and senses of possibility. *Second,* when this call-and-response relationship is going well, both types of political work and action (quotidian and evanescent) become more charged with energetic initiatives that deviate from hegemonic overworn grooves and begin to assemble alternative receptivities, relationships, movements, practices, and institutions. *Third,* as these alternatives develop, our heightened capacities for democratic receptivity to others and responsiveness to shifting events in the world enhance our resilience.

Of course, things can and do go awry. Patience can turn into narrow complacency, and intensities of the evanescent can fall in love with themselves in ways that are myopically self-righteous and increasingly isolated. I have spent the greater part of this book examining quotidian practices that I think avert these debilitating possibilities, but there are no guarantees. The best we can do is become very mindful of the risks involved in such politics, carefully work in both dimensions, reflect critically after each action, and learn as we go. Nevertheless, I believe these interanimations are indispensable to the flourishing of a radical and ecological democracy movement with any hope of addressing the urgencies of our time.

To further elaborate potential promises and pitfalls here, briefly consider the Occupy movement. There were some places where those focused on dramatic (and, so far, relatively brief) occupations and protests and those long engaged in more quotidian forms of community organizing began to explore collaborative relationships. In Boston, organizers and leaders in People Improving Communities through Organizing (PICO), a nationwide, broad-based organizing network, began to visit the Occupy Boston encampment in an effort to discuss possibilities for collaborating, and the Occupiers responded in kind.[22] In Brooklyn, Occupiers began to walk the neighborhoods in an effort to connect with community associations. Yet for the most part, this was not a priority, nor was it systematically and carefully pursued by the Occupiers.[23] Indeed, such efforts were often suspected of selling out and compromising the purity of Occupy's aspirations. From another side, leading organizers in one broad-based community organizing network showed a distinct lack of appreciation for the Occupy movement and concurred that "they don't understand power!"[24]

On one level, this accusation contains an important element of truth. Many—and perhaps most—in the Occupy movement likely have far too little knowledge of, let alone appreciation for and skill for, the radical, powerful, and resilient aspects of community organizing modes that nurture vital elements of political wisdom and power that Occupy lacked. Yet, at the same time, there is a stunning blindness in the community organizers' accusation, for Occupy might well be understood as an evanescent yet increasingly resilient strand of democratic protest that has been strengthening in a variety of locations since the "Battle of Seattle" in 1999.[25] With each of the intensifications of democratic energy in this strand, we have seen greater and greater cracks in the hegemonic common sense of global capitalism. In Occupy, radical critiques concerning inequality, systemic corporate corruption, and the need for radical democratic power were raised that began to expand the sphere of discourse and imagination far beyond the limits of anything seen in the United States since the early 1970s—and far beyond the achievements of most broad-based community organizing in this regard. This seems like power to me. So too does the dramatic enactment of audacious hope—even as its actions were also often profoundly disappointing.

Imagine a different scenario. Suppose that many people in Occupy had a keener sense for the modes, practices, and achievements of everyday organizing, and also for the potent micrological events of natality that happen there far in excess of the limits that press back so forcefully and disagreeably in much of our daily work. Suppose, too, that they had some sense that the grander surges of energy and radical imagination associated with Occupy were profoundly indebted to the imaginative agentic energies that fire up in relationships of everyday organizing and move below the radar of dominant public spheres and media most of the time. Suppose they understood their own dramatic enactments to be in no small part engendered by these energies and agencies—even as movements like Occupy amplify intensities and reconfigure possibilities in unexpected ways whose durability, in turn, requires the intentional cultivation of circuits that reconnect these with quotidian natalities and the practices wherein they are nurtured. Then, imagine cultures of community organizing that were profoundly cognizant of the myriad ways in which the spaces, textures, energies, paths, and newness of their quotidian political life are indebted to evanescent political intensifications that, though briefer according to some measures, nonetheless interanimate so many small surges of inventive democratic power that rework patterns of resonance, alter circulations of governmentality, and initiate new autocatalytic dynamics.[26] Imagine that such cultures of organizing were more welcoming of—and sought to work more with—these periods of dramatic democratic intensification.

In this context, I am not thinking of these two-way circuits primarily in terms of formal structures and relationships that give precise form to these articulations and interanimations, though these are utterly indispensable and must be very carefully considered and cultivated (as I have tried to do elsewhere in this book). Yet here I have in mind something equally indispensable that is more akin to a refined sense for the poetics of political engagement that acknowledges the diverse spatiotemporal dimensions in which political power, vitality, and natality are nurtured, and seeks to engender circuits of interaction across these different dimensions. People educating their sensibilities in these ways would tend to cultivate interanimating pathways between more ephemeral dramatic surges of political energy, power, and imagination, on the one hand, and those at play in smaller and more continuous sites of agentic political practice, on the other, thereby intensifying both. In so doing, this educated political sensibility might begin to cocreate textured networks and practices for the neurological regeneration of political bodies that become not only "shock-resistant" but also capable of radical democratic revitalization that can "take back the night" currently colonized by the unblinking beams, bullhorns, and circulations of neoliberal governmentality.

Is this no more than an impossible fantasy? In earlier chapters, I have suggested that the first half-dozen years of our radical and ecological democratic pedagogy movement at NAU and in Northern Arizona disclose an emergent habitus in which textured practices of interanimation are beginning to demonstrate powerful effects and possibilities. In ARTS around issues and problems such as immigration, climate change and alternative energy, gender and sexuality, and others, students, faculty, and community groups are collaborating in ways that diversely employ strategies of patient education and outreach, civil discourse, broad-based community organizing, lobbying and advocacy, aesthetic experimentation, and protest and disruption. Most focus their energies on doing good work and action in one or two of these modes. We are finite beings. Yet most become aware that there are many approaches at play and that these episodically collaborate quite closely. Many begin to learn the arts of such collaboration and come to see that these interactions are indispensable to the movement—far more powerful than any narrower range of strategies wholly on their own. Many are *animated and charged* by the interplays among the natalities that ignite betwixt and between these various modes. These charges stoke the fires of democracy. In this way, I believe, we are continuing along paths broached by the better periods in the best movements in the organizing traditions of democracy.

Of course there are tensions, moments when we approach the edge where things could devolve into chaos and come undone. This is an inescapable risk of radical democracy. Yet we are learning to negotiate these connections in ways that enhance transformative possibilities and reduce the risks. These achievements encourage us to pursue these directions, and this discussion is indebted—and meant as a contribution—to that project.

Visionary Pragmatism and Tragic Resilience for a Storm-Shocked Eaarth

I have called this emergent nexus of theory-practice, as well as the genre in which I discuss it, "visionary pragmatism." As noted in the introduction, the conjunction of these terms (commonly taken to be antonyms) refuses the choice between a "realist" pragmatism, which works within the limits of a present taken to be fixed, on the one hand, and a disconnected utopianism that criticizes and dreams without connections to the present that might engage and orient political pathways of work and action, on the other. Visionary pragmatism is *pragmatic* insofar as it relentlessly thinks, works, and acts on the limits of the present, drawing forth and engendering new resonances, receptivities, relationships, movements, dynamics, practices, powers, institutions, and forms of commonwealth, in an effort to contribute to desirable changes in our lived worlds. It seeks to be consequential—even if it is sometimes viewed as strangely so. Yet it is *visionary* in the sense that it maintains an intransigent practice of peering underneath, above, around, through, and *beyond* the cracks in the destructive walls of this world. It moves to the edges of the megaflows of contemporary power, slips beyond the currents, lingers in the eddies, catches crosscurrents, and cultivates new sorts of flows and solidarities. It has an unquenchable appetite for visions that come from beyond hegemonic common sense or exceed it from within, and it devotes itself to looking for clues of these, listening to whispers near and far that articulate suggestive possibilities beyond the assumed boundaries. The ways in which we think, work, and act are forever informed and inspired by visions—both immanent and transcendent—that again and again call us to "do a new thing" that nurtures democratic possibilities, ecological flourishing, and complex commonwealth.

As a genre, the textual practice of visionary pragmatism often cultivates hope with significant buoyancy. Let us call it futurity. It steers our glance toward the possibility that we can shift politics, economics, social life, and ecocidal dynamics in directions that will make our situation significantly better and engender game-transformative practices that coalesce to form a radical democratic habitus. Yes, difficult struggle, tragic remainders, significant setbacks, awful odds, and loss find expression here. Yet most often they are couched in a context where bodies remain springy and chins are up. There is already more than enough in the world to bend our heads and bodies despairing low, so in this genre we work to fashion an informed, inspired, and sometimes stubborn resolve, however fragile it may be.

In cycles and spirals of theory and practice, I pursue this project, this approach, and this genre. Sometimes, these are like vivifying vortices in which theory and praxis rapidly confirm, expand, and intensify glimpses of and movements toward radical democratic and ecological possibility. Other times, the cycles are more difficult, confronting nearly insurmountable challenges, failures, and turmoil, and they thus call us to tarry with profound critiques of modes, processes, and convictions we hold most dear—and then engage in difficult acts of radical reformation. There are occasions when this push-back can become so enormous that only the fiercest imagination, "wildest patience," and "optimism of will" may keep one from falling away from visionary pragmatism toward deep despair. Yet within the genre of theory-practice I have been discussing, these periods generally resolve into cocreative enactments in which theory and practice are revivified and pulled into new forms: these will suffer challenges and failures once again, but for the most part, precisely because of that, this is a vital and dynamic mode of being in the world.

Yet with the onset of anthropogenic climate change, *this world* is changing very dramatically and with increasing rapidity. In saying this, I am not insinuating a notion of wholly harmonious Earth from which we have fallen. For hundreds of millions of years our planet has been something like what Nietzsche, in *The Gay Science*, called the *rerum concordia discors* (discordant concord of things).[27] The Earth is a complex dynamical system, tipping from one equilibrium to another in processes that involve massive species extinction, ice ages, extreme droughts, and catastrophic rearrangements of vast ecosystems—often followed by new explosions of fecundity. Sometimes, Earth gets hit by asteroids or sometimes by solar flares. We live in a world of becoming, to be sure.

Yet we humans have begun to generate and amplify chaotic deformations of this world in ways that are clearly unprecedented during the comparatively short period of the Holocene, in which climatic and ecological dynamics have remained remarkably stable and within a range that has been highly conducive to the human flourishing of the past ten thousand years. Consider how this is playing out in Northern Arizona, in which my thinking and practice are most engaged on a daily basis.

As previous chapters have made clear, the initiatives at NAU with partners across the Colorado Plateau involve learning how to live well together *here*— whether that concerns how to grow food sustainably, or how we might live in hospitable solidarity and deep collaboration with people fleeing hardship and crossing the U.S.-Mexico border, or developing practices of cooperative economics involving diverse people, or divesting from the carbon economy and investing in distributed ownership and production of renewable energy, or teaching the arts of grassroots democracy to students at NAU and in K–12 schools in our community, or cultivating postcolonial, mutually beneficial relationships with indigenous peoples who have occupied this region for ages, or learning how to use precious waters of our arid region wisely and fairly. Our work is deeply connected with larger networks that often span and exceed national boundaries: networks involved in civic engagement and democracy education, sustainability, cooperative economics, immigration, water rights, climate change, postcolonial relationships, and so forth. Yet for all our collaboration and exchanges hither and yon, so much of our teaching and learning is informed by our daily work and action, *right here*, in this semiarid and utterly stunning land of the U.S. Southwest. So much of what we do is *rooting*, even when this involves—as it usually does—learning to move with and across the arbitrary and power-laden boundaries of this region in ways that are more conducive to engendering diverse and complex commonwealth.

But this place—always a precarious terrain—is beginning to undergo unfathomable changes due to global warming.[28] The fire seasons are growing longer, and the fires are growing in frequency, expanse, and intensity. Infernos increasingly burn at temperatures and geographic scales that diminish the chances of ecological regeneration.[29] Recent cutting-edge research on the surrounding (world's largest) ponderosa forest predicts that "water vapor deficits" will become permanent by no later than 2050.[30] The forest here (as is the case across so much of the western United States) is doomed within the next three or four decades. Increasing numbers of lightning storms will likely cause devastating fires and disastrous flooding, as hard rains strike barren earth. In spite of violent storms, current and projected drought makes it likely that the water in the Colorado River, upon which tens of millions of people in our region depend, will frequently be too low to flow beyond the dams that have created Lake Meade and Lake Powell. In Flagstaff, the water supply is projected to sink below demand by 2050.[31] The severe drought of the Dust Bowl lasted a few years. The megadroughts projected by the latest models for coming decades—even in scenarios in which we rapidly reduce carbon emissions—will regularly last a quarter of a century.[32] Climate change will intensify the dislocation of people in our region in ways that will pose profound challenges. As many who have stood among the Pueblo ruins that dot the landscape can attest, even relatively small concentrations of people were forced to flee their villages throughout the region within a few years when drought struck centuries ago. The archaeological evidence suggests that relatively peaceful people murdered their neighbors in large numbers when that happened.[33] This land of abandoned rock dwellings is haunted, and the precipitous future of climate change hangs over the present as an increasingly probable nightmare—to all who are not sleeping.

Some scholars in the sciences, humanities, and social sciences have begun to theorize the implications of climate change under the concept of the "Anthropocene."[34] Dipesh Chakrabarty uses this term to evoke the idea of a time in which the age-old distinction between human and natural history collapses: humans are no longer merely agents modifying a given environment but have become "geological agents" altering fundamental patterns on a planetary scale.[35] While there is a significant degree of truth to this claim, in some ways the term "Anthropocene" may obscure our condition by overhumanizing it. There is no serious scientific doubt that anthropogenic "forcing" (caused by greenhouse gas emissions) is pushing us toward a very proximate tipping point beyond which we will likely exit the relative stability of the Holocene and experience frequent and intense catastrophes. Yet the complex and auto-catalytic system dynamics that will likely be triggered may so overwhelm this initial forcing as to drown the label "Anthro" in roaring planetary laughter. Consider a brief summation of some key points in leading climatologist James Hansen's account in *Storms of My Grandchildren*.

Hansen notes that in the past five hundred million years there have been five massive extinctions, periods in which more than 50 percent of the planet's species died in a short span of time. In the "end-Permian" extinction, more than 90 percent disappeared. Some extinctions were associated with dramatic increases in atmospheric carbon composition and climate.[36] Yet the rate of current increases in atmospheric carbon is far greater than in those periods. Hansen estimates that by continuing on our current "business as usual" trajectory, "we will drive a large fraction of the species, conceivably all of the species, to extinction"—triggering a sixth mass extinction.[37]

The likely immediate cause of the previous dramatic rises in atmospheric carbon levels can be traced to the release of methane stored as ice up to that point in frozen tundra and sealed beneath the Arctic seafloor. It is not clear what triggered the release of the methane, though lava flows, carbon dioxide emissions from massive volcanic eruptions, and perturbations in the Earth's orbit are plausible suspects. Whatever the causes, it took Earth *fifty million years* to recover the diversity of life that had existed prior to the end-Permian extinction. The important thing to keep in mind is that once methane thawing and release gets beyond a certain point, an autocatalytic dynamic emerges and the methane keeps pouring into the atmosphere, with catastrophic consequences.

As Bill McKibben notes in *Eaarth*, one recent study predicts that by the end of the century, permafrost methane releases could pump the equivalent of 270 years of present-day levels of human-produced carbon into the atmosphere. Peat bog methane releases could add another 65 years or so. Seafloor methane would contribute an additional release of immense proportions.[38] Ominously, "temperatures over eastern Siberia [have] increased almost ten degrees in the last decade," and the melting tundra is releasing methane. Additionally, the relatively warm water now flowing into the Arctic Sea from this thawing may in turn already be melting the "icy seal over underwater methane" that would account for oceanic releases that have already been recorded.[39]

A warming planet will be one in which dying forests become carbon stacks instead of carbon sinks, while melting ice caps turn vast planetary heat-reflecting surfaces into heat absorbers. McKibben calls these and many other feedback loops "booby traps." In each case, "we're responsible . . . but we can't turn it off."[40] Mounting evidence from the past few years suggest that we are heading toward those traps far quicker than the worst-case models had predicted.

Let us put aside Hansen's "Venus" scenario in which Earth becomes utterly unlivable—a dead planet. What is clear is that for millennia we almost certainly—unless we take dramatic and effective action immediately—face a much more chaotic *storm-shocked* Earth. As McKibben puts it, "The stability that produced civilization has vanished."[41] We face a world of longer seasons of intensifying hurricanes, blistering lightning storms, ever-rising oceans, severe droughts, epic floods, devastating fires, massive species die-off, rapid disease migrations—the list is long and grim.

In my view, then, the "Anthropocene" frame obscures the likelihood that the planetary macro- and microdynamics we are beginning to trigger will place us in a world where our experience of being radically out of control and in the midst of disruptive chaos will greatly increase. It is a world in which billions of people (perhaps seven hundred million by midcentury)[42] will be hurled into diasporic conditions, and most of us will find these challenges at the center of our lives and communities—either among hordes of displaced or facing such hordes. Let us employ the term "storm-shocked" as a metaphor for this condition, which includes but exceeds stormy weather and evokes yet another set of shocks that radical ecological democracy will somehow have to learn to navigate if we are to cultivate communities of hopeful practice.

"Communities of hopeful practice" is a difficult phrase in this context, not only because of the sheer material challenges we will face but also and relatedly because we are likely to soon inhabit a world in which the spatiotemporal geographies where modern narratives and imaginaries of hope abide become severely challenged or evidently untenable. Modernist hope has been intimately linked with geographic imaginaries according to which we journey in landscapes conducive to progress—whether downhill slopes upon which our journey becomes easier and easier as we progress, or modestly uphill slopes with good traction that may require hard work yet consistently match such work with the probability of good prospects for forward movement. Amid these imaginaries there are, to be sure, steep, icy mountain ranges to be occasionally crossed, wars to be fought that are just barely won. Yet the overall bent of the terrain has enough stability to support broad visions of hope as a line, or a spiral, moving on the whole toward a horizon. Wallace Stegner brilliantly articulates the specifically temporal character of this "geography of hope" in his discussions of white people's movement into the West. Beyond what we can begin to see on the horizon, "western" is an *affective temporal topography* in which the new is anticipated with excitement as a coming abode of abundance.[43]

So many of the dominant imaginaries of hope in recent times hinge in some way upon a terrain that could become sufficiently stable and potentially fertile to support improved futurity. Even Walter Benjamin—one of the most profound critics of progressive narratives—when articulating a revolutionary history of episodic "weak messianic" explosions that might interrupt the continuous accumulation of historical destruction, did not imagine that the "straight gate through which the Messiah might enter" may topple on his or her head, nor that the city will be repeatedly flooded, or drought-starved and uninhabited the instant after the weak Messiah (or messianic) arrives.[44]

What might it mean to learn to cultivate practices of hope in a diasporic and more tenaciously tragic geography that may no longer sustain the stories we have projected and clung to thus far? And how might we ward off apocalyptic despair on what Bill McKibben calls Eaarth—a storm-shocked "uphill planet . . . where gravity exerts a stronger pull . . . [and] there's more friction than we're used to"?[45] On a planet like this, no testosterone fantasy of a "new Leninism" will do, for our capacities to navigate paths of flourishing will likely diminish (even more than this is already the case) in proportion to our efforts to try to impose the future. On Eaarth, our most necessary and highest vocation will often be to seek to negotiate new powers and configurations of community with receptive generosity and graceful vulnerability amid conditions that—and people who—arrive unexpectedly and pose great challenges, or among hordes of people arriving, or with those forced to move on, or with buried and unburied corpses.

Reimagining active hope for a storm-shocked Eaarth will undoubtedly be the modulating work of generations. Yet I suspect that the following two motifs—political imaginaries foregrounding temporal discontinuities and spatial dislocations—will be among those that are indispensable for future inhabitations and migrations to which our strange communities will be called.

The first motif discloses a temporal imaginary of ricocheting trajectories linking political struggles separated by vast stretches of time. I call this motif "wormhole hope." To my mind, one of the sharpest writers on this subject is Rebecca Solnit, whose *Hope in the Dark: Untold Histories, Wild Possibilities* explores discontinuous modalities of radical democratic and ecological hope.[46] "Hope in the dark" includes all of the kinds of work and action we have discussed in previous chapters, but Solnit suggests that it also requires a sensibility closer to *faith*. Inquiring, "What are the grounds for hope in this world full of wrecks?," she offers a hope akin to faith, in the sense that it "endures when there's no way to imagine winning in the foreseeable future . . . that you might live to see or benefit from."[47]

In the frequently interrupted but resurgent and resonant contestations of neoliberal capitalism from 1994 in Chiapas, to 1999 in Seattle, to iterations of the World Social Forum in the first decade of the twenty-first century, and most recently to Occupy, she discerns "something increasingly recognizable but yet unnamed, yet unrecognized—a new ground for hope." From these discontinuous eruptions (undergirded by but irreducible to the organizing-in-the-shadows without which they would not have been possible), she narrates much greater temporal and spatial discontinuities of political struggle in order to illuminate and encourage this new ground: "*the ricocheting trajectory* [of history] by which [e.g.] Thoreau, abolitionists, Tolstoy, women suffragists, Gandhi, Martin Luther King Jr., and various others had, over the course of more than a century, wrought a doctrine of civil disobedience and nonviolence that would become standard liberatory equipment in every part of the world."[48] It would be easy to extend these resonant ricocheting trajectories backward through the discontinuous eruptions of the Hebrew prophets and the radical democrats of ancient Athens, to the eruption of Jesus, the Talmudic contestations, kabbalistic mystics, the episodic tradition of radical Christianity from Saint Francis through Dorothy Day, the radical democratic revolutions of the seventeenth through twentieth centuries, and beyond. These ricocheting trajectories conjure a wormhole hope—always important, often unappreciated, but especially crucial for life on Eaarth, "when there is no way to imagine winning."

Wormhole hope can be seen *retrospectively* in narratives of ricocheting historical trajectories, and it manifests *prospectively* as an enlivening sense that our political work and actions, and that of those who have come before us, unfold in ways that frequently disappear but persistently reappear and reintensify across unfathomably vast stretches of space and time—beyond all the probabilities. Wormhole hope feels the wreckage of history and expects wreckage, long periods of defeat and retrenchment. Wormhole hope suspects that we think, work, and act in a darkness from which no enlightenment progress will enable us wholly or permanently to emerge. Nevertheless, wormhole hope remains intransigently faithful to work and action drawn by a sense that though we live amid temporal geographies riven by vast barrenness and tragic tidal waves, volcanic eruptions, earthquakes, and mass extinctions, they are nonetheless teeming with latencies stretching across millennia—partially incarnate and inextinguishable yearnings of immeasurable intensity that will reemerge and reignite when least expected, though we cannot prove it.

Briefly consider in this regard a Wiki account of astronomical wormholes as hypothesized by various astrophysicists:

> In physics, an Einstein-Rosen Bridge (or wormhole) is a hypothetical topological feature of spacetime that would be, fundamentally, a "shortcut" through spacetime. For a simple visual explanation of a wormhole, consider spacetime visualized as a two-dimensional (2D) surface. If this surface is folded along a third dimension, it allows one to picture a wormhole "bridge." (Please note, though, that this is merely a visualization displayed to convey an essentially *unvisualisable* structure existing in 4 or more dimensions. The parts of the wormhole could be higher-dimensional analogues for the parts of the curved 2D surface; for example, instead of mouths which are circular holes in a 2D plane, a real wormhole's mouths could be spheres in 3D space.) A wormhole is, in theory, much like a tunnel with two ends each in separate points in spacetime.[49]

Reading this in light of Solnit's account, wormhole hope is a political geographic sensibility and uncanny activating confidence that—even as long stretches of time unfold (depicted in figure 4.1 as the bent spatial surface) in which unfathomable retrenchment and wreckage prevail—"shortcuts" and "bridges" have and will repeatedly cut through the fabric of despairing spacetime and engender linkages and intensities of creative political engagement that seem impossible according to the normal coordinates we often take to exclusively define the real. Wormhole hope, then, names, solicits, and engenders the recurrence of miraculous connections among periods of intensive aspiration and struggle that we consider to be located across impossibly abyssal stretches of regular space and time. Like hypothesized astronomical wormholes, the wormholes of political space-time are "essentially unvisualisable." We can see and hear the narratives of such connective bridges storied by both actors and spectators, yet their emergence remains unanticipatable, and even our retrospective accounts harbor the significant opacity that must be part of any good wormhole narrative (emergences that cannot quite be visualized because they exceed the continuities of space-time contiguities and causality). This is part of what is evoked in different ways when Arendt writes of the

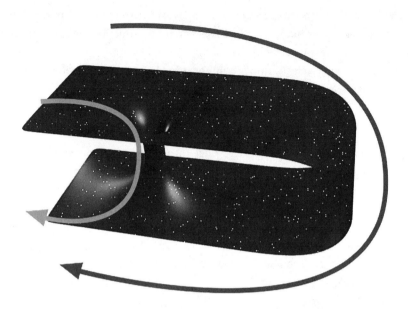

Figure 4.1. Two-dimensional analogical image of a wormhole (where the black surface represents the continuity of normal three-dimensional space-time and the hole represents connection across unfathomable three-dimensional distances). HTTP://COMMONS.WIKIMEDIA.ORG/WIKI/CATEGORY:WORMHOLES#/ MEDIA/FILE:WORMHOLE-DEMO.PNG. TEXT IS AVAILABLE UNDER THE CREATIVE COMMONS ATTRIBUTION–SHAREALIKE LICENSE. IMAGE SLIGHTLY ALTERED.

stimulated "miracle," Wolin evokes the "memory of the political," and Benjamin conjures "weak messianic power."

Let us further imagine this through another analogical flight in relation to hypotheses developing in theoretical physics from other summary Wiki discussions of wormholes, negative mass, and exotic matter: "The first type of wormhole solution discovered was the *Schwarzschild wormhole* which would be present in the Schwarzschild metric describing an eternal black hole, but it was found that this type of wormhole would collapse too quickly for anything to cross from one end to the other." Physicists theorize that wormholes sufficiently stable to enable such crossing—potentially in both directions—"would only be possible if exotic matter with negative energy density could be used to stabilize them." Exotic matter with negative energy density refers to hypothetical particles with properties that would "violate the known laws of physics, such as a particle having a negative mass." Or perhaps they would be within the realm of contemporary mainstream physics but "would have completely different properties than the regular chemical elements."[50] According to theoretical physics, negative mass would "show some *strange properties*, stemming from the ambiguity as to whether attraction should refer to force or the oppositely oriented acceleration" (my emphasis).[51] Yet it is thought that, "despite being completely inconsistent with a common-sense approach and the expected behavior of 'normal' matter, negative mass is completely mathematically consistent and introduces no violation of conservation of momentum or energy."[52]

Continuing our analogical line of flight, consider the possibility that events of radical democratic natality may be analogous to the negative mass and energy that make possible wormholes of sufficient duration to enable (uncanny) passage of political intensities across otherwise "impossible" spans of space-time. Events of intensity (these may be microquotidian or macroevanescent) may be thought of as energized assemblages and concentrations of natality, or what Benjamin referred to as weak messianic power. Natality is precisely the capacity to manifest "strange properties" that stem from the ambiguous futurity that emerges among us when we are no longer automatically propelled according to normalizing common sense, yet neither by a merely reactive opposition. Rather, through practices of radical receptivity we may, in our care for the world, articulate unpredictable gifts capable of breaking the chains of space-time—in the present or in some very distant future. I suggest that events like this manifest strange and intense powers for relationship, reflection, imagination, and action beyond the control of dominant powers and beyond the contiguities and regularities of hegemonic political space-time. "Miraculous" names their birth, but also the uncanny discontinuities of their strange life. They rise (or plunge? or leap?) beyond the normal contiguities of space-time to become exemplars of a pluralizing transtemporal collective natality. As such they may manifest an ethico-political exemplarity that partly exceeds the vulnerabilities to future moments to which they are in all other ways prone.

Walter Benjamin illuminates what I am calling "wormhole hope" when he writes that every revolutionary event (big or small) is itself made possible by an uncanny connection with a previous time that had a similar revolutionary charge or natal intensity. The connection is uncanny because it breaks with the hegemonic common sense of the present that stamps this past as irrelevant to those seeking to move beyond injustice, because it is outdated, overcome by progress, rightly defeated, or appears to be already assimilated. On Benjamin's reading, this strange connection receives its possibility in the charged intersection between two political intensities.

One of these intensities adheres to various revolutionary *pasts*. Such pasts are always at risk of being annihilated by the victors of "historical progress." Yet beyond the defeat of struggles for a better world, there remain the "spiritual things" of political work and action—partially incarnate yearnings of immeasurable intensity, which "manifest themselves in this struggle as courage, humor, cunning, and fortitude." Benjamin writes that "they have a retroactive force and will constantly call in question every victory, past and present, of the rulers. As flowers turn toward the sun, by dint of a secret heliotropism the past strives to turn toward that sun [of future time] which is rising in the sky of history."[53] For Benjamin, such times are "configuration[s] pregnant with tensions," and they carry a "charge" with vast powers—powers that can leap beyond seemingly impossible distances according to the commonsense continuities of "homogeneous, empty time" in which they have been thought to be imprisoned, in order to interrogate and disrupt such "progress" and beckon to future struggles.[54] The struggles of the present can connect with such charges because they turn toward us and beckon and are "filled with the presence of the now [Jestzeit]" that can "blast out the continuum of history."[55] They move us in ways we cannot know until we are charged by them.

Yet the possibility for wormhole bridges also hinges upon intensities of the *present* actively receiving and further enlivening those of the past. For though past intensities have this uncanny capacity to emerge full of life eons after this was declared to be impossible, on Benjamin's reading, they are also radically fragile: "For every image of the past that is not recognized by the present as one of its own concerns threatens to disappear irretrievably."[56] This sense of both the fragility and the uncanny powerful political potential of such pasts joins to intensify a redemptive receptive generosity—or "*weak* Messianic power"—according to which the possibility that we "will have the gift of fanning the spark of hope in the past" hinges on our being "firmly convinced that *even the* dead will not be safe from the enemy if he wins" (as when, for example, the slain Martin Luther King Jr. is woven into the temporal fabric of a celebratory imperialist neoliberal megastate).[57] Spurred by this sensibility, we may cultivate an acute receptivity toward miraculous quotidian and evanescent events of the past and seek solidaristic experiences in relation to how they arrested the automatic progressions of temporality. "Thinking involves not only the flow of thoughts, but their arrest as well."[58] In the latter vein, we seek to grasp the singularity of a time as a "monad" that radically deviates from the "homogenous course of history," to become a "configuration pregnant with tensions" harboring energy that can "blast out" of the oppressive fabric of progress and cocreate energetic bridges between points strewn across unfathomably vast stretches of hopelessness.

Sometimes Benjamin is read as fetishizing political "moments" in a way that I think misses the brilliance of his insight here. Rather, "now" does not refer to a moment but rather evokes any stretch of time that—with miraculous intensity—resists the "irresistible" and deviates from history as that which happens automatically.[59] This quality is evident in events of very diverse duration, as Benjamin clearly indicates in the examples he provides as signs of "a Messianic cessation of happening" that one ought to engage in order to deviate from the wretchedness of a time: "He takes cognizance of it in order to blast a specific *era* out of the homogeneous course of history—blasting a specific *life* out of the era or a specific *work* out of the life work."[60] Clearly there are continuities and transitions within any cessation of automaticity, whether this cessation occurs as an era, a life, a work, a brilliant morning when an artist finds the work's motif, or the instant a first-year college student at NAU musters the courage to make an empowering phone call that significantly shifts her life, the lives of others, and a movement. In each instance they are charged with natality and deviance, rather than being simply "progressive." When our work and action manifest such natality, and when we connect with the natality of other times that turn their active hope our way, political temporality becomes strange and strangely powerful. Retrospective experiences of this strange power in our lives, or what Solnit calls "ricocheting trajectories," tend to cultivate in us a more profoundly receptive attention to the natality of other times now and to come. They engender a stronger sense of possibilities for radical and ecological democracy in the present, and instill in us a more resilient faith that our own exemplary struggles may themselves reemerge beyond vast stretches of defeat to engage in revitalizing improbable futures long after we are gone.

The ricocheting trajectories of wormhole hope constitute the improbable wild time of radical and ecological democracy. Yet wild time repeatedly dislocates the domesticated contiguities and segregations of territorialized *space* as well, because our wormhole indebtedness to other times discloses how often the goods of any locality are commingled with those initiated in distant and most unwonted places. Because the governance of territory is tightly intertwined with powers to govern and narrate the continuous unfolding of time—origins, foundings, the emergence of borders, developments within and without, appropriate flows and exclusions, desirable futures, and so forth—the ricocheting trajectories of wild time tend repeatedly to disrupt and vitiate the dreams, powers, and policing of both sovereignty and governmentality in ways that confound hegemony. They repeatedly point to and energize other seductive possibilities. *This brings us to the second motif, likely indispensable for hope and flourishing on a storm-shocked Eaarth, the radical deterritorialization of environmentalism.* Let us call this the "hospitality for weightless seeds."

Consider, for example, the relatively short strand of Solnit's example cited earlier: powers of solidaristic and unwonted border crossings move from New England, to Russia, to India, to the U.S. South. If we extend the strand backward, it moves around the Middle East from Hebrew prophets to Jesus and far beyond. Extend the strand forward, and we see its influence in postcolonial struggles throughout Africa and Latin America. By pluralizing and proliferating our sense of spatiotemporal indebtedness and commingling possibilities across vast distances, wormhole hope may contribute to delinking environmentalisms from various forms of ugly and damaging territoriality.

Nothing will probably be more important on a storm-shocked Eaarth, where we will repeatedly find ourselves amid very challenging conditions facing people arriving from myriad dislocations, or as and among those who have been dislocated. Environmentalists have often espoused the virtues of *rooting*, developing deep relationships, attachments, and practices of care for the world in a specific place. I too think this is an indispensable responsibility, especially in the context of struggles to resist and cultivate alternatives to pervasive neoliberal dynamics of displacement and uprooting. Much of the theory and practice in previous chapters has focused on practices that involve such rooting, even as I have repeatedly sought to show how receptive *rooting* (even on the most microlevels) is bound up with *routing*, whether this takes the form of moving democracy or the mobile stewardship of polyface farming and a host of other receptive flows. Responsive routing, I have argued, is a practice without which rooting tends to become subjugative of the land and various peoples, other beings, and things on the undersides of power in any place. Stories of the ricocheting trajectories and commingling places of radical democracy give uncanny extension to James Clifford's sense in *Routes* that *both routing and rooting* are integral to how cultures form and negotiate futures. Such trajectories call us beyond territorializing impulses, practices, and institutions, as we deepen our awareness of the extent to which the goods of every place are and will in unexpected ways become indebted to initiatives and struggles of people in *other places*.

While I think people's sense of their unwonted indebtedness to the strange spatiotemporal journeys of the actions of others in other places is always vital to living well (e.g., with less xenophobia, greater hospitality), this sensibility will be especially important for living well on Eaarth—and perhaps most especially for radical and ecological democrats. Xenophobia has long haunted environmental movements, as foreigners have been perceived to be a threat to "our" national wilderness, healthy population levels, stewardship ethic, and so forth.[61] Combine this tendency with many forms of environmentalism today that accent rooting in ways that may be relatively oblivious to the also-important vitalities of translocal and planetary routing. Then, place this mixture in a context of growing numbers of "climate refugees" circulating under conditions of enhanced scarcity. Stir in the wide dispersion of arms from the legacy of the Cold War and the unprecedented pressures and displacements of neoliberalism, as Christian Parenti has insightfully analyzed in *The Tropic of Chaos*. What emerges is a situation that many military generals have repeatedly described as ripe for violent conflict and fascistic formations and disintegrations.

In contrast, a heightened sense for how every time and place is profoundly indebted to a multitude of ricocheting spatiotemporal trajectories of wormhole hope and struggle can contribute to an ethos of receptive generosity and enhanced hospitality toward those coming unexpectedly into the places we are trying to make home. It better disposes and enables us to anticipate abundance in relation to those who move beyond borders. Benjamin closed his "Theses on the Philosophy of History" by reflecting on how, for Jews focused on remembering, every future instant is nevertheless "the straight gate through which the Messiah might enter" (keeping in mind that for him this meant *weak* messianic powers).[62] Giving this thought a spatial twist, we would do well to dispose our oft-rooting ecological selves and political cultures to view people who are dislocated and tossed into ricocheting trajectories across myriad borders by storms, droughts, crop failures, rising tides, or the suffering-strewn topographies of neoliberalism and violent conflict, less as threats and much more as possible occasions for democratic relationships of natality, or weak messianic power. We would do well to cultivate arts of hospitality and generous political interaction to help midwife such emergence.

Every ecosystem hinges on those "weightless seeds"—birds, insects, sea life, waters, winds, warmth, coolness—moving across unfathomable distances according to complex flows of planetary respiration.[63] Just as this dynamic ecological commingling among nearby and vastly separated places is now understood by ecologists to be absolutely indispensable to the distinctive fertility of each and every place, so too I suggest that human beings' capacities to understand, care for, and cocreatively enact the political and ecological goods of any place will hinge on nothing so much as our strenuously cultivated ability to receive and generate abundance among those tossed into routing on a storm-shocked Eaarth: it will depend on nothing so much as the *hospitality for weightless seeds*. This will not be easy, but we will make every place an ecological and political wasteland if we fail to do so, and we must begin our efforts now.

What might this look like? As I have discussed earlier, the radical and ecological democracy movement at NAU and in Northern Arizona consists of collaborations among students, faculty, and myriad community partners on a growing number of action research teams that address challenges in our region and far beyond. From the very beginning, we pursued a variety of approaches to problems around immigration as an elemental part of the ecology of concerns, pedagogies, and political modalities through which we are attempting to cocreate what it might mean to live well, here in the U.S. Southwest. Just as we must learn to receive and care for sunshine, wind, water, soil, compost, seeds, and so forth, as possibilities for cocreating abundance, similarly and relatedly, we must learn to respond to the untold numbers of people crossing beyond what Margaret Randall calls "these molecules of hate" (that many would insidiously call the "fences" of national borders), with hospitality and a studied anticipation that together we can cocreate democratic mutualism and ecological vitality.[64] In our search for practices through which we—people living legally and illegally in Northern Arizona—might teach and learn together how we might live well and cocreate commonwealth, we pursue a variety of strategies: education and outreach, civil discourse, humanitarian, broad-based organizing, and abolitionist politics that confrontationally refuse the legitimacy of any infringement on "the right to live, love, and work wherever you please" with justice.

Through all this work, we are attempting to cultivate a radical and ecological democracy in which borders and discrimination against those who journey illegally across them are thrown into question, challenged, and disrupted. We do this not as an "afterthought," nor as an "add-on" issue, but rather because this thinking, work, and action are integral to the vision that is developing among us concerning what it means to live well here and now, and what is most important to teach and learn for our rapidly approaching future on storm-shocked Eaarth.

In similar fashion, the present discussion of wormhole hope and the hospitality for weightless seeds is not an afterthought either. Nor should we think of these virtues merely in terms of what will be necessary to struggle, live well, and persevere on a storm-shocked Eaarth. Rather, I would argue that what appears to be required on the screen of this projected future is actually what is now and always has been indispensable to any hope and action that is genuinely radically democratic and ecologically viable.

To learn and teach and struggle to live well has always involved a work and action informed by an uncanny faith in improbable futures, as well as a profound sense that the ecologies of what has been, is now, and will be good are utterly strewn with myriad "weightless seeds" blown in from other times, places, and peoples. This is to say, then, that what moves to the foreground on the screen of Eaarth is first and foremost the fact that truly visionary pragmatism has always required an intense receptive generosity in relationship to that which and those who greatly exceed our horizons of vision. Visionary pragmatism, as Maurice Merleau-Ponty certainly understood, is thus utterly contingent upon our sense of and taste for the invisible. This is true on an increasingly devastated planet that will likely take away so much of what we love to see and make seen. It is also the condition of any gift—the condition of any democratic and ecologically flourishing community worthy of becoming real.

EPILOGUE

_____

I began *Visionary Pragmatism* in significantly quieter political times. It was before Occupy and the antiausterity movements, before the campus divestment organizing associated with 350.org, before the growing protests around racist police violence, and during the very early stages of the increasingly networked resistance to the fossil fuel extraction industry called "Blockadia." Each of these movements has shown that the episodic democratic tradition of protest and disruption is more alive and subject to renewal than many had believed. Hopeful suspicions that we may be entering a new era of protest politics are not unreasonable in light of these events.

At the same time, there is a sense among many that the radical democratic capacities manifest in these movements—particularly in the United States—remain far short of what will be needed to radically transform neoliberal capitalist trajectories that are rapidly dismantling democracy, expanding horrific inequalities, resurrecting Jim Crow, and careening toward planetary ecological catastrophe. So far the "No!" is much more audible and articulated than the "Yes!" The prefigurative enactments are often problematic. The powers of durability are not yet terribly impressive. The connections to broader organizing efforts tend to be weak, and the capacity to translate discontents into systemic political economic transformation remains to be seen. These weaknesses are common to most young movements, and sometimes, organizing efforts ascend steep learning curves. It would be ridiculous to expect that after decades of quiescent democracy, those beginning to rise up would be great at it. And who among the critics has figured out how to build broad, durable, and powerful movements for change?

Nevertheless, unless such movements can connect with and generate quotidian practices and cultures of radical and ecological democracy, there is little reason to be hopeful about the prospects for transformation. Neoliberal capitalism is organized to deploy and utilize shocks with increasing frequency and effect; our world, lives, and bodies are awash in and proliferate mega-circulatory powers of governmentality; our senses are bombarded and overwhelmed by its resonance machines; the system dynamics of corporate capitalism continue to amplify at rates that exceed those of even the most promising democratic and ecological justice movements to date. Our sensibilities, identities, affect, and orientations are made and unmade daily in this dense and multifaceted matrix. Institutions of higher education, still harboring some of the freer spaces in our polity where legacies of previous movements carry on, are rapidly collapsing and reconfiguring to corporate imperatives.

Visionary Pragmatism has worked the generative intersections between theory and practice—particularly in the movement for democratic action research at Northern Arizona University—in order to explore and advance several interrelated dimensions of what I have called a radical democratic habitus. The aim has been to discern, cocreate, and amplify horizons of transformative aspiration. Thinking between research on mirror neurons and relational practices of resonant receptivity, I have suggested paths for beginning to cultivate alternatives to today's dominant resonance machine. Reflecting on emergent flows of humans, things, and other beings that have proliferated in the alternative agriculture and food justice movements, I have suggested possibilities for profoundly challenging and displacing the mega-circulations that are re-creating and imperiling life across the planet. I have argued that complexity theory offers an important heuristic lens for generating autocatalytic dynamics with substantial capacities to co-opt some elements of the current order in transformative ways. Finally, I have argued for the importance of generating alternating currents between the political energies and natality stimulated in quotidian organizing and those that are fostered in the more episodic events of shock democracy. Together, these may constitute a hopeful mix.

———————

I awake to the hum of the jet in which I have been sitting for ten hours and lift a window shade. Between the black ocean below and the still starry sky above, a brilliant yellow-orange line begins to crack open the day on the horizon behind us. We continue to race away toward the night, but soon morning catches us over a strange sea. In a few hours we'll be landing in Sydney, Australia, shortly to be my new home.

Half awake, I recall parts of the westward journey I recounted in the beginning of this book, heading away from what I felt was an overly professionalized academic environment, hungering toward new articulations of theory, pedagogy, and political practice. The following six years have far exceeded my wildest imagination of what might be possible in terms of institutional transformation and relationships. And however modest our work may be, I am unfathomably grateful to so many people—and for the constant presence of the peaks and canyons—for the collaborations we engaged in and the many possibilities we opened together. My theory and sense of political hope are indelibly shaped by those years. Much we began continues to develop, extending many paths and venturing in some new directions.

Yet if no place has quite grabbed my heart the way Flagstaff did, my sense of vocation calls me in some new directions. I have reached a point where precisely what has nourished me in our increasingly altered academic habitus has engendered interests, passions, and aspirations that have exceeded these spaces in which they developed. I seek a space in which to try to bring this movement into conversations and collaborations among larger networks—global networks, even—to explore possibilities for creating greater transformations in what increasingly appears to be the last decade in which we might avert the worst of climate catastrophe and ruthless oligarchy. I have been wondering if it might be possible to form a new PhD program that would combine serious theory and action research in ways that would continue to experiment with and disseminate the sorts of academic habitus that we have begun at NAU.

At the same time these dreams began to emerge, a new Institute for Social Justice (ISJ) was formed at Australian Catholic University that shares many similar aspirations and has substantial resources. The ISJ seeks to cogenerate vast networks of theoretical reflection and collaborative interaction among scholars and people organizing on the ground around the planet—and those of us engaged in both—for radical democracy, social justice, and ecological survival. Its evolving vision incorporates action research into the new modes of critical and generative scholarship that will form a core of its PhD program. It is an initiative that fires enthusiasms in me in ways I feel drawn to explore.

Enthusiasms, yes, and questions that sometimes make me tremble. Aboriginal people have been living in Australia continuously for forty thousand years and struggling for centuries against colonialism. Will I be able to listen and practice receptivity half as well as I need to—especially at this moment? What will it be like to theorize and organize in such a different context, far from people and places I have come to love, in a land that is very foreign to me? The vulnerable relationships, genuinely reflective conversations, collaborative public work, and political action to which we are called are hard enough to generate in a single university and in a small city. How will we manage to do analogous things on much larger scales?

The horizons I believe we must explore and the paths we must create if there is to be any hope are vast and fragile. It will be easy to get lost. Yet we are already lost, are we not? It will take countless collective democratic efforts to "do a new thing," to paraphrase the prophet Isaiah, if we are to patch this sinking ship and sail it toward better futures. Visionary Pragmatism *has given expression to some of the transformative possibilities of a few such efforts. Even more than that, however, it is a call to others in and beyond institutions of higher education to embark on new modes of inhabiting and transfiguring how we cocreate knowledge and practice. There is much to be done. We have very little time. Yet we have much to offer if we lend ourselves to the teeming potentials for game-transformative practice. What will we do?*

NOTES

Introduction

1 See Euben, "Creatures of a Day," for an incisive discussion of the connections between travel and theory.

2 The issue here is one of *how* we dwell, as much as it is one of where we move. Attentive stillness can be a mode of moving into where one already is in new and disclosive ways, as John Paul Lederach conveys in his discussion of the "Zen of going nowhere" in *The Moral Imagination.*

3 I develop this argument a bit more in "'It's the "We," Stupid.'"

4 See, for example, Bourdieu, *Outline of a Theory of Practice.*

5 For Foucault's discussion of "limit ethos," see "What Is Enlightenment?"

6 Ganz, *Why David Sometimes Wins,* 14, 12.

7 Ganz, *Why David Sometimes Wins,* 13.

8 Arreguin-Toft, *How the Weak Win Wars.*

9 Malcolm Gladwell, "How David Beats Goliath: When Underdogs Break the Rules," *New Yorker,* May 11, 2009.

10 Ganz, *Why David Sometimes Wins.*

11 The consortium Imagining America: Artists and Scholars in Public Life has begun to explore and advance some of these ideas. See http://imagining america.org/.

12 Richard Rorty's *Achieving Our Country* is a good example of this tendency.

13 Wendy Brown, in *Politics Out of History,* provides a classic articulation of this perspective. I am significantly closer to Brown than I am to Rorty, yet I think that things missing in her argument may enable poor readings that reinforce a rather hermetically sealed scholarly habitus—even as her own rich work always avoids this trap.

14 See Connolly, *Capitalism and Christianity American Style.*

15 I refer here to the works gathered in Coole and Frost, *New Materialisms,* as well as Jane Bennett's *Vibrant Matter.*

16 See my *Beyond Gated Politics.*

17 My argument here has, of course, significant debts to James Clifford's *Routes.*

18 Meadows, *Thinking in Systems,* ix.

19 McKibben, *Eaarth.*

20 Ellison, *Invisible Man,* xx.

1. Neuropolitical Habitus

1 Connolly, *Capitalism and Christianity American Style*, 11.
2 The expression "capitalist axiomatic" comes from Connolly, *Capitalism and Christianity American Style*, 11.
3 Connolly, *Capitalism and Christianity American Style*, 40.
4 Connolly, *Capitalism and Christianity American Style*, 15.
5 Wooten, *The Music Lesson*, 127.
6 Prigogine and Stengers, *The End of Certainty*, 71.
7 Holland, *Emergence*, 5.
8 Holland, *Emergence*, 7.
9 Bloch, *Principle of Hope*.
10 Prigogine and Stengers refer to resonant energy as "nonlocal," insofar as it emerges *between* beings. It is thus perhaps emblematic that the discovery of "mirror neurons"—the energetic receptors involved in such resonance—likely happened not as a result of the intentionality of a subject-researcher, nor even within that locality we designate as the "human," but rather accidentally in a chance observation of resonance between a macaque monkey and a human. As Vittorio Gallese, a neuroscientist deeply indebted to Merleau-Ponty, reached for something during a break in his research on a brain-wired monkey, he heard the computer unexpectedly register monkey-brain grasping activity even though the monkey was entirely still. (There are other versions of this "origin" story involving other researchers, yet all seem to point toward "nonlocal" interspecies serendipity.) Gradually, Gallese and numerous other scientists working in Giacomo Rizzolatti's laboratory in Parma were drawn to investigate this seemingly impossible transbeing neurological activity, and from this work eventually a whole field of inquiry emerged for which Rizzolatti received a Nobel Prize many years later. Iacoboni, *Mirroring People*, 10–11.
11 Iacoboni, *Mirroring People*, 152, 55.
12 Iacoboni, *Mirroring People*, 133–34.
13 The dynamical interactive biocultural character of this development is further indicated by the growth of "new properties" in monkeys' mirror neurons as a result of their repeated exposure to humans using tools that the monkeys do not yet use or comprehend (Iacoboni, *Mirroring People*, 42). It is also indicated by the changes in mirror neurons that occur in relation to practices, as I discuss later.
14 Carl Zimmer discusses the complexity of smiling and interpretations of smiling in "More to a Smile Than Lips and Teeth," *New York Times*, January 25, 2011. Smiles are not simply about harmony and love: they can be about happy emotion, relations of power, embarrassment, and so forth. Chris Huebner brought this article to my attention, which was published the day after I presented a shortened version of this essay at Canadian Mennonite University and he was pushing me to discuss additional complexities involved in resonance and mir-

ror neurons. On this latter point, see my discussion of (and additional note on) political resonance below.

15 Iacoboni, *Mirroring People*, 111.

16 Rizzolatti and Sinigaglia, *Mirrors in the Brain*, 48.

17 Rizzolatti and Sinigaglia, *Mirrors in the Brain*, 50.

18 Changeux and Ricoeur, *La nature et la règle*, 137.

19 Gallese, "The 'Shared Manifold' Hypothesis." In general, Gallese's writing appears to be the most "philosophical" of the group of scientists in Parma and is deeply influenced by Merleau-Ponty.

20 Rizzolatti and Sinigaglia, *Mirrors in the Brain*, 137.

21 Rizzolatti and Sinigaglia, *Mirrors in the Brain*, 117.

22 Iacoboni, *Mirroring People*, 26.

23 Holland, *Emergence*, 5.

24 These words are an approximate rendering based on my notes and memory of this discussion rather than the student's exact words.

25 The vitality of these relationships and the way in which we are disposed to enter them are further indicated by the fact that our pleasure is profoundly oriented to this interworld, as is manifest by the great joy babies, children, and adults take in imitation games.

26 Blackmore, *The Meme Machine*, and Dennett, *Consciousness Explained*, 207, as quoted in Iacoboni, *Mirroring People*, 51.

27 Kilner, Marchant, and Frith, "Modulation of the Mirror System by Social Relevance," 147.

28 Kourtis, Sebanz, and Knoblich, "Favouritism in the Motor System," 760.

29 Arendt, *Lectures on Kant's Political Philosophy*.

30 Bourdieu, *Outline of a Theory of Practice*, 167.

31 Liepelt, Von Cramon, and Brass, "How Do We Infer Others' Goals from Non-stereotypic Actions?," 785; Brass et al., "Investigating Action Understanding."

32 Boyte, *Commonwealth*; Boyte, *Everyday Politics*.

33 Foucault, "What Is Enlightenment?," 50.

34 Amos Oz and Fania Oz-Salzberger brilliantly evoke this sort of resonance in *Jews and Words*.

35 Bourdieu, *Outline of a Theory of Practice*, 72.

36 Bourdieu, *Outline of a Theory of Practice*, 94.

37 Bourdieu, *Outline of a Theory of Practice*, 2.

38 Bourdieu, *Outline of a Theory of Practice*, 1.

39 Bourdieu, *Outline of a Theory of Practice*, 72.

40 Wolin, *Politics and Vision*, 601–6; Wolin, "Fugitive Democracy."

41 This is a crucial theme when considering complicated and critical questions, challenges, and possibilities regarding the capacity of the virtual sphere to extend, intensify, amplify, and modulate the resonance machine I have sketched in this chapter in democratic ways. Yet it is beyond the scope of this inquiry and beyond the realm in which I am presently prepared to offer substantial insight.

2. Mega-circulatory Power

1 A few important exceptions include Panagia, *The Political Life of Sensation*; Honig, *Emergency Politics*; and Bennett, *Vibrant Matter*.

2 Foucault, *Security, Territory, Population*, 66.

3 Bloch, *The Principle of Hope*, 6.

4 Foucault, *Security, Territory, Population*, 18.

5 See, for example, Brown, *Walled States, Waning Sovereignty*.

6 Foucault, *Security, Territory, Population*, 344.

7 They operate by "standing back," "letting things happen," in order to grasp events and circulations "at the level of their effective reality," and then "work on the basis of this reality, by trying to use it as a support and make it function, make its components function in relation to each other." Foucault, *Security, Territory, Population*, 47.

8 Foucault, *Security, Territory, Population*, 6.

9 Foucault, *Security, Territory, Population*, 47.

10 Foucault's account here has similarities with Polanyi's account of the commodifying circulations of labor resulting from post-Speenhamland poor laws. Polanyi, *The Great Transformation*.

11 One might elaborate a similar functional analysis in relation to schools that consistently fail to serve a portion of their students—to the benefit of McDonald's and Walmart; nations that consistently fail to "protect their borders"— without which many agricultural, construction, and service operations would become cost-prohibitive; states that allow counterpolitics while regulating and nullifying it with responses that insert state power into such activities through tax codes, nonprofit regulations, public (non)participation spaces, laws regulating street protests, and trivializing media productions—to maximize legitimacy and minimize its costs; states that guide the discursive order not by disallowing free speech but by subsidizing it in hyperprofessionalized "transgressive" academic practices. To enhance power, states now arouse, facilitate, and manage circulations whose vitality and power hinge on substantial degrees of autonomy.

12 Foucault, *Security, Territory, Population*, 73.

13 Foucault, *Security, Territory, Population*, 45.

14 Foucault, *Security, Territory, Population*, 350.

15 Foucault, *Security, Territory, Population*, 48–49.

16 Polanyi, *The Great Transformation*.

17 Wolin, *Politics and Vision*, chaps. 16 and 17.

18 Nace, *Gangs of America*.

19 See Wolin, *Politics and Vision* and *The Presence of the Past*, chap. 9. See also Klein, *The Shock Doctrine*.

20 Wolin, *Politics and Vision*, 563.

21 Key texts here would be Foucault's *Birth of Biopolitics*, as well Paul Apostolidis's insightful discussion of how race, class, and nation modulate this schema in *Breaks in the Chain*.

22 Pollan, *The Omnivore's Dilemma*, 60.

23 Pollan, *The Omnivore's Dilemma*, 65.

24 USDA, "Corn: Trade," accessed April 15, 2015, http://www.ers.usda.gov/topics /crops/corn/trade.aspx.

25 Pollan, *The Omnivore's Dilemma*, 19.

26 Pollan, *The Omnivore's Dilemma*, 26.

27 Pollan, *The Omnivore's Dilemma*, 90.

28 Pollan, *The Omnivore's Dilemma*, 58–59.

29 Pollan, *The Omnivore's Dilemma*, 39.

30 Worse still, Monsanto has designed a "terminator seed," which, if ultimately deemed legally marketable, would be wholly sterile and risk contaminating nearby related non–terminator seed species with such sterility. See Mushita and Thompson, *Biopiracy of Biodiversity*.

31 Pollan, *The Omnivore's Dilemma*, 63.

32 Pollan, *The Omnivore's Dilemma*, 107.

33 Berry, *What Are People For?*, 146.

34 Apostolidis, *Breaks in the Chain*, xxviii, xxix.

35 Esteva, *Grassroots Postmodernism*, 31.

36 See Inglehart, *Modernization and Postmodernization*.

37 There are affinities between the lines of critique and initiative under discussion here and significant streams of theorizing that have been coined "new materialism." See Coole and Frost, *New Materialisms*. Though new materialism contains numerous themes and strands of inquiry, Coole and Frost discern three "interrelated but distinctive themes." First, there is a shift from subjectivist paradigms that privilege human cognition and valuation, to "an orientation that is posthumanist in the sense that it conceives of matter itself as lively or as exhibiting agency." This matter, as we have argued earlier, includes but exceeds human bodies that are themselves immersed in broad flows of biotic and physical materiality which has various sorts and degrees of agency. Human agency is increasingly understood as indebtedly networked with complex and dynamic agentic systems. Second, this fact raises a host of "biopolitical and bioethical issues concerning the status of life and of the human"—in conjunction with which we are drawn into a thicket of crucial questions concerning human responsibility with and for the more than human world (Coole and Frost, *New Materialisms*, 7). Finally, "new materialist scholarship testifies to a critical and nondogmatic reengagement with political economy, where the nature of, and relationship between, the material details of everyday life and broader geopolitical and socioeconomic structures is being explored afresh." All three emphasize "materialization as a complex, pluralistic, relatively open

process" and insist "that humans, including theorists themselves, be recognized as thoroughly immersed within materiality's productive contingencies" (7). Particularly promising in the context of a critique of power and the initiatives of new social movements is the extent to which new materialism is "bringing biopolitics, critical geopolitics, and political economy together with genealogies and phenomenologies of everyday life" (28). See Schlosberg and Coles, "The New Environmentalism of Everyday Life."

38 Longhofer, Golden, and Baiocchi, "A Fresh Look at Sociology Bestsellers."

39 "Farmers Markets and Local Food Marketing," USDA, accessed August 16, 2013, http://www.ams.usda.gov/AMSv1.0/farmersmarkets.

40 Petrini, *Slow Food*, xiii.

41 Winne, *Food Rebels, Guerrilla Gardeners, and Smart-Cookin' Mamas*, 158–59.

42 Winne, *Food Rebels*, 22.

43 "Garden Resource Program," Detroit Agricultural Network, accessed August 16, 2013, http://detroitagriculture.net/urban-garden-programs/garden-resource -program/.

44 David Whitford, "Can Farming Save Detroit?," *Fortune Magazine*, December 9, 2009, accessed March 30, 2015, http://archive.fortune.com/2009/12/29/news /economy/farming_detroit.fortune/index.htm. For a fuller account, see Boggs, *The Next American Revolution*.

45 See Cavanaugh, *Being Consumed*.

46 Gottlieb and Joshi, *Food Justice*, 144.

47 Petrini, *Slow Food*, xvii–xviii. See also the Slow Food Foundation's Tierra Madre communities project, http://www.slowfoodfoundation.com /athousandgardens.

48 For a global analysis, see Shiva, *Manifestos on the Future of Food and Seed*.

49 As is insightfully discussed by Schurman and Munro, *Fighting for the Future of Food*.

50 See Alcon and Agyeman, *Cultivating Food Justice*.

51 Danielle Kurzleben, "Farmers' Market Boom Not Reaching Many Food Stamp Users," *U.S. News and World Report*, August 6, 2012, accessed March 30, 2015, http://www.usnews.com/news/articles/2012/08/06/farmers-market-boom-not -reaching-many-food-stamp-users.

52 Gottlieb and Joshi, *Food Justice*.

53 Scott Scanlon, "Doubling Up on Food Stamps and Nutrition," *Buffalo News*, June 22, 2014, accessed March 30, 2015, http://www.buffalonews.com/city -region/doubling-up-on-food-stamps-and-nutrition-20140622. See also "Double Up Food Bucks," Fair Food Network, accessed March 30, 2015, http:// www.doubleupfoodbucks.org/about/.

54 "NYC Food by the Numbers: Farmers' Markets," New York City Food Policy Center, accessed November 7, 2014, http://nycfoodpolicy.org/nyc-food -numbers-farmers-markets/.

55 Winne, *Food Rebels, Guerrilla Gardeners, and Smart-Cookin' Mamas*.

56 "About Us," Women Food & Ag Network, accessed March 30, 2015, http://wfan.org/about/.

57 Gottlieb and Joshi, *Food Justice.*

58 On the latter, see Apostolidis, *Breaks in the Chain.*

59 Sirriani, *Investing in Democracy.* See also my critical engagement in "Collaborative Governance and Civic Empowerment."

60 On these possibilities, see Gottlieb and Joshi, *Food Justice.*

61 On environmentalism, nativism, xenophobia, and racism, see Park and Pellow, *The Slums of Aspen*, especially chap. 4; Gottlieb, *Forcing the Spring*, especially chap. 7; and John Hultgren's insightful *Border Walls Gone Green.*

62 Benyus, *Biomimicry*, 23.

63 Benyus, *Biomimicry*, 54, quoting Wes Jackson.

64 Berry, *The Way of Ignorance and Other Essays*, 47.

65 Wolin, *The Presence of the Past,* 119. See also my extensive discussion of this theme in the work of Wolin, in Hauerwas and Coles, *Christianity, Democracy, and the Radical Ordinary*, chap. 6.

66 Joel Salatin himself has written many books, perhaps the most pertinent in this context being *The Sheer Ecstasy of Being a Lunatic Farmer.*

67 Pollan, *The Omnivore's Dilemma*, 187.

68 Pollan, *The Omnivore's Dilemma*, 186.

69 Pollan, *The Omnivore's Dilemma*, 190.

70 Pollan, *The Omnivore's Dilemma*, 206.

71 Pollan, *The Omnivore's Dilemma*, 150.

72 Pollan, *The Omnivore's Dilemma*, 211–13.

73 Pollan, *The Botany of Desire.*

74 Pollan, *The Omnivore's Dilemma,* 214, 219.

75 Levinas, *Totality and Infinity.*

76 Pollan, *The Omnivore's Dilemma*, 150.

77 Petrini, *Slow Food,* xvii, xix. For an excellent discussion of *convivium*, see Panagia, *The Political Life of Sensation*, chap. 5.

78 Petrini, *Slow Food*, 16, 17, 8, 19.

79 Petrini, *Slow Food*, 33.

80 Petrini, *Slow Food*, xxiv.

81 Borrowing loosely from Isaiah 43:19, changing "I" to "we."

82 Gottlieb and Joshi's *Food Justice* is among the best compilations and analyses of the initiatives. See also J. K. Gibson-Graham's *A Postcapitalist Politics*, a highly provocative theorization of action research around similar initiatives worldwide.

83 Orr, *Down to the Wire*, 182.

84 Mark Winne, keynote speech at Flagstaff Food Film Festival, February 18, 2011.

85 See Pollan, *The Omnivore's Dilemma.*

86 Stephanie Strom, "Has 'Organic' Been Oversized?," *New York Times,* July 7, 2012.

87 For a sobering overview of these challenges, see Bren Smith, "Don't Let Your Children Grow Up to Be Farmers," *New York Times*, August 9, 2014.

88 See John Gallagher's series of reports and analyses: *Reimagining Detroit*; "Detroit Residents Speak Out against Project, City Council at Hantz Woodlands Hearing," *Detroit Free Press*, December 10, 2012, accessed May 16, 2013, http://www.freep.com/article/20121210/NEWS01/121210076/Detroit-residents-speak-out-against-project-City-Council-Hantz-Wodlands-hearing; "Critics Say Hantz Getting Unfair Advantage as Detroit Council Prepares to Revisit Plan for Land Sale," *Detroit Free Press*, December 10, 2012, accessed May 16, 2013, http://www.freep.com/article/20121210/BUSINESS06/312100041/critics-say-hantz-getting-unfair-advantage-as-detroit-council-prepares-to-revisit-plan-for-land-sale; "Hantz Woodlands Gets Green Light from Detroit City Council," *Detroit Free Press*, December 12, 2012, accessed May 16, 2013, http://www.freep.com/article/20121212/BUSINESS06/312120058/Hantz-Woodlands-gets-green-light-from-Detroit-City-Council. See also Alethia Carr, "Detroit: The Business of Urban Agriculture," *The Boggs Blog*, July 2010, accessed May 16, 2013, https://conversationsthatyouwillneverfinish.wordpress.com/2010/08/11/detroit-the-business-of-urban-agriculture/.

89 Monte Reel, "Saving Detroit, One Tree at a Time," *Bloomberg Businessweek*, September 2, 2014, accessed November 26, 2014, http://www.businessweek.com/articles/2014–09–02/detroits-john-hantz-plants-tree-farm-to-fight-urban-decay#p1.

90 Lovins, *Soft Energy Paths*.

91 Kruse and Maegaard, "An Authentic Story," 263.

92 Kruse and Maegaard, "An Authentic Story," 257–58.

93 Midnight Notes Collective and Friends, "Promissory Notes."

94 Kruse and Maegaard, "An Authentic Story," 260.

95 Kruse and Maegaard, "An Authentic Story," 261.

96 Maegaard, "Denmark," 491.

97 "Wind Power in Denmark," Wikipedia, accessed February 12, 2015, http://en.wikipedia.org/wiki/Wind_power_in_Denmark.

98 "Social Acceptance of Wind Energy Projects: 'Winning Hearts and Minds,' State-of-the-Art-Report," country report of Denmark, International Energy Agency, accessed February 12, 2015, http://en.wikipedia.org/wiki/Wind_power_in_Denmark.

99 Oceransky, "Fighting the Enclosure of Wind," 515.

100 Oceransky and Yansa Community Interest Company, "The Yansa Group," 611.

3. System Dynamics

1 Ani DiFranco, "In or Out," *Imperfectly*, Righteous Babe Records, 1992, CD.

2 The long tradition of revolutionary reform stretching back to Karl Marx (in some texts, in reference to some places), and finding articulations in the past several decades in scholars such as Gorz, *Ecology as Politics*, and Alperovitz, *America beyond Capitalism*, is often ignored.

3 This is especially odd, as this dialectic—or "generative themes"—was at the heart of Paulo Friere's dialogical organizing. See *Pedagogy of the Oppressed*.

4 Lederach, *The Moral Imagination*.

5 E.g., see Habermas, *Reason and the Rationalization of Society* and *Lifeworld and System*. In his engagement with Niklas Luhmann, Habermas articulates the tripartite model of the bureaucratic system, the economic system, and the life-world of civil society. Numerous thinkers adopted this framework, including Cohen and Arato, *Civil Society and Political Theory*, and it went viral from there. I critically engage Habermas's conceptualization of systems in *Rethinking Generosity*.

6 One of the most important and now classic efforts to theorize this idea is Unger, *False Necessity*. William Connolly insightfully pursues proximate themes in *Capitalism and Christianity, American Style* and *A World of Becoming*, drawing upon the work of complex dynamical systems theorists to whom I am indebted as well.

7 Gibson-Graham, *A Postcapitalist Politics*. See also Alperovitz, *America beyond Capitalism*, and Lew and Conaty, *The Resilience Imperative*.

8 Brown, *States of Injury*.

9 Gottlieb, *Forcing the Spring*, chap. 4. For an excellent discussion of radical democratic environmentalism that developed in the 1980s, at the same time the mainstream movement was professionalizing, see Szasz, *Ecopopulism*.

10 Kauffman, *At Home in the Universe*, 300. For a much more interesting set of reflections on the interplay between metaphor and modeling, see Holland, *Emergence*.

11 Hope, as social movement organizer and theorist Marshall Ganz says, quoting Moses Maimonides, is belief in the "plausibility of the possible" as opposed to the "necessity of the probable." Marshall Ganz, "What Is Public Narrative?" (manuscript, 2008), http://wearesole.com/What_is_Public_Narrative.pdf.

12 Kauffman, *At Home in the Universe*, 49.

13 Kauffman, *At Home in the Universe*, 60–61.

14 Kauffman, *At Home in the Universe*, 62.

15 Kauffman, *At Home in the Universe*, 63.

16 Kauffman, *At Home in the Universe*, 62.

17 For an insightful analysis of the discourse of "enthusiasm" in relation to radical democratic politics, see Frank's "'Besides Our Selves'" and *Constituent Moments*.

18 I have simplified aspects of Kauffman's account in the following discussion in order to foreground those aspects that I find to be most suggestive for questions of radical democracy. See Kauffman, *At Home in the Universe*, for a fuller discussion.

19 See Kauffman, *At Home in the Universe*, chaps. 4 and 5.

20 Kauffman, *At Home in the Universe*, 89.

21 Kauffman, *At Home in the Universe*, 90.

22 This has strong affinities with Walker and Salt's argument for the importance of "modularity" for resilient systems. In contrast to chaotic systems where everything is highly connected to everything else and shocks zoom through

the entire system, "systems with subgroups of components that are strongly linked internally, but only loosely connected to each other, have a modular structure. A degree of modularity in the system allows individual modules to keep functioning when loosely linked modules fail, and the system as a whole has a chance to self-organize and therefore a greater capacity to absorb shocks." *Resilience Thinking*, 69–71.

23 Kauffman, *At Home in the Universe*, 90.

24 Kauffman, *At Home in the Universe*, 91.

25 Kauffman, *At Home in the Universe*, 182.

26 See Gitlin's analysis in *Occupy Nation*. See also Frank, "To the Precinct Station," which suffers greatly from its own modes of dismissiveness but is nevertheless provocative and important on this issue.

27 Whether or not peaks are isolated from each other, or connected by thin ridges (which means that a being can get from one to another via paths that do not involve leaping across ontological gaps—even if they may often involve leaping across cognitive gaps, in the case of the evolution of human learning), is disputed by evolutionary biologists. See Gavrilets, "Evolution and Speciation on Holey Adaptive Landscapes," and Kaplan, "The End of the Adaptive Landscape Metaphor."

28 Kauffman, *At Home in the Universe*, 252.

29 Kauffman, *At Home in the Universe*, 252–53.

30 Kauffman, *At Home in the Universe*, 265.

31 Kauffman, *At Home in the Universe*, 271.

32 See, e.g., Connolly, *A World of Becoming*.

33 Another initiative, to generate cooperative economic networks, institutions, and practices in Northern Arizona, is similarly promising in this regard and the subject of ongoing experimentation and research.

34 For a sharp analysis of these processes, see Brown's "Governmentality in the Age of Neoliberalism" and *Undoing the Demos*.

35 Marc Bousquet provides an excellent analysis of many of these neoliberal and corporatizing trajectories in *How the University Works*. See my more extensive analysis of our radical democratic pedagogy movement as a powerful response to neoliberalism in "Transforming the Game."

36 Michelle Miller, "Assessment Report for AY 2012–2013 First Year Seminar/ FYSeminar-ARTS" (The First Year Seminar Program, Northern Arizona University, May 2013). The study carefully controlled its comparison sample in order to avoid "propensity biases," according to which those who self-selected into the FYS-ARTS might be expected to have higher rates of retention on this basis alone. To avoid such bias, FYS and non-FYS student samples were matched and equivalent on the following characteristics: ethnicity, gender, Arizona residency, FAFSA/PELL eligibility, attended previews, high school deficiencies (math, English, lab science), declared college, ACT/SAT scores, high school CORE GPA, and student success inventory (six scales).

37 Republican Party of Texas, 2012 State Republican Party Platform, 11–13, accessed March 30, 2015, http://www.texasgop.org/wp-content/themes/rpt/images/2012Platform_Final.pdf.

38 For my analysis of some of the implications of this argument for political theory and politics, see "'It's the "We," Stupid.'"

4. Shock Democracy

1 Klein, *The Shock Doctrine*.

2 Klein, *The Shock Doctrine*, 29.

3 Klein, *The Shock Doctrine*, 31.

4 Klein, *The Shock Doctrine*, 71.

5 "Blockadia" is the term Klein uses for climate protests around the world resisting the regime of carbon extraction in *This Changes Everything*. This excellent book appeared after I had finished this manuscript, yet I engage it in another book I am writing, tentatively titled "Of Line Drawing and Web Weaving."

6 Naomi Klein, "Latin America's Shock Resistance," *Nation*, November 26, 2007, http://www.thenation.com/article/latin-americas-shock-resistance#.

7 "Naomi Klein," interview, *Occupy Wall St. Grounded TV Network*, video 7, October 12, 2011, accessed September 7, 2013, http://www.youtube.com/watch?v=BaEeeLOB5IA.

8 Benjamin, *Selected Writings*, 402.

9 Benjamin, *Illuminations*, 262, 263.

10 I discuss questions of violence in relation to a broader range of movements and contexts in a book manuscript in progress tentatively titled "Of Line Drawing and Web Weaving." Here I confine my discussion to nonviolent modes of shock politics.

11 See Laura Grattan's excellent discussion of this type of shocking politics and its (dis)connections with quotidian forms and radical democracy in "Pierre Bourdieu and Populism" and *Populism's Power*; and also my argument concerning the intertwinement of both modes in "The Wild Patience of Radical Democracy."

12 Beltrán, *The Trouble with Unity*.

13 Beltrán, *The Trouble with Unity*, 143.

14 Beltrán, "Everyday Acts of Greatness," 880.

15 I strongly disagree with many of these common readings of Wolin, as I argue at length in chapter 6 in Hauerwas and Coles, *Christianity, Democracy, and the Radical Ordinary*.

16 Beltrán, *The Trouble with Unity*, 52.

17 Beltrán, *The Trouble with Unity*, 52.

18 Beltrán, "Everyday Acts of Greatness," 880.

19 Paul Apostolidis insightfully discusses such events in *Breaks in the Chain*. See my transfigurative reading of his account in terms of natality in "Paul Apostolidis' *Breaks in the Chain*."

20 Arendt, *The Human Condition*, 246, 177.

21 See Theoharis's account in *The Rebellious Life of Rosa Parks*.

22 See, for example, Lewis Finfer, executive director of Massachusetts Communities in Action Network, "Report from Occupy Boston: 'We Are Still a Generous and Hopeful People,'" October 12, 2011, http://blog.piconetwork.org/index.php /report-from-occupy-boston-"we-are-still-a-generous-and-hopeful-people-"/.

23 See, for example, Gitlin, *Occupy Nation*, and Frank, "To the Precinct Station." While there is much with which I disagree in the latter essay, there remains much to consider seriously in relation to the present issue.

24 The source and the specific network must remain anonymous.

25 See Rebecca Solnit's incisive account of intermittent yet persistent traditions of resistance in *Hope in the Dark*, about which I have more to say later.

26 I think that Charles Payne's *I've Got the Light of Freedom* powerfully illustrates this interanimation between dramatic protest actions and quotidian organizing in the Student Nonviolent Coordinating Committee (SNCC) in the years between 1960 and 1965, as well as the lack of explicit theory and political education that was one ingredient in SNCC's devolution after that.

27 Nietzsche, *The Gay Science*, 76.

28 See Stuart, *Anastazi America*, and DeBuys, *The Great Aridness*.

29 DeBuys, *The Great Aridness*.

30 Williams et al., "Temperature as a Potent Driver."

31 Bureau of Reclamation, Coconino Plateau Water Advisory Council, "North Central Arizona Water Supply Study," 2006, http://www.usbr.gov/lc/phoenix /reports/ncawss/NCAWSSP1NOAPP.pdf.

32 Cook, Ault, and Smerdon, "Unprecedented 21st Century Drought Risk."

33 See Stuart, *Anastazi America*, and DeBuys, *The Great Aridness*.

34 For an overview of the development of this term and pertinent references, see "Anthropocene," Wikipedia, accessed November 10, 2013, http://en.wikipedia .org/wiki/Anthropocene.

35 Chakrabarty, "The Climate of History," 206.

36 Hansen, *Storms of My Grandchildren*, 146–47.

37 Hansen, *Storms of My Grandchildren*, 147.

38 McKibben, *Eaarth*, 22.

39 McKibben, *Eaarth*, 21.

40 McKibben, *Eaarth*.

41 McKibben, *Eaarth*, 27.

42 McKibben, *Eaarth*, 83. This figure is estimated to be billions by the end of the twenty-first century with a warming of four to five degrees Celsius—a likely scenario. See also Parenti, *Tropic of Chaos*, for a broader overview and analysis of this topic in relation to neoliberalism and militarism.

43 See "Introduction" (drawn from a lecture entitled "The Geography of Hope") in Stegner, *Where the Bluebird Sings*.

44 Benjamin, *Illuminations*, 264.

45 McKibben, *Eaarth*, 86.

46 Jonathan Lear's *Radical Hope* is another text that is richly suggestive in relation to the issue at hand, even as his text travels toward a liberalism I seek to contest.

47 Solnit, *Hope in the Dark*, 233, 63.

48 Solnit, *Hope in the Dark*, 32. See also Rebecca Solnit, "Occupy Your Victories," *Nation*, September 17, 2012, accessed November 10, 2013, www.thenation.com /article/169976/occupy-your-victories.

49 "Wormhole," Wikipedia, accessed March 6, 2013, http://en.wikipedia.org/wiki /Wormhole.

50 "Exotic Matter," Wikipedia, accessed March 9, 2013, http://en.wikipedia.org /wiki/Exotic_matter.

51 "Negative Mass," Wikipedia, accessed March 9, 2013, http://en.wikipedia.org /wiki/Negative_mass.

52 "Exotic Matter," Wikipedia, accessed March 9, 2013, http://en.wikipedia.org /wiki/Exotic_matter.

53 Benjamin, *Illuminations*, 255.

54 Benjamin, *Illuminations*, 262.

55 Benjamin, *Illuminations*, 261.

56 Benjamin, *Illuminations*, 256.

57 Benjamin, *Illuminations*, 255.

58 Benjamin, *Illuminations*, 262.

59 Benjamin, *Illuminations*, 260.

60 Benjamin, *Illuminations*, 263.

61 See Gottlieb, *Forcing the Spring*, chap. 7; Park and Pellow, *The Slums of Aspen*; and Hultgren, *Border Walls Gone Green*.

62 Benjamin, *Illuminations*, 264.

63 This expression is Solnit's, *Hope in the Dark*, 40.

64 This phrase is from Margaret Randall's poem (brilliantly performed with Glenn Weyant) "Offended Turf," *Border Songs: A Collection of Music and Spoken Word to Benefit No More Deaths / No Mas Muertes*, produced by Robert Neustadt and Chuck Cheeseman, 2012, CD. Many of the songs, poems, and stories on this CD powerfully exemplify the ethos I seek to advance here.

BIBLIOGRAPHY

Alcon, Alison, and Julian Agyeman. *Cultivating Food Justice: Race, Class, and Sustainability*. Cambridge, MA: MIT Press, 2011.

Alperovitz, Gar. *America beyond Capitalism: Reclaiming Our Wealth, Our Liberty, and Our Democracy*. Hoboken, NJ: Wiley, 2005.

Apostolidis, Paul. *Breaks in the Chain: What Immigrant Workers Can Teach America about Democracy*. Minneapolis: University of Minnesota Press, 2010.

Arendt, Hannah. *The Human Condition*. 2nd ed. Chicago: University of Chicago Press, 1998.

———. *Lectures on Kant's Political Philosophy*. Edited by Ronald Beiner. Chicago: University of Chicago Press, 1982.

Arreguin-Toft, Ivan. *How the Weak Win Wars: A Theory of Asymmetric Conflict*. Cambridge: Cambridge University Press, 2005.

Beltrán, Christina. "Everyday Acts of Greatness: Reply to Boyte." *Political Theory* 38 (2010): 877–83.

———. *The Trouble with Unity: Latino Politics and the Creation of Identity*. Oxford: Oxford University Press, 2010.

Benjamin, Walter. *Illuminations: Essays and Reflections*. Edited by Hannah Arendt. Translated by Harry Zohn. New York: Schocken Books, 1969.

———. *Selected Writings*. Vol. 4. Edited by Howard Eiland and Michael W. Jennings. Cambridge, MA: Belknap Press, 2006.

Bennett, Jane. *Vibrant Matter: A Political Ecology of Things*. Durham, NC: Duke University Press, 2010.

Benyus, Janine. *Biomimicry: Innovation Inspired by Nature*. New York: HarperCollins, 2002.

Berry, Wendell. *The Way of Ignorance and Other Essays*. Berkeley: Counterpoint, 2006.

———. *What Are People For?* 2nd ed. Berkeley: Counterpoint, 2010.

Blackmore, Susan. *The Meme Machine*. Oxford: Oxford University Press, 1999.

Bloch, Ernst. *The Principle of Hope*. Vol. 1. Translated by N. Plaice. Cambridge, MA: MIT Press, 1995.

Boggs, Grace Lee. *The Next American Revolution: Sustainable Activism for the Twenty-First Century*. Berkeley: University of California Press, 2012.

Bourdieu, Pierre. *Outline of a Theory of Practice*. Cambridge: Cambridge University Press, 1977.

Bousquet, Marc. *How the University Works: Higher Education in the Low-Wage Nation*. New York: NYU Press, 2008.

Boyte, Harry. *Commonwealth: A Return to Citizen Politics*. New York: Free Press, 1989.

———. *Everyday Politics: Reconnecting Citizens and Public Life*. Philadelphia: University of Pennsylvania Press, 2005.

Brass, Marcel, Ruth M. Schmitt, Stephanie Spengler, and György Gergely. "Investigating Action Understanding: Inferential Processes versus Action Simulation." *Current Biology* 17 (2007): 2117–21.

Brown, Wendy. "Governmentality in the Age of Neoliberalism." Paper presented at the Pacific Centre for Technology and Culture, Victoria, BC, Canada, March 18, 2014.

———. *Politics Out of History*. Princeton, NJ: Princeton University Press, 2001.

———. *States of Injury: Power and Freedom in Late Modernity*. Princeton, NJ: Princeton University Press, 1995.

———. *Undoing the Demos: Neoliberalism's Stealth Revolution*. Cambridge, MA: Zone Books, 2015.

———. *Walled States, Waning Sovereignty*. Cambridge, MA: Zone Books, 2010.

Cavanaugh, William T. *Being Consumed: Economics and Christian Desire*. Grand Rapids, MI: Eerdmans, 2008.

Chakrabarty, Dipesh. "The Climate of History: Four Theses." *Critical Inquiry* 35 (2009): 197–222.

Chambers, Edward. *Roots for Radicals: Organizing for Power, Action, and Justice*. New York: Bloomsbury, 2003.

Changeux, Jean-Pierre, and Paul Ricoeur. *La nature et la règle: Ce qui fait que nous pensons*. Paris: Odile Jacob, 1998.

Clifford, James. *Routes: Travel and Translation in the Late Twentieth Century*. Cambridge, MA: Harvard University Press, 1997.

Cohen, Jean, and Andrew Arato. *Civil Society and Political Theory*. Cambridge, MA: MIT Press, 1994.

Coles, Romand. *Beyond Gated Politics: Reflections for the Possibility of Democracy*. Minneapolis: University of Minnesota Press, 2005.

———. "Collaborative Governance and Civic Empowerment: A Discussion of *Investing in Democracy*." *Perspectives on Politics* 8 (2010): 601–4.

———. "'It's the "We," Stupid,' or Reflections toward an Ecology of Radical Democratic Theory and Practices." *Theory and Event* 16 (2013). http://muse.jhu.edu/login?auth=0&type=summary&url=/journals/theory_and_event/v016/16.1.coles.html.

———. "Paul Apostolidis' *Breaks in the Chain: What Immigrant Workers Can Teach America about Democracy*." *Contemporary Political Theory* 12 (2013): 71–77.

———. *Rethinking Generosity: Critical Theory and the Politics of Caritas*. Ithaca, NY: Cornell University Press, 1997.

———. *Self/Power/Other: Political Theory and Dialogical Ethics*. Ithaca, NY: Cornell University Press, 1992.

———. "Transforming the Game: Democratizing the Publicness of Higher Education and Commonwealth in Neoliberal Times." *New Political Science* 36 (2014): 622–39.

———. "The Wild Patience of Radical Democracy: Beyond Žižek's Lack." In *Radical Democracy: Politics between Abundance and Lack*, edited by Lars Tønder and Lasse Thomassen, 68–85. Manchester: Manchester University Press, 2006.

Connolly, William. *Capitalism and Christianity, American Style*. Durham, NC: Duke University Press, 2008.

———. *A World of Becoming*. Durham, NC: Duke University Press, 2011.

Cook, Benjamin I., Toby R. Ault, and Jason E. Smerdon. "Unprecedented 21st Century Drought Risk in the American Southwest and Central Plains." *Science Advances* 1 (2015). doi: 10.1126/sciadv.1400082.

Coole, Diana, and Samantha Frost, eds. *New Materialisms: Ontology, Agency, and Politics*. Durham, NC: Duke University Press, 2010.

DeBuys, William. *The Great Aridness: Climate Change and the Future of the American Southwest*. Oxford: Oxford University Press, 2011.

Dennett, Daniel. *Consciousness Explained*. Boston: Back Bay Books, 1991.

Ellison, Ralph. *Invisible Man*. New York: Vintage, 1995.

Esteva, Gustavo, and Madhu Suri Prakash. *Grassroots Postmodernism: Remaking the Soil of Culture*. London: Zed Books, 1998.

Euben, J. Peter. "Creatures of a Day: Thought and Action in Thucydides." In *Political Theory and Praxis: New Perspectives*, edited by Terence Ball, 28–56. Minneapolis: University of Minnesota Press, 1977.

Foucault, Michel. *The Birth of Biopolitics: Lectures at the College de France 1978–1979*. Translated by G. Burchell. Hampshire, England: Palgrave Macmillan, 2008.

———. *Security, Territory, Population: Lectures at the College de France*. Translated by G. Burchell. Hampshire, England: Palgrave Macmillan, 2009.

———. "What Is Enlightenment?" In *The Foucault Reader*, edited by P. Rabinow, 32–50. New York: Random House, 1984.

Frank, Jason. "'Besides Our Selves': An Essay on Enthusiastic Politics and Civil Subjectivity." *Public Culture* 17 (2010): 371–92.

———. *Constituent Moments: Enacting the People in Postrevolutionary America*. Durham, NC: Duke University Press, 2010.

Frank, Thomas. "To the Precinct Station: How Theory Met Practice . . . and Drove It Absolutely Crazy." *The Baffler* 21 (2012). http://www.thebaffler.com/salvos/to-the-precinct-station.

Friere, Paulo. *Pedagogy of the Oppressed*. New York: Herder and Herder, 1970.

Gallagher, John. *Reimagining Detroit: Opportunities for Redefining an American City*. Detroit, MI: Wayne State University Press, 2010.

Gallese, Vittorio. "The 'Shared Manifold' Hypothesis: From Mirror Neurons to Empathy." *Journal of Consciousness Studies* 8 (2001): 33–50.

Ganz, Marshall. "What Is Public Narrative?" 2008. http://grassrootsfund.org/docs/WhatIsPublicNarrative08.pdf.

———. *Why David Sometimes Wins: Leadership, Organization, and Strategy in the California Farm Worker Movement*. Oxford: Oxford University Press, 2010.

Gavrilets, S. "Evolution and Speciation on Holey Adaptive Landscapes." *Trends in Ecology and Evolution* 12 (1997): 307–12.

Gibson-Graham, J. K. *A Postcapitalist Politics*. Minneapolis: University of Minnesota Press, 2006.

Gitlin, Todd. *Occupy Nation: The Roots, the Spirit, and the Promise of Occupy Wall Street*. New York: HarperCollins, 2012.

Gorz, Andre. *Ecology as Politics*. London: Pluto, 1983.

Gottlieb, Robert. *Forcing the Spring: The Transformation of the American Environmental Movement*. Washington, DC: Island, 2005.

Gottlieb, Robert, and Anupama Joshi. *Food Justice*. Cambridge, MA: MIT Press, 2010.

Grattan, Laura. *Populism's Power: Radical Grassroots Democracy in America*. Oxford: Oxford University Press, 2016.

———. "Pierre Bourdieu and Populism: The Everyday Politics of Outrageous Resistance." *The Good Society* 21 (2012): 194–218.

Habermas, Jürgen. *Lifeworld and System: A Critique of Functionalist Reason*. Vol. 2 of *Theory of Communicative Action*. Boston: Beacon, 1985.

———. *Reason and the Rationalization of Society*. Vol. 1 of *Theory of Communicative Action*. Boston: Beacon, 1985.

Hansen, James. *Storms of My Grandchildren: The Truth about the Coming Climate Catastrophe and Our Last Chance to Save Humanity*. London: Bloomsbury, 2010.

Hauerwas, Stanley, and Romand Coles. *Christianity, Democracy, and the Radical Ordinary*. Eugene, OR: Cascade Books, 2008.

Holland, John. *Emergence: From Chaos to Order*. New York: Basic Books, 1998.

Honig, Bonnie. *Emergency Politics: Paradox, Law, Democracy*. Princeton, NJ: Princeton University Press, 2011.

Hultgren, John. *Border Walls Gone Green: Nature, Sovereignty and Anti-immigrant Politics in the United States*. Minneapolis: University of Minnesota Press, 2015.

Iacoboni, Marco. *Mirroring People: The Science of How We Connect with Others*. New York: Farrar, Straus and Giroux, 2008.

Inglehart, Ronald. *Modernization and Postmodernization: Cultural, Economic, and Political Change in 43 Countries*. Princeton, NJ: Princeton University Press, 1997.

Kaplan, J. "The End of the Adaptive Landscape Metaphor." *Biology and Philosophy* 23 (2008): 625–38.

Kauffman, Stuart. *At Home in the Universe: In Search of the Laws of Self-Organization and Complexity*. Oxford: Oxford University Press, 1996.

Kilner, James M., Jennifer L. Marchant, and Chris D. Frith. "Modulation of the Mirror System by Social Relevance." *Social Cognitive and Affective Neuroscience* 1 (2006): 143–48.

Klein, Naomi. *The Shock Doctrine: The Rise of Disaster Capitalism*. New York: Picador, 2008.

————. *This Changes Everything: Capitalism versus the Climate*. New York: Simon and Schuster, 2014.

Kourtis, Dimittrios, Natalie Sebanz, and Günter Knoblich. "Favouritism in the Motor System: Social Interaction Modulates Action Simulation." *Biology Letters* 6 (2010): 758–61.

Kruse, Jane, and Preben Maegaard. "An Authentic Story of How a Local Community Became Self-Sufficient in Pollution-Free Energy from Wind and Created a Source of Income for the Citizens." In *Sparking a Worldwide Energy Revolution*, edited by Kolya Abramsky, 256–63. Oakland, CA: AK Press, 2010.

Lear, Jonathan. *Radical Hope: Ethics in the Face of Cultural Devastation*. Cambridge, MA: Harvard University Press, 2006.

Lederach, John Paul. *The Moral Imagination: The Art and Soul of Building Peace*. Oxford: Oxford University Press, 2005.

Levinas, Emmanuel. *Totality and Infinity: An Essay on Exteriority*. Translated by A. Lingus. Pittsburgh: Duquesne University Press, 1969.

Lew, Michael, and Patrick Conaty. *The Resilience Imperative: Cooperative Transitions to a Steady-State Economics*. Gabriola Island, BC: New Society Publishers, 2012.

Liepelt, Roman, D. Yves Von Cramon, and Marcel Brass. "How Do We Infer Others' Goals from Non-stereotypic Actions? The Outcome of Context-Sensitive Inferential Processing in Right Inferior Parietal and Posterior Temporal Cortex." *NeuroImage* 43 (2008): 784–92.

Longhofer, Wesley, Shannon Golden, and Arturo Baiocchi. "A Fresh Look at Sociology Bestsellers." *Contexts* 9 (2010). http://contexts.org/articles/spring-2010/a-fresh-look-at-sociology-bestsellers/.

Lovins, Amory. *Soft Energy Paths: Toward a Durable Peace*. New York: Harper Colophon, 1977.

Maegaard, Preben. "Denmark: Politically-Induced Paralysis in Wind Power's Homeland and Industrial Hub." In *Sparking a Worldwide Energy Revolution*, edited by Kolya Abramsky, 489–94. Oakland, CA: AK Press, 2010.

McKibben, Bill. *Eaarth: Making a Life on a Tough New Planet*. New York: St. Martin's Griffin, 2011.

Meadows, Donella H. *Thinking in Systems: A Primer*. White River Junction, VT: Chelsea Green, 2008.

Midnight Notes Collective and Friends. "Promissory Notes: From Crisis to Commons." In *Sparking a Worldwide Energy Revolution*, edited by Kolya Abramsky, 32–59. Oakland, CA: AK Press, 2010.

Miller, Michelle. "Assessment Report for AY 2012–2013 First Year Seminar/FYSeminar-ARTS." First Year Seminar Program, Northern Arizona University, May 2013.

Mushita, Andrew, and Carole B. Thompson. *Biopiracy of Biodiversity: Global Exchange as Enclosure*. Trenton, NJ: Africa World Press, 2007.

Nace, Ted. *Gangs of America: The Rise of Corporations and the Disabling of Democracy*. San Francisco: Berrett-Koehler, 2005.

Nietzsche, Friedrich. *The Gay Science: With a Prelude in Rhymes and an Appendix of Songs*. Translated by W. Kauffman. New York: Vintage, 1974.

Oceransky, Sergio. "Fighting the Enclosure of Wind: Indigenous Resistance to the Privatization of the Wind Resource in Southern Mexico." In *Sparking a Worldwide Energy Revolution*, edited by Kolya Abramsky, 505–22. Oakland, CA: AK Press, 2010.

Oceransky, Sergio, and Yansa Community Interest Company. "The Yansa Group: Renewable Energy as a Common Resource." In *Sparking a Worldwide Energy Revolution*, edited by Kolya Abramsky, 608–27. Oakland, CA: AK Press, 2010.

Orr, David. *Down to the Wire: Confronting Climate Collapse*. Oxford: Oxford University Press, 2009.

Oz, Amos, and Fania Oz-Salzberger. *Jews and Words*. New Haven, CT: Yale University Press, 2012.

Panagia, Davide. *The Political Life of Sensation*. Durham, NC: Duke University Press, 2006.

Parenti, Christian. *Tropic of Chaos: Climate Change and the New Geography of Violence*. New York: Nation Books, 2012.

Park, Lisa Sun-Hee, and David Naguib Pellow. *The Slums of Aspen: Immigrants vs. the Environment in America's Eden*. New York: NYU Press, 2011.

Payne, Charles. *I've Got the Light of Freedom: The Organizing Tradition and the Mississippi Freedom Struggle*. Berkeley: University of California Press, 1995.

Petrini, Carlo. *Slow Food: The Case for Taste*. New York: Columbia University Press, 2004.

Polanyi, Karl. *The Great Transformation: The Political Economic Origins of Our Time*. Boston: Beacon, 2001.

Pollan, Michael. *The Botany of Desire: A Plant's-Eye View of the World*. New York: Random House, 2001.

———. *The Omnivore's Dilemma: A Natural History of Four Meals*. New York: Penguin, 2007.

Prigogine, Ilya, in collaboration with Isabelle Stengers. *The End of Certainty: Time, Chaos, and the New Laws of Nature*. New York: Free Press, 1997.

Rizzolatti, Giacomo, and Corrado Sinigaglia. *Mirrors in the Brain: How Our Minds Share Actions and Emotions*. Translated by Frances Anderson. Oxford: Oxford University Press, 2008.

Rorty, Richard. *Achieving Our Country*. Cambridge, MA: Harvard University Press, 1999.

Salatin, Joel. *The Sheer Ecstasy of Being a Lunatic Farmer*. Swoope, VA: Polyface, 2010.

Salinas, Pedro. *The Love Poems of Pedro Salinas and Letter Poems to Katherine*. Translated by W. Barnstone. Chicago: University of Chicago Press, 2010.

Schlosberg, David, and Romand Coles. "The New Environmentalism of Everyday Life: Sustainability, Material Flows, and Movements." *Contemporary Political Theory*. Advance online publication, June 30, 2015.

Schurman, Rachel, and William A. Munro. *Fighting for the Future of Food: Activists versus Agribusiness in the Struggle over Biotechnology*. Minneapolis: University of Minnesota Press, 2010.

Shiva, Vandana, ed. *Manifestos on the Future of Food and Seed*. Boston: South End, 2007.

Sirriani, Carmen. *Investing in Democracy: Engaging Citizens in Collaborative Governance*. Washington, DC: Brookings Institution Press, 2009.

Solnit, Rebecca. *Hope in the Dark: Untold Histories, Wild Possibilities*. New York: Nation Books, 2005.

Stegner, Wallace. *Where the Bluebird Sings to the Lemonade Springs: Living and Writing in the West*. New York: Modern Library Classics, 2002.

Stuart, David E. *Anastazi America: Seventeen Centuries on the Road from Center Place*. Albuquerque: University of New Mexico Press, 2000.

Szasz, Andrew. *Ecopopulism: Toxic Waste and the Movement for Environmental Justice*. Minneapolis: University of Minnesota Press, 1994.

Theoharis, Jeanne. *The Rebellious Life of Rosa Parks*. Boston: Beacon, 2013.

Unger, Roberto Mangabeira. *False Necessity: Anti-necessitarian Social Theory in the Service of Radical Democracy*. Cambridge: Cambridge University Press, 1987.

Walker, Brian, and David Salt. *Resilience Thinking: Sustaining Ecosystems and People in a Changing World*. Washington, DC: Island, 2006.

Williams, A. Park, et al. "Temperature as a Potent Driver of Regional Forest Drought Stress and Tree Mortality." *Nature Climate Change* 3 (2013): 292–97.

Winne, Mark. *Food Rebels, Guerrilla Gardeners, and Smart-Cookin' Mamas: Fighting Back in an Age of Industrial Agriculture*. Boston: Beacon, 2011.

Wolin, Sheldon. "Fugitive Democracy." In *Democracy and Difference: Contesting Boundaries of the Political*, edited by Seyla Benhabib, 31–45. Princeton, NJ: Princeton University Press, 1996.

———. *Politics and Vision*. Expanded edition. Princeton, NJ: Princeton University Press, 2006.

———. *The Presence of the Past: Essays on the State and the Constitution*. Baltimore: Johns Hopkins University Press, 1990.

Wooten, Victor. *The Music Lesson: A Spiritual Search for Growth through Music*. New York: Penguin, 2008.

INDEX

capitalism (*continued*)
  power and, 74–84; and shock politics,
  164–65
Cargill, 80–81
causality, evangelical-capitalist resonance
  machine and, 38–40
Chakrabarty, Dipesh, 178–79
challenge, radical democratic habitus and,
  68–69
chaotic systems: autocatalytic dynamics
  and, 133–46; visionary pragmatism and,
  177–91
Chicana feminism, food justice and, 89–91
circulatory power: contentious struggle
  and, 107–14; corporate power and,
  79–84; decentralized receptive circulation and, 84–91, 97; engaged pedagogy
  and, 68–69; governmentality and, 75–84;
  mega-circulatory power and, 72–74;
  politics and, 26–27; resonant relations
  and, 51–58
citizenship, engaged pedagogy vs.
  state-sanctioned forms of, 59–60
Civic Agency Initiative, 150
civil society, "three-sector" model of systems and, 120
class structure, food politics and, 87–91
Clifford, James, 188
climate change: radical democratic theory
  and, 27–30; soft energy production
  and, 113–14; visionary pragmatism and,
  177–91
coevolutionary relations, Kauffman's autocatalytic dynamics and, 142–46
collective action, plural ecologies of practice and, 54–58
communities of hopeful practice, 180–91
community gardening, polyface rooting
  and routing and, 102–7
community organizing: autocatalytic
  systems and, 129–46; engaged pedagogy
  and, 59–69; imagined ethical communities as, 91–102
community-supported agriculture (CSA)
  farming, 86–91, 105–7

complex system dynamics: autocatalytic
  systems and, 124–46; co-optive radical
  democracy and, 147–59; radical democracy and, 119–23; receptive intercorporeal resonance and, 40–49; theories of,
  95–97; "three-sector" model, 120
Congregations, Associations, and Neighborhoods (CAN), 23
Connolly, William, 36–40, 121
contentious circulations, root/route struggles and, 107–14
contingency, systems theory and, 121–23
co-optive systems dynamics, 25–26; radical
  democratic power and, 146–59
corporate structures: superpower development and, 77–84; "three-sector" model
  of systems and, 120
counterconducts, governmentality and,
  76–84
counterpublics, shock politics and, 168–69
cycle of organizing, autocatalytic systems
  and, 129–46

David and Goliath narrative, radical democratic theory and, 9–12, 27–30, 161–63
decentralized receptive circulation, 84–91;
  autocatalytic dynamics and, 142–46;
  wind energy distribution and, 110–14
Deleuze, Gilles, 37
democracy education, co-optive dynamics
  and promotion of, 150–59
Denmark, wind energy in, 110–14
Dennett, Daniel, 46
Detroit Agricultural Network, 87
Detroit food justice movement, 109–14
disaster capitalism, Klein's discussion of,
  164–75
disciplinary power: Foucault on, 74–75;
  governmentality and, 75–84; at Northern
  Arizona University (NAU), 148–49
Double Up Food Bucks, 88
Dust Bowl era, 93

Eaarth (McKibben), 179–81
East India Company, 77

eccentricity, resonant circulation and, 98–102

ecologies of practice, 54–58

ecology of differences, democratic habitus and, 68–69

economic theory: co-optive systems dynamics and, 147; food politics and, 87–91; governmentality and, 75–84; non-capitalist community economy, 121–23

Economistes movement, 75–76

edge of chaos, in autocatalytic systems, 134–46

electronic media, evangelical-capitalist resonance machine and, 38–40

Ellison, Ralph, 29–30

embodiment, resonant receptive democracy and, 54–58

emergence: in autocatalytic systems, 134–46; of behavior patterns, 41–42; in complex systems, 122–23; possibility and, 56–58, 62–69; radical democratic theory and, 21–30

"emergency brake" tactics, shock politics and, 167–68

environmentalism, professionalism and market logic in, 123

Esteva, Gustavo, 85, 87

evanescence, shock politics and, 171–75

evangelical-capitalist resonance machine, 36–40

evolutionary theory, phase transition in, 132–33

extraterritoriality, corporate power and, 78–84

Fair Food Network (Detroit), 88

farmers' markets: income barriers in, 87–88; proliferation of, 86–91

feedback loops, in autocatalytic systems, 126–46

First Year Seminars (FYS) Program (NAU), 151–53

fitness landscapes, Kauffman's concept of, 122, 137–46

Flagstaff Farmers Market, 105–7

food-body-desire nexus, agri-security apparatus and, 81–84

food justice initiatives, 88–91; Detroit food justice movement, 109–14

Foucault, Michel: on governmentality, 75–84, 90; on power, 22–23

fugitive democracy, Wolin's concept of and resilient emergence, 123–26, 169

futurity: engaged pedagogy and, 62–69; "not yet" and, 43–44, 53

Gallese, Vittorio, 198n10

game changers, alternative definitions of, 11–12

game-transformative practices, 11–18, 27–30; complex system dynamics and, 122–23; co-optive dynamics and, 150–59; engaged pedagogy and, 63–69; resonant receptive democracy and, 51–58; visionary pragmatism and, 175–91

Ganz, Marshall, 9–12

Gay Science, The (Nietzsche), 177

genetically modified organisms (GMOs), resistance to, 91

Gibson-Graham, J. K., 121–23

Gladwell, Malcolm, 10–11

Goodwyn, Larry, 3

Gottlieb, Robert, 88, 123

governmentality: corporate power and transformation of, 78–84; decentralized receptive circulation and, 84–91; mega-circulatory power and, 74–84; neoliberal regime of, 23; wind energy distribution and, 112–14

Gramsci, Antonio, 84–85

grassroots democratic practice: autocatalytic systems and, 130–46; engaged pedagogy and, 59–69; intertwining quotidian organizing and shock democracy and, 161–75; receptive intercorporeal resonance and, 45–49

Grassroots Postmodernism: Remaking the Soil of Cultures (Esteva and Prakash), 87

mirror neurons: intercorporeal resonances and, 99; receptive intercorporeal resonance and, 40–49, 198n13

molecular systems, autocatalytic dynamics and, 124–27, 140–46

movement, resonance and, 50–58, 72–74

moving democracy, theory of, 23

Nace, Ted, 77

natality, 17, 102; persistence and, 26; phase transition and, 133, 136; radical democratic theory and, 27–30; shock politics and, 27, 168–71; wormhole hope and, 185–91

National Immigration Rally, 168–69

National Science Foundation, 151

neoliberal power: in Arizona politics, 148–59; complex system dynamics of, 119–23; co-optation of, 149–59; shock politics of, 164–75

neuroscience: movement and, 72–74; radical receptivity and, 34–37; receptive intercorporeal resonance and mirror neurons, 40–49

new materialism: biopolitics and, 75–84, 201n37; mega-circulatory power and, 112–14; resistance to governmentality and, 89–91, 201n37

Newtonian causality, radical democracy and, 40–41, 118–19

Nietzsche, Friedrich, 177

No More Deaths advocacy group, 136–37

nonhuman encounters, intercorporeal resonances and, 98–102

Northern Arizona Institutions for Community Leadership (NAICL), 60, 129–32

Northern Arizona Interfaith Council, 136–37

Northern Arizona University (NAU): autocatalytic dynamics in radical democracy at, 129–46; democratic habitus and engaged pedagogy at, 58–69; dropout rates and, 152; neoliberal culture of assessment at, 148–49; polyface routing and rooting at, 102–7; Program for

Community, Culture, and Environment at, 15–21

Occupy movement, 165–66, 173–75, 182

Omnivore's Dilemma, The (Pollan), 79–80, 86

organic agriculture, agri-food corporation co-optation of, 108–14

Ottoman Empire, Bedouin uprising against, 10–11

Panopticon, Bentham's concept of, 74–75

Parenti, Christian, 189

"patch procedures," Kauffman's autocatalytic dynamics and, 141–46

Payne, Charles, 208n26

People Improving Communities through Organizing (PICO), 173

Petrini, Carlo, 87, 100–102

phase transition, in autocatalytic systems, 126–29

Poincaré, Henri, 41, 69, 72

Polanyi, Karl, 77, 200n10

political theory, radical democracy and, 1–30

Pollan, Michael, 79–84, 86; Joel Salatin and, 95–97

polycultural perennial farming, 94–95

poly-eccentricism, resonant circulation and, 98

polyface flows, 23–24; contentious circulations and, 108–14; imagined ethical communities and, 91–102; routing and rooting at NAU, 102–7

possibility: democratic resonance and, 62–69; habitus and, 56–58

Prakash, Madhu Suri, 87

preplowed prairies, root clod of, 94

President's Innovation Fund (NAU), 151

Prigogine, Ilya, 40–41, 45, 53, 69, 72, 198n10

Program for Community, Culture, and Environment (Northern Arizona University), 15–21, 151

Public Achievement (PA), 59–69, 143–46

Pueblo culture, routing in, 93

quotidian politics: countershocks and, 163, 168–70; natality and, 27, 171–75

radical and ecological democracy: autocatalytic dynamics in, 123–46; co-opting dynamics in, 146–59; countershock politics and, 163–75; engaged pedagogy and, 62–69; imagined ethical communities and, 91–102; resonance machine for, 53–58; shock politics and, 166–75; theories and practices for, 1–30; wormhole hope and, 181–91

receptivity: alternative farming and, 96–102; autocatalytic systems and, 127–29; decentralized receptive circulation and, 84–91; democratic habitus and, 68–69; intercorporeal resonance and, 40–49; natality and, 171–75

Repeal Coalition, 137

resistance: circulatory power and, 107–14; shock politics and, 163–64, 167–68

resonance: circulatory power and, 22–23; evangelical-capitalist resonance machine and, 38–40; movement and, 118–19; receptive intercorporeal, 40–49; shock politics and, 166–75

revolutionary pasts, Benjamin's concept of, 185–87

Rizzolatti, Giacomo, 198n10

root clod: of alternative farming, 94–102; vs. malignant tree of mega-circulatory power, 83–84

Rorty, Richard, 197nn12–13

Route 66, connectedness of, 92

routing practices: imagined ethical communities and, 93–102; polyface flows and, 102–7; in Pueblo culture, 93; radical democracy and, 24–30; visionary pragmatism and, 188–91

rugged fitness landscapes, Kauffman's concept of, 122, 137–46

Salatin, Joel, 23, 95–97

Salatin's Polyface Farm, 95–102

School Gardens ARTS program, 71–72

Schwarzschild wormhole, 184–85

security, as centrifugal force, 83–84

self-organization: autocatalysis in radical democracy and, 123–46; Kauffman's theory of, 25–26

Shiva, Vandana, 87

shock politics: alternating currents in, 164–75; neoliberal doctrine of, 146, 164–75; radical democratic theory and, 26–30; resistance and, 163–75; *The Shock Doctrine: The Rise of Disaster Capitalism* (Klein), 164–67

Siemens Wind Power, 112–14

simulated annealing, autocatalytic dynamics and, 141–46

Sirriani, Carmen, 75

Slow Food movement, 87–91, 100–102

soft energy, contentious circulations and, 110–14

Solnit, Rebecca, 29–30, 181–83, 187–88

Southeast Industrial Areas Foundation, 7–8

Stegner, Wallace, 181

Stengers, Isabelle, 40–41, 45, 53, 72, 198n10

Storms of My Grandchildren (Hansen), 179

Student Nonviolent Coordinating Committee (SNCC), 208n26

Students for Sustainable Living and Urban Gardening (SSLUG) (NAU), 71–72, 105–7

subcritical systems, autocatalytic dynamics and, 134–46

"SunnyCider" cooperative enterprise, 106–7

Sunnyside Neighborhood Association, 106–7

Supplemental Nutrition Assistance Program (SNAP), 88

Sustainable Food Center, 89

sustainable materialism, contentious circulations and, 108–14

technopolitical resonance, evangelical-capitalist resonance machine and, 38–40

terroir, alternative farming and, 100–102

Thatcher, Margaret, 120